Wire and Cable For Electronics

A User's Handbook

Neil Sclater

FIRST EDITION
FIRST PRINTING

© 1991 by **McGraw-Hill, Inc.**.

Printed in the United States of America. All rights reserved. The publisher takes no
responsibility for the use of any of the materials or methods described in this book,
nor for the products thereof.

Library of Congress Cataloging-in-Publication Data

ISBN 0-8306-7787-9(H)

For information about other McGraw-Hill materials,
call 1-800-2-MCGRAW in the U.S. In other countries
call your nearest McGraw-Hill office.

Vice President and Editorial Director: Larry Hager
Book Editor: Andrew Yoder
Production: Katherine G. Brown
Book Design: Jaclyn J. Boone   TPR4

Contents

Acknowledgments

Many different companies sent me catalogs, technical literature, user guide books, internal training documents, and other current references that were invaluable in the preparation of this handbook.

I especially thank Mr. Lowell S. Lisker, Chief Engineer of the American Insulated Wire Corp., Pawtucket, RI, for reviewing the manuscript, suggesting necessary changes, and providing additional references from his personal library.

I also acknowledge the manuscript review and additional information provided by various people at Underwriters Laboratories Inc. in Melville, NY and Northbrook, IL.

I thank the companies that sent me catalogs and literature and those that also gave me permission to reproduce either published tables or illustrations:

- American Insulated Wire Corp., Pawtucket, RI
- Belden Wire and Cable, Richmond, IN
- Brand-Rex Cable Systems Div., BRINntec Corp., Willimantic, CT
- Carol Cable Co., Inc., Pawtucket, RI
- Daburn Electronics & Cable Corp., Northvale, NJ
- General Cable Co., Greenwich, CT
- Madison Cable Corp., Worcester, MA
- Methode Electronics, Inc. Rolling Hills, IL
- Manhattan Electric Cable Corp., Rye, NY

A basic reference widely used in this handbook is the National Electrical Code (NEC) 1990, published by the National Fire Protection Association (NFPA), Quincy, MA.

Introduction

This handbook is a user-friendly guide to the sometimes confusing world of wire and cable for electronics. Until now, the best sources of practical information on the subject have been the supplier catalogs, which include engineering data that relates to the product lines. However, these catalogs are sales tools for actual or prospective customers with sufficient technical background and experience to understand the code designations and references to standards and specifications. They are not intended as educational texts or comprehensive references.

By contrast, this handbook was prepared for the reader who might not have this "hands-on" experience or might not have kept up to date with the recent changes in codes, standards, specifications, and materials. This book serves these readers who "need to know" for business or personal reasons. It contains many pages of useful reference information that transcend the catalogs and general engineering texts. It will be of value to both seasoned and entry-level professionals, whether in manufacturing, engineering, marketing, purchasing, sales, or distribution. In addition to its coverage of conventional wire and cable, it is an informational source for fiber-optic cable.

The handbook is intended as a reference for identifying, selecting, and purchasing wire and cable for many electronic applications. It discusses the many conductor and insulation materials, as well as the design, manufacture, and performance of wire and cable that conform to accepted standards. Considerable coverage is given to national and international standards and codes.

This handbook supplements and enhances information on wire and cable that is available in electronics textbooks, general engineering handbooks, and the manufacturers' catalogs. However, it is not cluttered with references to proprietary insulation materials and trade-named products, which limit the usefulness of catalogs as references. Included are: standard wire tables, conversion tables, wire and cable design formulas, and performance data that is found in some of the more general electrical and electronic engineering handbooks.

Wire and cable has been manufactured for many years to meet the specific requirements of the electronics industry, as distinguished from consumer and commercial/industrial electric wiring, electrical power distribution, and telephony. Some wire and cable products, such as flat cable, coaxial cable, and fiber-optic cable are inseparable from electronics applications. However, other conductors and power cords find use outside of strictly electronics applications in appliances, building services, process controls, and fire alarm systems.

In the era of the vacuum-tube radios, most electronic wiring was point-to-point positioning of color-coded hook-up wire to interconnect discrete components within a metal chassis. Most of the wiring was done by hand between the component sockets. Today, large-scale integrated circuits and sophisticated circuit boards have replaced the "spaghetti-bowl" jumble of discrete wires in virtually all electronic products, except laboratory prototypes.

The rise of computer-based systems with many enclosures for separate components and peripherals has shifted the emphasis of electronic wiring from internal to external connections. Specialized wires and cables now interconnect computers with peripherals and benchtop computers in vast networks. Specialized wire and cable has evolved for audio systems, musical instruments, TV and radio broadcast equipment, process controls, instrumentation and security systems, to mention but a few.

New and improved wires and cables are continually added to the inventories and catalogs of commercial wire and cable vendors. Some of these were originally custom-designed cables that met applications specific system requirements. Because of general acceptance, they have evolved into standard products. Changes in the electrical code and the requirements for doing business overseas have also had an impact on inventories and standard product lines.

Demand for new and modified wire and cable is driven by:

- Circuit and system operation at ever higher frequencies and data rates—particularly in computers and telecommunications equipment.

- Trends toward product miniaturization and weight and power reduction. Some examples are the shrinking desktop and laptop computers and smaller audio and stereo systems.

- Imposition of stricter national and international codes and standards that govern product safety, fire prevention, and EMI/RFI suppression.

- Ongoing developments in material technology—particularly in insulation and dielectric materials.

All new wire and cable products must maintain standards for reliability and durability set by earlier generations and still be available at prices appropriate with their intended applications.

Connectors form an integral part of electronic system interconnections. However, the discussion of connectors in this handbook is limited to those styles that depend on precise dimensioning of mating wire or cable: flat cable connectors, coaxial cable connectors, fiber-optic cable connectors, and to some extent, multiconductor circular connectors.

Ten subjects of special interest to users

1. Background information on conductor materials including wire drawing and stranding.

2. An overview of primary insulation and jacket materials. Text and tables cover the physical and electrical properties and compare the relative merits.

3. Background information on insulation extrusion, conductor testing, color coding, and shielding.

4. Descriptions of multiconductor and multipair cables, including conductor gauges, number of conductors, insulation, shielding, jacketing and applicable standards, and UL/NEC codes.

5. A discussion of the principal industrial and military standards and specifications that apply to manufacturing and testing wire and cable.

6. Information on military and commercial coaxial cables, including a list of the principal characteristics of RG/U-style cables.

7. A collection of reference tables on conductor and insulation properties and the conversion of measurement units.

8. An introduction to fiber-optic networking, the theory of light wave communication, and the fundamentals of optical guides.

9. A discussion of certain important connectors that are designed to meet specific cable styles: flat, coaxial, and multiconductor/multipair cable.

10. A complete and updated glossary of wire and cable terminology.

1

Conductor materials

To select the most appropriate wire and cable for electronics applications, you must carefully consider the many options available in conductors, insulation, shielding, and jacketing. The wire and cable industry has kept pace with advances in electronics, so a bewildering choice of products is now available as standard catalog items. If, for some reason, the design engineer is unable to find a satisfactory product in the catalogs, unusual requirements can be met by custom manufacture.

This book distinguishes between wire and cable for electronics and wire and cable used primarily for the conduction of electrical power (in such applications as power distribution, home and building service, and appliance and machine wiring). Although the products for these two general applications areas are quite similar, wires and cables for electronics must be functional over a wide range of frequencies—from direct current well into the millimeter wavelengths. By contrast, electrical wire and cable is primarily intended to carry direct current or alternating current at 50/60 Hertz.

Certain kinds of products (such as flat ribbon cable, coaxial cable, and fiber-optic cable) are used exclusively in the domain of electronics, and power cords are common to both market divisions. However, as electronics invades more products and applications, the distinctions begin to blur as cables that carry both power and signals become more prevalent.

In most wire and cable electronics applications, the designer and engineer are likely to be concerned about transmitting weak signals that might be subject to distortion by crosstalk or other interference within the cable. They might also be concerned about the effects of externally generated electromagnetic and radio frequency interference (EMI and RFI). In addition, a real concern exists for the suppression of signals that originate within the cable. In instances where these signals are 10 kHz or higher, laws restrict this radiation. These signals could possibly interfere with sensitive systems and equipment

1

nearby. These requirements are more comprehensive in the home and office than in the factory.

Because of rapid strides in electronics, particularly in such areas as satellite communication ground links and computer networks, certain wire and cable configurations that were available only as custom products a few years ago are now standard items. Some wire and cable manufacturers now refer to their products under names derived from end-use applications, rather than in terms of their construction. Thus, some companies now refer to computer cables, local-area network (LAN) cables, and telecommunications cables. These classifications can be confusing because they include single conductors, twisted pairs, coaxial cables, multiconductor cables, and even fiber-optic cables (covered in a separate chapter in this book).

Conductor materials selection

The selection of conductor materials for electronics applications has been limited to a relatively few metals: copper, copper-coated steel, and high-strength copper alloys. Aluminum is unsatisfactory for most electronic wire and cable applications for a number of reasons that will be discussed later in this chapter.

Bare copper is widely used as a conductor in both electrical and electronic applications. However, it is often coated with tin to improve solderability and inhibit corrosion. Silver and nickel coatings are specified if it is necessary to use the wires and cables at higher than normal operating temperatures. Copper-covered steel has higher tensile strength than annealed copper, although its conductivity is lower. Although, high-strength copper alloys have about the same strength as copper-covered steel, they weigh less and are smaller in diameter.

Conductors can be solid wires or bundles of stranded wires. Stranded conductors are specified in diameters or gauge sizes that are equivalent to solid-wire diameters or gauge sizes. Cross-section area (CSA) equivalence can be achieved with a relatively small number of strands (7 or 10) or a larger number (65 or more) of finer strands, if greater flexibility is required.

The basic requirements for the conduction of electricity through any conductor include:

- A gauge or diameter large enough to handle the signal or power conducted for the intended service environment.

- Physical properties (such as conductivity, ductility, corrosion resistance, strength, hardness, and flexibility) that are suitable for the application.

The acceptable conductor materials, forms, and physical properties are governed by commercial/industrial and government standards and specifications, as well as by electrical codes. The burden for compliance with these documents is on the product or equipment designer, systems integrator, and all those who are responsible for wire and cable replacement during equipment maintenance and update work.

Conductor types and uses

The size, weight, cost, method and ease of termination, corrosion resistance, strength, and flex life of conductors are related to five characteristics:

- Material selection
- Size or gauge of conductor
- Stranded versus solid
- Stranding method
- Coating or plating

Suitable electrical conductors are available as bare or plated solid and stranded wire. Copper, the most commonly used conductor for both electrical and electronics applications, can be annealed, medium hard drawn, or hard drawn. For electronics applications, it can be plated with tin, silver, or nickel. Copper-covered steel and high-strength copper alloys can also be silver coated.

Solid wire

Solid wire is available commercially with round, square, and rectangular cross sections, but round conductors predominate. Wire and cable manufacturers might draw their own solid wire from bar stock or purchase it either bare or plated. Solid wire is advantageous because it can conduct high current or high frequencies more efficiently than stranded wire. Silver-plated solid copper wire is also more efficient than tinned copper wire at high frequencies.

However, the major disadvantage of solid wire is its lack of flexibility; it is susceptible to cracking or fracture when under stress or after repeated bending. Moreover, a slight nick in a solid wire, during wire stripping, can become a fracture site when the wire is flexed or vibrated.

Stranded wire

Stranded wire is recommended over solid wire for most general-purpose applications because it is more flexible. It can easily be bent and formed into wire and cable harness assemblies. In addition, stranded wire is less likely to fracture during jacket or insulation removal and when a conductor must be unsoldered from a terminal or connector. Stranded conductory flexibility at all gauge sizes is directly related to the number of strands and their individual gauge sizes.

Wire size

No legal standard exists for wire gauges in the United States. However, as a result of general industrial and commercial acceptance, the American Wire Gauge (AWG) is accepted as the standard. It was devised by J.R. Brown in 1857, and was formerly called the Brown and Sharpe (B&S) Gauge.

The sizes of this gauge relate to the number of successive drawing operations or passes that are needed to reach the desired diameter—starting with a copper rod about 5/16 (0.312) inch in diameter. The final wire size is obtained by continuously drawing the rod at high speed through successive dies—each smaller than the preceding one. Thus, AWG size numbers are retrogressive; the larger the number, the smaller the diameter.

The gauge is formed by assigning size 36 to a 0.0050-inch diameter and 0000 (4/0) to 0.460-inch diameter. The intermediate diameters are formed by a geometric progression. Because 39 intermediate sizes exist, the ratio of the diameters of any two successive sizes is given by:

$$\sqrt[39]{92} = 1.123$$

The square of this ratio is 1.261 or approximately 1¹/₄. Because resistance, weight, and cross section vary with the square of the diameter, these values can be determined for any size, from the next size above or below, by multiplying or dividing by 1¹/₄. The sixth power of the ratio (i.e., the ratio of any diameter to the diameter of the sixth greater gauge number) is 2.005. Because this value is approximately two, it is the basis for several simple wire computations.

- An increase of three gauges, from thin to thicker wire (i.e., 22 to 19 AWG), doubles the cross section area (CSA) and the weight of the wire and halves its direct current resistance.

- An increase of six gauge numbers, from thin to thicker wire (i.e., 22 to 16 AWG), doubles the diameter.

- An increase of 10 gauge numbers, from thin to thicker wire (i.e., 22 to 12 AWG), multiplies the cross section area (CSA) and weight by 10 and divides the resistance by 10.

A knowledge of these relationships and reference to basic data on 10 AWG wire permits the approximate calculation of data on all other wire sizes without reference to wire tables.

Wire size:	10 AWG
Diameter:	0.1 inch
Resistance:	1 ohm /1000 feet
Weight:	31.4 pounds/1000 feet

Wire is specified in AWG sizes or by diameter in either decimal parts of an inch, or in mils (0.001 inch). For example, 22 AWG has a diameter of 0.0253 inch. By moving the decimal point three places to the right, the value in mils is obtained: 25.3.

The circular mil is defined as the area of a circle that is one mil in diameter. This unit is used to determine the equivalent gauge of a stranded conductor. A circular mil equals $\pi/4$ or 0.785 of a square mil. The area of a solid conductor in circular mils is the square of its diameter in mils.

Conductor materials

Three classes of conductor materials are detailed in this chapter: copper, copper-covered steel, and high-strength copper alloys. The following properties will be considered:

- Minimum conductivity
- Tensile strength
- Maximum continuous operating temperature
- Relative weight

TABLE 1-1 lists the physical properties of materials commonly used in electronics applications.

Copper

The outstanding physical properties of copper that make it so well suited as an electrical conductor are:

- High electrical conductivity (low resistivity).
- High thermal conductivity.
- Ductility (ability to be drawn without fracture).
- Malleability (ability to be formed into thin sheets).
- Ease of solderability.

Improved smelting methods have made it possible to economically produce satisfactory electrical conductors from low-grade ore with less than 1 percent copper content. After concentration and smelting, the ore that is intended for use as electrical conductors is refined to a purity of at least 99.9 percent. The resulting electrolytic tough pitch (ETP), still contains small amounts of copper oxide that make it brittle. This copper oxide is removed in further processing to yield oxygen-free, high-conductivity (OFHC) copper. Although the conductivity is only slightly improved, the *ductility* (ability to be drawn, stretched, or hammered into thin sheets without breaking) is appreciably greater. This decreased brittleness also improves the flex life of the copper.

Electrolytically refined copper is cast into bars before it is hot rolled and cold drawn to a final wire size. In the hot-rolling process, the bars are first heated to as high as 927 °C (1700 °F) and then passed through grooved rolls to make approximately 5/16-inch diameter rods. The CSA of the rod is then progressively reduced until the desired gauge is reached.

Even OFHC copper becomes brittle during these drawing operations, so the rods must be annealed to obtain the required temper. Annealed copper conductors are better able to withstand the flex and vibration stresses of normal use. They are less susceptible to damage during later insulation stripping and termination than medium hard-drawn or hard-drawn copper. However, there is a ductility/tensile strength trade-off.

The nominal tensile strength of annealed copper (TABLE 1-1) is 36,000 psi. By contrast, medium hard-drawn copper has nearly twice that tensile strength (60,000 psi) and hard-drawn copper has nearly three times that tensile strength (97,000 psi).

Bare copper is considered to have a minimum conductivity of 100 percent. Tin coating does not change the conductivity, but silver coating improves it by about 2 percent. However, nickel coating decreases the conductivity by about 4 percent.

Copper wire tables are based on standard values for density, conductivity, or resistivity, and the temperature coefficient of resistance of copper. The complete tables are located in the appendix because of their lengths. These values have been accepted by the American Society for Testing and Materials (ASTM) and the American National Standards Institute (ANSI).

Copper-covered steel

Copper-covered steel combines the conductivity and corrosion resistance of copper with the strength of steel. Three different manufacturing methods are used to bond a copper layer to steel:

- Molten welding
- Electroplating
- Metallurgical bonding

A copper-clad rod is rolled and drawn to the desired wire size by conventional methods and a predetermined copper-to-steel thickness ratio is maintained. The wire is normally furnished in:

- Two tempers: annealed and hard drawn
- Two conductivity grades: 30 and 40 percent

The annealed form of copper-clad steel is specified where flexibility is required. Although the soft steel core is nearly as pliable as annealed copper, it has almost twice the tensile strength of copper. (55,000 psi). This value is comparable to that of medium hard-drawn copper (60,000 psi).

Hard-drawn, copper-covered steel is selected where greater strength is required and slightly stiffer wire is acceptable. Hard-drawn, 40-percent-conductivity copper-covered steel has more than three times the tensile strength of annealed copper (115,000 psi vs. 36,000 psi). However, this value increases to 127,000 psi for hard-drawn 30-percent-conductivity copper-covered steel.

Note that the actual conductivity of copper-covered steel depends on the frequency of the signal being conducted. At high frequencies, its conductivity is comparable to copper because electron conduction occurs through the copper-coated "skin" on the surface of the conductor, rather than in the steel core of the wire. This phenomenon is known as the "skin effect." However, at low 50/60 Hertz line power frequencies, conduction occurs through the steel core, which has a conductivity that is only 30 to 40 percent of equivalent AWG copper wire.

To convert the weight and resistance of copper wire to values for equivalent-sized copper-covered steel (CCS) wire, multiply the copper weight and resistance by the following factors:

Weight: 0.93

Resistance of CCS (30 percent conductivity): 3.3

Resistance of CCS (40 percent conductivity): 2.5

The appendix contains a table of properties of high-strength copper-covered steel.

High-strength alloys

High-strength copper alloy wires are used in applications where high strength is required. However, copper-covered steel would be unsatisfactory; for equivalent conductivity, the diameter would be too large and the weight excessive. As can be seen from TABLE 1-1, these alloys offer higher tensile strength than copper-covered steel. Also, the conductivity of these alloys is only about 15 to 20 percent lower than copper.

However, these alloys are more expensive than copper-covered steel wires. Because of their superior size/weight characteristics, these alloys are most likely to be specified for military aerospace applications. The high-strength alloys include:

- Cadmium-chromium copper.
- Cadmium copper.
- Chromium copper
- Zirconium copper.

Of these, cadmium-chromium copper has the highest conductivity, 85 percent. The properties of this alloy remain substantially unchanged after exposure to temperatures as high as 313 °C (600 °F) and it is capable of continuous operation at temperatures up to 260 °C (500 °F). The alloy retains its tensile strength, conductivity, and ductility at 400 °C (752 °F).

As can be seen in TABLE 1-1, the tensile strength of high-strength copper alloy conductors is comparable to that of copper-covered steel, but it is superior to reinforced wire—made either as one steel wire in seven copper strands or as three steel wires in 19 copper strands.

Cadmium copper is satisfactory for low-temperature applications because it softens on prolonged exposure to temperatures of about 175 °C (345 °F). Cadmium copper, chromium copper, and zirconium copper are usually silver coated.

Table 1-1. Physical Properties of Conductor Materials.

Conductor Material	Conduct. Min. (%)	Tensile Strength (psi)	Continuous Operating Temp. C	Relative Weight
Copper				
Annealed, bare	100	36,000	150	1.00
Annealed, T.C.	100	36,000	150	1.00
Annealed, S.C.	102	36,000	200	1.00
Annealed, N.C.	96	36,000	260	1.00
Med.Hrd.drawn, bare	97	60,000	150	1.00
Hd.drawn, bare	96	97,000	150	1.00
Copper-covered steel				
Annealed bare	40	55,000	200	.93
Annealed, S.C.	40	55,000	200	.93
Hard drawn, bare	40	115,000	200	.93
Hard drawn, bare	30	127,000	200	.93
High-strength alloy				
Cadmium chrome cu.	85	58,000	200	.98
Cadmium cu., S.C.	80	55,000	200	.98
Chrome, cu., S.C.	85	58,000	200	.98
Zirconium cu., S.C.	85	55,000	200	.98

T.C. - Tin coated   S.C. - Silver coated   N.C. - Nickel coated

Aluminum

Aluminum has many properties that are similar to copper: ductility, malleability, and thermal conductivity. However, its electrical conductivity is only about 60 percent of copper. Nevertheless, aluminum is rarely used as a conductor in electronics, except for noncritical ground-wire applications.

Because of its lower conductivity, aluminum wires must be about 50 percent larger in diameter than equivalent copper wires. This drawback is partially offset by the reduced weight of aluminum. However, aluminum conductors cannot be bonded with conventional lead-tin eutectic soldering methods. In addition, aluminum poses a constant threat of galvanic corrosion.

Properties of conductor materials

Density is a material property that is measured in weight per unit volume. For example, the density of annealed copper is 8.89 grams per cubic centimeter or 0.321 pounds per cubic inch.

Resistivity is the electrical resistance of a conductor of unit length and unit cross-sectional area (volume resistivity) or unit length and unit weight (mass resistivity). Resistivity units are based on the International Annealed Copper Standard (IACS), which was adopted by the International Electrotechnical Committee (IEC) in 1913.

100% Conductivity $= 1/58$ ohm-millimeter^2/meter at 20 °C (68 °F)

Volume resistivity $= 0.017241$ ohm-millimeter^2/meter

Mass resistivity $= 0.15328$ ohm-grams/meter^2

As a result of these definitions, a copper wire that is one meter long and weighs one gram would have a resistance of 0.15328 ohm. Volume and mass resistivity at 20 °C in various units are listed in TABLE 1-2.

Table 1-2. Volume and Mass Resistivity Units at 20°C.

Volume Resistivity	Mass Resistivity
0.017 ohm-mm² / meter	0.153 ohm-gram/meter²
1.724 microhm-cm	875.20 ohm-pound/mile²
0.679 microhm-inch	
10.371 ohm-circular mil/ft	

Temperature coefficient of resistance

The direct current resistance of copper wires varies with temperature, in accordance with the formula:

$$R_t = R_o [1 + \alpha (t - t_o)]$$

where: R_t = Resistance measured at temperature t
   R_o = Resistance at reference temperature t_o

α = Temperature coefficient of resistance at t_o
t_o = Reference temperature

α = 0.0039 per degree C (0.0022 per degree F) for copper with 100 percent conductivity at 20 °C (68 °F). Because the temperature coefficient is proportional to conductivity, it can be calculated for any temperature or for copper of any conductivity from the following formulas:

$$\alpha t = \frac{0.0407}{\text{ohms (mil, foot) at } t\,°C}\,/°C \quad \text{or} \quad \frac{0.0226}{\text{ohms (mil, foot) at } t\,°C}\,/°F$$

TABLE 1-3 shows the multiplying factor to be used when converting the resistance value at the measured temperature to the corresponding resistance value at 20 °C.

Table 1-3. Multiplying Factors To Convert Resistance Values.

	To reduce resistance to 20°C (68°F)				
Copper temp. °C	°F	Multiplying Factor	Copper temp. °C	°F	Multiplying Factor
0	32	1.084	45	113	0.912
5	41	1.061	50	122	0.896
10	50	1.040	55	131	0.881
15	59	1.020	60	140	0.866
20	68	1.000	65	149	0.852
25	77	0.981	70	158	0.838
30	86	0.963	75	167	0.825
35	95	0.945	80	176	0.812
40	104	0.928			

Current carrying capacity

Current carrying capacity (ampacity) is the current that a conductor can carry before its temperature rise exceeds a preset limit. It is influenced by many factors including:

- *Conductivity of the conductor material.* Steel is 30 to 40 percent as conductive as the same AWG-size copper wire; a high-strength copper alloy is 80 to 85 percent as conductive.

- *Cross-sectional area of the conductor.* The larger the conductor diameter, the greater its current-carrying capacity. Stranded and solid conductors of the same gauge have slightly different current-carrying capacities because of differences in their circular mil areas.

- *Ambient temperature or temperature of the surrounding air.* A high ambient temperature reduces the amount of heat required for the conductor to reach the maximum temperature rating of the insulation. Thus, the ampacity is lowered.

- *Insulation type.* The heat conductivity of the insulation varies with the material. Conductor temperatures should not be allowed to exceed the insulation's maximum temperature rating. A higher rated insulation should be specified where the ambient temperature could be within 10 °C of the insulation's rated temperature.

- *Number of conductors.* Single conductors have a higher ampacity rating than the same AWG conductors in multiconductor cable. Insulated wires and jacketing can limit the circulation of cooling air around each conductor.

- *Installation environment.* Heat dissipation by convection or radiation can be assisted with fans, blowers, or air conditioning.

- *Installation method* (suspension in air, location in conduit, tray or plenum, or direct burial in the earth). Bundling, stacking, and spacing affect the conductor's heat dissipation.

- *Amperage.* Heat increase is a function of the square of the applied current. Thus, the more the current, the more the heat.

TABLE 1-4 shows the approximate amperage required to raise the temperature of a single copper conductor in free air from a 30 °C ambient to the temperature rating of commonly used wires and cables. So many possible variations exist when calculating ampacities that no single table or graph can encompass them all.

Table 1-4. Current-Carrying Capacity of Copper Conductors.
(Single Conductor in Free Air @ Ambient Temperature 30°C)

AWG Size	80 °C	90 °C	105 °C	125 °C	200 °C
30	2	3	3	3	4
28	3	4	4	5	6
26	4	5	5	6	7
24	6	7	7	8	10
22	8	9	10	11	13
20	10	12	13	14	17
18	15	17	18	20	24
16	19	22	24	26	32
14	27	30	33	40	45
12	36	40	45	50	55
10	47	55	58	70	75

(Amperes per conductor, Copper temperature)

Figure 1-1 is an alternate method for calculating current-carrying capacity. It shows the current necessary to raise the temperature of copper conductors in free air at an ambient temperature of 25 °C by a fixed increment. These values are an approximation because actual temperature rise is influenced by insulation heat transfer characteristics.

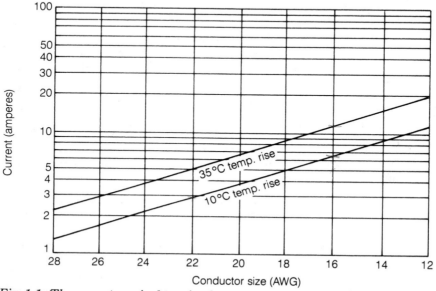

Fig. 1-1. The current required to raise the temperature of copper conductors in air to an ambient temperature of 25 °C by a fixed amount.

TABLE 1-5 lists the correction factors to be used when estimating the current carrying capabilities of cables. As the number of conductors in a cable increases, current-carrying capacity increases.

Table 1-5. Correction Factors for Current-Carrying Capacity.

Number of Conductors	Multiplying Factor
1	1.6
2-3	1.0
4-5	0.8
6-15	0.7
16-30	0.5

Note: Shields count if they are used as
      conductors

Rating the ampacity of a conductor is an inexact procedure. Any values that are obtained by tables, graphs, and empirical data can be further derated to provide an even greater margin of service life for the cable in the end-use equipment or system. Values should be established only after a conductor is considered in a specific environment.

Stranded conductors

Most of the conductors used in electronic wire and cable today are stranded; two or more thin wires are twisted together to form a unit with a larger cross-section area. Three practical considerations for specifying stranded conductors are:

1. *Conductor flexibility.* Stranded wire is more flexible than solid wire of equivalent size, which makes installation easier.

2. *Flex life.* Stranded wire can withstand far more vibration and bending before fracture than solid wire.

3. *Surface damage.* Scratches or nicks on one or more strands of a stranded conductor are less likely to become sites for conductor fracture than in a solid wire.

The stranded conductors used in electronic applications where they are subjected to little or no flexing have 7, 10, 16, or 19 strands. Those that will be subjected to moderate flexing have 7, 10, 16, 19, 26, 41, or 65 strands. TABLE 1-6 shows how the number of strands relates to the severity of the cable duty. The number of strands increases significantly with AWG, but the strand gauge increases at a slower pace. At any given wire gauge, the greater the number of strands (with a corresponding decrease in the individual strand diameters), the more flexible and costly the conductor.

Table 1-6. Stranding Related to Severity of Conductor Duty.

AWG	Fixed Service	Moderate Flexing	Severe Flexing	Most Severe
26	7 × 34	7 × 34	10 × 36	Braid
24	7 × 32	7 × 32, 10 × 34	19 × 36, 45 × 40	Braid
22	7 × 30	7 × 30, 19 × 34	19 × 34, 26 × 36	Braid
20	7 × 28, 10 × 30	7 × 28, 10 × 30 19 × 32, 26 × 34	26 × 34, 42 × 36	105 × 40
18	7 × 26, 16 × 30	16 × 30, 41 × 34	41 × 34, 65 × 36	63 × 36
16	19 × 29	19 × 29, 26 × 30	65 × 34, 104 × 36	105 × 36
14	19 × 27	19 × 27, 41 × 30	104 × 34	168 × 36
12	19 × 25	65 × 30	165 × 34	259 × 36

The table also shows some alternatives for achieving equivalent AWG for the most commonly used conductor sizes. For severe flexing applications, 104 or even 165 strands might be used. Nevertheless, with the most widely used gauge sizes, conductors with 7 or 19 strands are usually specified. Because the insulation type and thickness also affect flexibility, this factor must be considered when selecting a conductor for any specific application.

Effects of stranding

Slight changes in the properties of conductors result from the stranding operation:

- Work hardening can increase resistance.
- Stretching can reduce diameter and increase resistance.
- The helical paths of the strands increase conductor length; thus, both resistance and weight increase.

In all conductors, weight and resistance are proportional to the circular mil area. In stranded conductors, weight and resistance depend on the number and diameter of component strands. Because the circular mil areas of stranded wires only approximate the solid wire equivalents, these properties are approximations. Concentric stranding, based on the bundling of 7, 19, 37, or 61 strands, will show greater deviations in weight and resistance than bundled-wire conductors, consist of a solid wire whose number can be adjusted to produce a nearly equal area.

The following formulas are useful when calculating stranded conductor weight and maximum resistance:

$$\text{Weight:} \quad W = wKN$$

$$\text{Resistance:} \quad R = \frac{10.37K}{10NC\,(d^2)}$$

where: C = Minimum conductivity (in percentage) permitted by the applicable ASTM specification for the diameter and material involved.

d = Minimum single-strand diameter (in inches) permitted by the applicable ASTM specification.

K = Stranding factor (TABLE 1-7)

N = Number of strands in the conductor.

R = Maximum conductor resistance of stranded conductor (in ohms/1000 feet).

w = Nominal weight of a single strand (in pounds /1000 feet).

W = Nominal weight of finished conductor (in pounds /1000 feet).

Strand construction

Equivalent gauge

To determine the gauge of a stranded conductor, multiply the circular mil area of an individual strand by the number of strands. The total circular mil area should be at least 98 percent of the circular mil area of the equivalent solid wire size.

Lay

The *lay* of any helical element of a conductor is the axial length of a turn of the helix of that element. Thus, if a single conductor component strand is unwound, the lay in inches will be that length—measured along the axis of the conductor that is required for that wire to make one complete turn around the axis of the conductor. Usually the number of turns in one foot of conductor is measured to allow for normal manufacturing variations. Lay lengths are expressed as decimals or fractions (e.g., 0.33 or 1/3).

In general, the lay lengths of most wire and cable made in the United States conform to the latest revision of ASTM specification, B-286. Conductors with short lay lengths are less likely to untwist or flare when the insulation is stripped.

The outer layer of stranded conductors is usually left-hand lay (FIG. 1-2). The direction of lay is the lateral direction in which the strands of the conductor run over the top of the conductor as they recede from an observer who

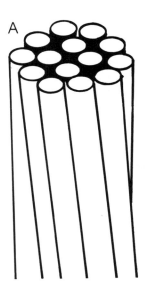 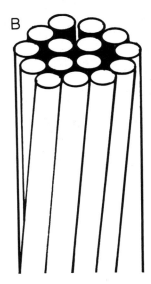

Fig. 1-2. Cable lay, left hand (A) and right hand (B).

looks along the axis of the conductor. Right-hand lay conductors usually must be requested.

Physical properties

The component conductor wire strands are twisted so that the length of an individual strand is greater than the length of the conductor. As a result, the weight and resistance of stranded conductors are greater than the equivalent AWG size of solid wire as shown in TABLE 1-7. A higher resistance is conspicuous in very flexible conductors, which have large numbers of tin-coated strands, because of the significant increase in the tin-to-copper ratio.

Stranded conductor construction

Bunch stranded conductors consist of many wire strands (with the same diameter) twisted together in the same direction, without regard to the geometric arrangement of the individual strands. This conductor is not likely to have a uniform cross section because the strands tend to cross over each other and migrate from one layer to another during the twisting operation. As shown in TABLE 1-6, common constructions have 7, 10, 16, 19, 26, 41, and 65 strands. Bunch stranding, as shown in FIG. 1-3, is used where low cost is important.

Table 1-6.
Stranding Factors.

No. Strands	Factor
7	1.03
19	1.04
37	1.05
133	1.06
>133	1.07

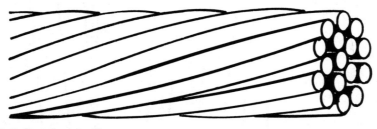

Fig. 1-3. Bunch stranding.

True concentric stranded conductors (FIG. 1-4) consist of a central wire that is surrounded by one or more layers of helically laid strands with a reversed direction of lay, and an increased length of lay, for each successive layer.

Equilay stranded conductors (FIG. 1-4) consist of more than one layer of helically laid strands, with a reversed direction of lay and the same length of lay for each successive layer.

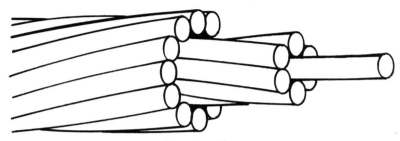

Fig. 1-4. True concentric and equilay stranding.

Unidirectional concentric stranded conductors (FIG. 1-5) consist of a central wire, surrounded by one or more layers of helically laid strands, with the same direction of lay, and an increased length of lay, for each successive layer.

Unilay stranded conductors (FIG. 1-5) consist of more than one layer of helically laid wires, with the same direction of lay, and the same length of lay, for each successive layer.

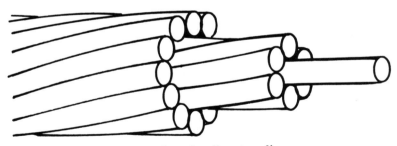

Fig. 1-5. Unidirectional concentric and unilay stranding.

The four types of stranding described (true concentric, equilay, unidirectional concentric, and unilay) have helically laid cores that are surrounded by layers of helically laid wires. Their similarities and differences are more easily understood by referring to TABLE 1-8 on helically laid stranded-conductor construction.

True concentric, unidirectional concentric, equilay, and unilay stranded-conductor construction are more expensive than bunch-stranded. True con-

Table 1-8. Helically Laid Stranded Conductor Construction.

| | Successive layers over core | | | |
| | Lay direction | | Lay length | |
Type	Same	Reversed	Same	Increased
True concentric		X		X
Equilay		X	X	
Unidirectional concentric	X			X
Unilay	X		X	

centric and equilay stranded (with reversed direction) conductors have the greatest mechanical strength and best crush resistance. Unilay stranding provides the smallest diameter at the least weight.

All four of these conductors have a nearly circular cross section so they can be more uniformly centered in the insulation than bunched wire. True concentric stranding, with a cross section that is closest to circular, is recommended for high-voltage cables because the high-strand concentricity reduces inter-strand corona.

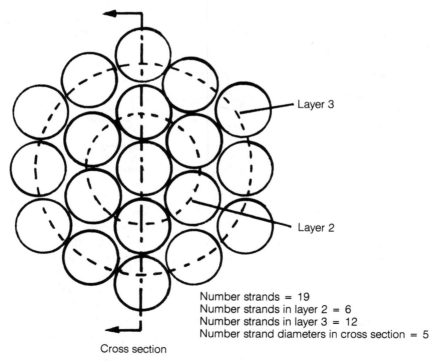

Layer 3

Layer 2

Number strands = 19
Number strands in layer 2 = 6
Number strands in layer 3 = 12
Number strand diameters in cross section = 5

Cross section

Fig. 1-6. Sectional view of a 19-strand helically laid conductor.

In these constructions, each successive layer has six wires more than the preceding layer. Figure 1-6 is a cross section of a 19-strand helically laid conductor with a central conductor (first layer), six strands in the second layer, and 12 strands in the third layer. It also shows that a vertical line drawn through the figure would intersect the five-strand diameter. TABLE 1-9 lists the relationships between the total number of strands, the number of strands per layer, and the number of strand diameters in cross section. Constructions with 7, 19, and 37 strands are most frequently specified.

Table 1-9.
Numerical Relationships among Helically Laid Conductors.

| | | Number of | |
Layer	Strands	Strands/Layer	Strands/Section
1	1	1	1
2	7	6	3
3	19	12	5
4	37	18	7
5	61	24	9
6	91	30	11
7	127	36	13

Conductor coatings

Bare copper oxidizes slowly at room temperature to form an outer skin of red-brown copper oxide. This reaction can be accelerated by increasing the ambient temperature. At temperatures above 180 °C (356 °F), the bright surface of clean copper wire blackens in minutes. Copper oxide film poorly conducts electricity and acts as a resistance element. Oxide on bare copper can be tolerated in many applications where the ambient temperature does not exceed 100 °C (212 °F) and current passing through the conductor is sufficient to overcome the resistance of the oxide. However, the oxide must be removed for effective solder adhesion.

In many other applications, the oxides must be prevented from forming to ensure reliable connections. The copper wire is coated with another metal that oxidizes more slowly at operating and processing temperatures to:

- Facilitate termination by soldering.
- Prevent copper oxidation at the high ambient temperatures permitted by the use of such high-temperature insulation materials as Teflon TFE.
- Lower resistance for such applications as termination by wire wrapping.

Tin is the most widely used coating for copper conductors, but silver and nickel are also employed. Occasionally other coatings, such as combinations of silver and nickel, are specified. Stranded copper wires are available with tin, silver, and nickel coatings. TABLE 1-10 summarizes the available protective metal coatings.

Table 1-10. Protective Conductor Metal Coatings.

Material	Bare	Tinned	Silver	Nickel
Copper	X	X	X	X
Copper-covered steel	X		X	
High-strength copper alloy	X		X	X

Tin coating

Tinning the surface of copper conductors helps to make a sound lead-tin solder bond. *Tinned wires* are usually specified in applications where the wire is to be terminated by some soldering method. Tin coatings are suitable for conductors that are expected to function at temperatures less than 150 °C (302 °F). Although tin-coated copper wires are slightly more expensive than bare copper wires, this cost can be offset by time and labor savings in wire termination. For example, it might not be necessary to twist the strands manually and dip the ends in a pot of molten solder prior to soldering a termination in place.

Tin coatings increase the resistance of the finished wire because the tin thickness is constant for all wire sizes. Thus, the tin-to-copper ratio increases as wire size decreases.

Tinned copper

Tinned stranded copper wire is the most widely produced tinned conductor. Each strand of copper has a nominal coating of 40 microinches (0.000040 in.) of tin. This conductor meets ASTM specification B-33 and Federal Specification QQ-W-343. In this conductor, the individually tinned strands are twisted together.

Although tinned copper costs less than any other tin-coated conductors, it usually needs to be twisted and soft-solder dipped prior to termination. This coating is acceptable under UL, CSA, military, and most industrial specifications.

Silver coating

Silver-coated wires start as 18 AWG wires that have been electroplated with pure silver. The plated wire is then cold drawn to size and annealed. The minimum silver thickness on this conductor is 40 microinches. More expensive than tinned copper conductors of equivalent size, silver-coated conductors are recommended for wires that operate at temperatures of 150 to 200 °C (302-

392 °F). They are also useful in high frequency-applications because the higher conductivity of silver enhances the "skin effect"—the tendency of electron conduction to occur at the conductor's surface.

Silver-coated conductors are readily wet by soft lead-tin eutectic solder, which permits rapid soldering with handheld soldering irons and guns. However, prevent molten solder from *wicking* (when solder creeps under the insulation of the stranded conductor) because this action can reduce conductor flex life. Silver coatings will oxidize after a few hundred hours of exposure to temperatures of 250 °C (482 °F) or greater.

Nickel coating

Conductors that have been plated with a minimum of 50 microinches of nickel are recommended for Teflon TFE insulated hookup wire, which can operate for prolonged periods at temperatures from 200 to 260 °C (392-500 °F). Nickel coatings can also be used where silver coatings are objectionable because of possible lead-tin solder wicking. Ordinary lead-tin soft solder does not wet nickel as readily as it does tin or silver. Although lead-tin solder adhesion is good enough to make a satisfactory termination, the solder will not wick into the stranded conductor beyond the soldered joint. As a result, the flexibility of the conductor will not be impaired.

Nickel-coated conductor connections that are exposed to temperatures above the melting point of lead-tin solder, 400 to 420 °C (753-788 °F), require special soldering techniques. The term *nickel-clad* refers to conductors that have a much thicker coating of nickel—from 10 to 30 percent of the radius of the strand.

2

Insulation materials

Conductor insulation is *primary insulation* if it is applied directly over a conductor and it is a *jacket* or *sheath* if it is used to enclose and protect one or more insulated conductors. Primary insulation can be extruded as a viscous liquid over the conductor or it (in the form of tape) can be wrapped around the conductor. Primary insulation can be solid cellular or foamed plastic.

All suitable insulation materials are tough, flexible, and waterproof. These materials offer a relatively high dielectric strength and insulation resistance. Insulation materials that cover metallic conductors perform some or all of the following functions:

- Prevent accidental short circuiting of the bare conductor as a result of contact with an external conductor, either solid, liquid, or vapor.

- Isolate and physically separate two or more parallel conductors.

- Shield personnel and animals from accidental contact with live bare conductors.

- Eliminate possible damage and fire hazards to property by preventing contact with bare live and/or heated conductors.

- Protect metallic conductors from cut-through, abrasion, and crushing as a result of damage and degradation from externally applied heat, flame, oxidation, chemical reaction, and exposure to ultraviolet light.

- Form a rigid low-loss dielectric to separate conductors carrying high-frequency signals.

- Provide for conductor and cable flexibility at low ambient temperatures.

Solid insulating materials include natural materials (rubber) and synthetic polymers (polyvinyl chloride, polyethylene, polypropylene, polyamide, elastomers, and fluorocarbons). Synthetic polymers have been widely used to replace natural rubber as primary insulation on conductors for more than a half century. The use of these materials has continued to grow.

Cables that are insulated with synthetic polymers are tougher and have better high and low temperature properties than those that are insulated with rubber or other natural materials. Assuming that conductors have the same diameter or AWG, those with synthetic polymer insulation will have smaller outside diameters, will be lighter in weight, and will be able to carry higher current (higher ampacity); all of these qualities are desirable.

This chapter covers the properties of the various synthetic polymers and why some are preferable for primary insulation, some are preferable for jackets, and some are satisfactory in both applications. Some synthetic polymers are also used as separators and as substrates for aluminized foil that is used as shielding.

The electronic product packaging engineer or systems designer must consider the many requirements for wire and cable that have a direct impact on the choice of primary insulation, intermediate insulation, and jacketing. The circuitry or system must operate reliably when subjected to:

- High humidity
- High ambient temperature
- Thermal cycling
- Contact with chemically corrosive liquids
- Extreme mechanical stresses
- Possible electrical overloads

Nevertheless, even after the designer finds the best insulation for a specific cable application, this choice is usually reviewed for cost. The general rule for purchasing the most cost-effective wire and cable is to obtain the least expensive product that will perform the task reliably. This system might require compromises on insulation materials or even the acceptance of less-than-optimum insulation.

Every synthetic polymer has both desirable and undesirable characteristics. However, the most desirable properties are usually the most expensive. So, anyone who chooses cable should be familiar with the favorable and unfavorable characteristics of all widely used insulation materials.

In some cases, the best insulation is a composite of two or more synthetic polymers to benefit from the best properties of each. Examples are polyvinyl chloride (PVC) blended with polyamide (nylon) or Teflon TFE blended with polyamide. These composites can provide better performance than either polymer used by itself. Composite are compromises between what is theoretically possible and what is commercially available at reasonable cost.

Commercial wire and cable manufactures blend generic materials to form

Table 2-1. Properties of Conductor and Jacket Insulation.

Material	Max. Oper. Temp. °C	Dielectric K @ 1MHz	Specific Gravity
Polyvinyl chloride (PVC)			
Conventional	105	2.7	1.38
Semi-rigid	80	4.3	1.38
Irradiated	105	2.7	1.38
Polyethylene (PE)			
Low-density	80	2.3	0.92
Flame Retardant	80	2.5	1.30
Cellular	80	1.5	0.50
High-density	80	2.3	0.95
Cross-linked	150	2.5	1.20
Polypropylene			
Solid	90	2.3	0.91
Cellular	90	1.5	0.50
Fluorocarbons			
Teflon TFE	260	2.1	2.15
Teflon FEP			
Solid	200	2.1	2.15
Cellular	200	1.4	1.10
Teflon PFA	250	2.1	2.17
Tefzel ETFE	150	2.6	1.70
Kynar PVDF	135	6.4	1.76
Halar ECTFE	150	2.5	1.68
Hypalon	90	-	1.40
Kapton	200	2.4	1.67
Neoprene	90	-	1.45
Nylon	105	4.0	1.10
Polyester	150	2.8	1.40
Polysulfone	130	3.1	1.24
Polyurethane	80	-	1.12
Surlyn A	75	2.4	0.96
Silicone rubber	200	3.1	1.30
Thermoplastic elastomer	125	2.2	0.89

proprietary materials. These are given trade names, but the exact composition might not be identified. References to these materials are seen in wire and cable catalogs.

The many different materials discussed in this chapter are characterized by "typical" values in the tables and text. These values, which are based on laboratory tests, permit valuable comparisons to be made between plastic materials. The materials covered in this chapter are also subject to variations that are introduced when the materials are formulated. Thus, the values might vary in the literature. However, these comparisons are not necessarily valid under all field conditions. TABLE 2-1 lists four important properties of a wide selection of materials to convey the most significant differences in an easy-to-understand form restricted to:

- Maximum operating temperature, °C
- Dielectric constants @ 1 MHz
- Specific gravity

However, for more detailed information on the properties of any insulation material, the designer and engineer should examine data sheets that present more physical, thermal, and electrical data. Call or write the manufacturers of the materials or the wire and cable manufacturer.

The important physical properties of insulation are:

- Specific Gravity or weight per unit volume
- Durometer (hardness)
- Tensile Strength, psi (minimum)
- Elongation, percent (minimum)
- Abrasion resistance
- Cut-through resistance
- Water resistance

The important thermal properties are:

- Maximum operating temperature (°C)
- Solder iron resistance
- Flame resistance

The important thermal properties of insulation are:

- Dielectric constant (@ 1 MHz)
- Dissipation factor (@ 1 MHz)
- Volume resistivity (ohm-cm)
- Dielectric strength (volts/mil)
- Insulation resistance (megohms/1000 ft)

Insulation is subjected to many physical variables when it is applied to conductors or cables during the manufacture and later during the installation. As a result, the nominal characteristic values that are listed in the tables of this chapter are subject to change. Users should be aware of the kinds of changes in insulation properties that can occur when they are exposed to environmental extremes. It might be necessary, in some cases, to perform independent tests on samples of the insulated conductors and cable before deciding to purchase in volume. When possible, the tests should closely approximate the anticipated operating environment.

Definitions

Wire and cable manufacturers use many different terms to describe insulation materials in their catalogs and literature. Because some of the insulation materials are identified only by manufacturers' trade names, it might be necessary to call or write the company for the desired specifications. By contrast, technical information is readily available on the trade-named materials (e.g., Tefzel, Kynar, Halar) that are sold in bulk to the wire and cable companies.

The wire and cable glossary in this book contains the definitions of many of the terms that are used in the formulation and application of insulation. However, as an aid to readers, the most frequently used chemical terms are:

Plastics   Synthetic organic materials (resins or polymers) that soften under heat and pressure. Plastics can be extruded and molded to form protective insulation.

Monomer   A basic chemical unit that is used to form a polymer. Monomers appear repetitively, usually linearly, in the molecular structure of a polymer.

Polymer   A synonym for plastic, it is the result of a chemical union of one or more monomers.

Homopolymer   A chemical combination of the same kind of monomer. Two examples are polyethylene and Teflon TFE.

Copolymer   The chemical combination of two different monomers. The resulting substance has properties that differ from those obtained by mechanically mixing monomers. Two examples are Tefzel ETFE and Teflon FEP.

Polyallomer   A crystalline polymer that is produced from two or more monomers. Polyallomers differ from copolymers in physical structure and they require different polymerization techniques. For example, when prepared by standard methods, the ethylene propylene copolymer is an amorphous, rubber-like material. By contrast, the crystalline polyallomer can be easily extruded as a primary insulation over small-gauge conductors.

Terpolymer   The chemical combination of three different kinds of monomer. An example is ethylene-propylene terpolymer (EPT or EPDM).

Thermoplastics   Thermoplastics soften and flow when heated to a definite melting point. They become rigid when they are cooled. These plastics can be molded and shaped repeatedly by heating and cooling. This property permits the reuse of scrap, reject, and defective products, which minimizes waste from the molding process and reduces the cost of plastic products. Compared with thermosets, thermoplastics exhibit the following advantages:

- Have better electrical properties
- Accept brighter coloring in a wider range of shading

- Weigh and cost less
- Form thinner walls

However, the drawbacks of thermoplastics are that they:

- Are stiffer and less flexible than thermosets
- Are more brittle at low temperatures

Two thermoplastic materials are polyvinyl chloride (PVC) and polyethylene.

Thermosets Plastic materials that are soft and pliable during processing and can be molded and extruded. However, after molding or extrusion the materials set or cure, usually at a higher temperature. After curing or cross-linking, they cannot be softened by reheating and they become insoluable in most solvents. One thermoset material is Kapton Type F film.

Elastomer Plastic materials that can be stretched to at least twice their length and will snap back to original form at room temperature. Elastomers are an intermediate material class between thermosets and thermoplastics. They flow during forming operations, but are changed to an elastic or rubber-like state after curing or vulcanization. One elastomer is neoprene.

Cross-linking A bonding that occurs between polymer chains, which improves most mechanical and thermal properties of the material. Thermosets are cross-linked by curing. In addition, some thermoplastics commonly used as insulation on conductors have been improved by cross-linking. This process transforms thermoplastics into thermosets. Cross-linking is performed by two methods:

- Chemical reaction that increases electrical loss
- Irradiation with a high-energy electron beam

Cross-linking improves the following properties of plastics:

- Resistance to high temperature, including contact with molten lead-tin solder
- Flexibility at low temperatures
- Tensile strength
- Resistance to cut-through and chemical solvents

Polyethylene is most commonly cross-linked chemically, and polyvinyl chloride (PVC) is the most commonly cross-linked by irradiation.

Irradiation response Thermoplastics can be classified into three groups, based on their reaction to radiation:

1. Properties enhanced (PVC and both solid and cellular polyethylene).
2. Properties unchanged (polysulfone and composites of polyethylene and polyester).
3. Properties degraded (polypropylene, Teflon TFE, Teflon FEP, and nylon).

Oxygen index A percentage that indicates the concentration of oxygen in a material. Air at sea level contains about 21 percent oxygen, so any material with an oxygen index of less than 21 will burn readily in air. An oxygen index of 27 or greater is generally considered to be high enough to pass the UL Vertical Flame Test VW-1. Materials considered to be flammable that should be protected by proper jacketing include:

- Low-density, high-density, and cellular polyethylene with oxygen indexes of 18.
- Solid and cellular polypropylene with oxygen indexes of 18.

Materials with oxygen indexes high enough to pass standard flame tests include all of the fluorocarbon insulations, but specifically:

- Semi-rigid polyvinyl chloride with an oxygen index of 36
- Solid Teflon FEP with an oxygen index of 95
- Cellular Teflon FEP with an oxygen index of 40
- Kynar with an oxygen index of 44

Insulation classifications

Extrudable primary insulation Materials used as primary insulation combine good or excellent electrical properties with good or excellent mechanical properties. These materials can be extruded directly over the conductor. Examples are PVC, polyethylene, and fluorocarbons (such as Teflon FEP and Teflon PFA).

Jacket or sheath insulation Materials that provide secondary mechanical and chemical protection over insulated conductors, textile braid, metallic braid, foil shields, and other components (including fillers). Outer jackets can also cover inner jackets in breakout cables (see *jacket materials* in this chapter). Extrudable plastics, most widely used as jackets, include neoprene, Hypalon, ethylene-propylene rubber (EPR), polyurethane, thermoplastic elastomer (TPE), and polyamide (nylon).

Insulating tapes Insulating tapes are used as primary insulation on conductors in some telephone and power cables, but they are not generally used in
electronic cables. Tapes can also be used as separators in certain types of
cables. The plastics used to make these tapes include polyester, Kapton Type
F, and Teflon TFE.

Extrudable primary insulations

Polyvinyl chloride (PVC) Polyvinyl chloride (also called vinyl or PVC)
has become the standard insulation for wire and cable rated for less than 1000
volts. It is recommended for use under normal environmental conditions,
where cost is a consideration. TABLE 2-2 lists the typical properties of PVC
insulations. It is used for power supply and portable cords on consumer, commercial, and industrial electrical appliances and line-powered electronic equipment. It is also used in control and communications cables. Three types of
PVC are available:

1. Conventionally plasticized
2. Semi-rigid for use in thin-wall products
3. Irradiated cross-linked

Table 2-2. Typical Properties of Polyvinyl Chloride Insulation.

Property	Standard	Semi-rigid	Irradiated
Physical			
Specific gravity	1.38	1.38	1.38
Durometer hardness	A85-90	A90-96	A94-96
Tensile strength, psi	2100-2700	3200-4000	4500
Elongation, % (min.)	250-350	150-250	150-200
Abrasion resist.	Good	Good	Excell.
Cut-through resistance	Good	Good	Excell.
Thermal			
Max operating temp., C	105	80	105
Solder iron resist.	Poor	Poor	Excell.
Electrical			
Dielec. Const. @ 1 MHz	2.7	4.3	2.7
Volume resist. ohm-cm	5×10^{13}	1×10^{14}	2×10^{12}
Dielec. strength, V/mil	800-900	800-900	800-900

Benefits of all vinyl compounds are:

• Moderately high dielectric strength and insulation resistance
• Dielectric constant values from 3.5 to 6.5
• Tough with high-impact and tensile strength
• Resistant to abrasion, moisture, and flame

- Outstanding resistance to ozone, acids, alkalis, alcohols, most solvents, oils, gasoline, greases, and waxes
- Service temperatures from -55 to $+105\,°C$

Disadvantages of all vinyl compounds are:

- High capacitive and loss properties
- Tendency of plasticizers to migrate into adjacent insulations, degrading their properties
- Hardening and cracking as a result of plasticizer loss
- Poor flexibility at temperatures below $-50\,°C\ (-58\,°F)$

Vinyls can be formulated for required or optimum values to critical variables, without neglecting less-important qualities. These compounds are mechanical mixtures of resin, plasticizers, stabilizers, fillers, and modifiers. The quality and type of each of these ingredients affect the properties of the compound. The average vinyl compound consists of 50 percent resin and 25 percent plasticizer; the remaining 25 percent consists of other additives (stabilizers, fillers, and modifiers).

Resin used in PVC is usually a homopolymer of vinyl chloride, although copolymers of vinyl chloride and vinyl acetate are often used. The resin is transparent and rigid, so it must be plasticized to make it flexible. PVC compounds contain from 40 percent to 79 percent resin by weight. High percentages of resin yield tougher compounds, but high percentages of plasticizer result in more elastic compounds.

Plasticizers are used to soften rigid PVC resin for flexibility and workability or distensibility. Plasticizers have the greatest influence on:

- Cold bending
- Insulation resistance
- Elongation retention with aging
- Flame resistance

Plasticizers are grouped in families to provide the following characteristics:

- Phthalates provide high dielectric properties
- Adipates and sebacates enhance cold bending
- Phosphates enhance flame resistance
- Polymeric or resinous plasticizers (such as epoxies) provide better high-temperature aging

In practice, two or more plasticizers are used in varying proportions to achieve the desired qualities.

Stabilizers, including lead salts, retard or counteract any chemical degradation that occurs if the compound oxidizes during processing at elevated temperature.

Modifiers improve the insulation's qualities:

- Lubricants (such as stearic acid) improve the surface appearance of insulation and permit higher speed extrusion.
- Fillers (such as clay) improve the insulation's electrical properties and its resistance to abrasion and cut-through.
- Additives (such as carbon black) improve the insulation's conductivity and resistance to damage by ultraviolet rays.
- Pigments add color and are selected so they do not impair the insulation's electrical properties.
- Flame retardants (such as alumina trihydrate, antimony oxide, bromine, and chlorine) resist the spread of flame.
- Fungicides discourage the growth of mold.

Polyolefins

Polyolefins are polymers and copolymers of the ethylene family of hydrocarbons, including polyethylene (PE) and polypropylene. The term today generally refers to high- and low-density polyethylene and copolymers of ethylene and propylene.

Polyethylene (PE) Polyethylene is available in low and high-density, flame retardant, and cellular (foamed) forms. It is used as both primary insulation and as a jacket material in telephone, control, high-voltage, coaxial, submarine, and power cables; as well as in antenna lead-in wire. A wide selection of polyethylene has been developed to perform optimally in different applications. TABLE 2-3 lists the typical properties of polyethylene insulation. Low-density and high-density polyethylene exhibit the following desirable properties:

- Low dielectric constant that is stable over a broad range of frequencies (typically 2.3 in low-density and high-density, about 2.5 in flame retardant and cross-linked, and as low as 1.5 in flame retardant).
- Very high insulation resistance (typically above 10^{16} compared with 10^{12} to 10^{14} for PVC).
- Higher dielectric strength than PVC: 1000 – 1200 vs. 800 – 900.
- Flexibility; it can be prepared to range in stiffness from flexible to very hard, depending on molecular weight and density (low-density PE is most flexible).
- Good weathering if the PE compound is pigmented with carbon black or another material that blocks ultraviolet light.
- Outstanding resistance to acids, alkalies, and most organic chemicals.

- Resistant to moisture, so it is a suitable sealant against water, vapor, and gas.
- Lighter weight than PVC.
- Easily colored with pigments.

The disadvantages of polyethylene include:

- Support of combustion (it has a low oxygen index of 18, but additives can improve its flame-retardant properties—with some sacrifice in electrical and physical properties).
- Poor weathering or resistance to ultraviolet light if unpigmented. This results in crazing, cracking, and loss of flexibility after long-term exposure to sunlight.
- Higher cost per pound than PVC.
- Even low-density PE is stiffer than PVC.

Table 2-3. Typical Properties of Polyethylene Insulation.

Property	Low Density	High Density	Flame Density	Cross-Link	Cellular
Physical					
Specific gravity	0.92	0.95	1.30	1.26	0.50
Durometer hardness	D45	D58	D55	D51	-
Tensile strength, psi	2200	3000	1800	2200	600
Elongation, % (min.)	600	250	250	500	300
Abrasion resist.	Good	Good	Good	Fair	Poor
Cut-through resist.	Good	Good	Good	Fair	Poor
Thermal					
Max operating temp. °C	80	80	80	150	80
Solder iron resist.	Poor	Poor	Poor	Good	Poor
Electrical					
Dielec. const. @ 1 MHz	2.3	2.5	1.5	2.3	2.5
Volume resist. ohm-cm	$>10^{16}$	$>10^{16}$	$>10^{16}$	10^{13}	-
Dielectric, V/mil	1200	1200	1000	1000	500

Low-density polyethylene compared with high-density polyethylene has the following characteristics:

- Tough and flexible in thin sections
- Less prone to stress fracture

High-density polyethylene (formed by low-pressure processing) compared with low-density polyethylene has the following characteristics:

- More rigidity
- Greater surface hardness, tensile strength, and toughness

- Better resistance to chemicals and abrasion
- Less permeability to water vapor
- Lower temperature coefficient (expansion)

Flame-retardant polyethylene contains additives to counteract its poor flame resistance. These additives reduce tensile strength by about 30 percent. They slightly increase the dielectric constant.

Cross-linked polyethylene (XLPE, XLP, X-Link PE) uses both chemical and irradiation methods to change it from a thermoplastic to a thermoset without altering most of its characteristics. As compared with standard polymers, it has the following advantages:

- Maximum operating temperature is increased to 150 °C from 80 °C (302 °F from 176 °F)
- Greater resistance to stress fractures, ozone, cut-through, solvents, and soldering iron temperatures
- Permits thinner conductor walls

Cross-linked polyethylene has the following disadvantages:

- Stiff, compared to neoprene and Hypalon
- Subject to fine-line rupture in high-voltage application

Cellular (foamed) polyethylene is produced by generating an inert gas within the compound during the extrusion process. Foaming can be controlled to yield a material with the lowest dielectric constant for any of the primary insulations. With a gas volume of 55 percent, a dielectric constant of 1.5 can be obtained (compared to a dielectric constant of 2.2 for Teflon TFE). The lower dielectric constant in coaxial cable, which is obtainable with cellular polyethylene, permits:

- Lower attenuation (while retaining characteristic impedance) and smaller outside diameter (by increasing the inner conductor diameter).
- Reduction in the outer diameter of the cable (while retaining its characteristic impedance and attenuation) by reducing the core diameter.

The disadvantage of cellular polyethylene is its ability to retain moisture, thus degrading attenuation. Cables with cellular PE must be adequately protected by a moisture barrier, such as aluminum conduit or an aluminum jacket.

Polypropylene Propylene-ethylene copolymer or polypropylene has electrical properties that are similar to polyethylene. Propylene, like ethylene, is a member of the olefin (alkene) family and has similar characteristics. TABLE 2-4 lists the typical properties of polypropylene insulation. Solid polypropylene exhibits the following physical properties:

- The dielectric constant of 2.3 is stable over a wide range of frequencies and temperatures
- Lowest density of all thermoplastics (0.9)
- Coefficient of friction equal to that of nylon (0.12)
- Highly resistant to cracking from environmental stress
- Constant dissipation factor over the operating temperature range that varies only slightly with frequency
- Maximum operating temperature rating of 80 °C (176 °F)

Table 2-4. Typical Properties of Polypropylene Insulation.

Property	Solid	Cellular
Physical		
Specific gravity	0.91	0.45 - 0.80
Durometer hardness	—	D58
Tensile strength, psi	3600	600 - 1000
Elongation, % (min.)	>600	100 - 200
Abrasion resist.	Good	Poor
Cut-through resist.	Good	Poor
Thermal		
Max operating temp. °C	80	80
Solder iron resist.	Poor	Poor
Electrical		
Dielec. const. @ 1 MHz	2.3	1.45 - 1.75
Volume resist. ohm-cm	10^{17}	$>10^{16}$
Dielectric, V/mil	850	200 - 500

Polypropylene offers qualities that are superior to high-density polyethylene including:

- Hardness, making it suitable for thin-wall insulations
- Better resistance to heat, moisture, abrasion, and chemicals
- Higher tensile strength

No known solvents exist for polypropylene at room temperature. At high temperatures, it remains resistant to acids, alkalies, and base solutions. However, some chemicals (such as chlorinated hydrocarbons) can soften polypropylene and cause it to swell slightly at high temperatures.

Ultraviolet radiation will degrade unpigmented polypropylene, but the addition of carbon black will screen it out. Polypropylene will burn, but flame-retardant formulations exist. However, additives to reduce the spread of flames also reduce its dielectric strength and heat resistance, and limit the application of these compounds.

Cellular (foamed) polypropylene is used to insulate telecommunication and coaxial cable because it has approximately 50 percent of the capacitance and attenuation of comparable polyethylene-insulated cable. Cellular polypropylene also has the following desirable properties:

- Dielectric constant of 1.45 to 1.75 at 1 MHz that is stable over a wide range of frequencies and temperatures.
- Permits either reduction of cable diameter or reduction of larger diameter central conductors in coaxial cable to hold electrical characteristics constant.

Fluorocarbons

Fluorocarbons are resins that contain fluorine in their molecular structures. Fluorine replaces the hydrogen atoms in the ethylene monomer. This replacement is complete in the Teflon polymers—DuPont's trade name for its fluorocarbon resins Teflon TFE, FEP, and PFA. In Kynar and Tefzel (other DuPont fluorocarbons) the hydrogen atoms are partial replaced. Fluorocarbons generally have excellent electrical characteristics. However, they are not suitable for long-term operation at voltage stress levels high enough for corona discharge to occur; their performance is poor in ionizing fields. TABLE 2-5 lists typical properties of the fluorocarbon insulations.

Table 2-5. Typical Properties of Fluorocarbon Insulation.

Property	Teflon TFE	Teflon FEP	Teflon PFA	Tefzel ETFE	Kynar PVDF	Halar ECTFE
Physical						
Specific gravity	2.25	2.15	2.17	1.70	1.76	1.68
Durometer hardness	D52	D59	D60	D75	D80	D75
Tensile strength, psi	4500	3100	3500	6000	5000	7000
Elongation, % (min.)	300	300	300	150	250	200
Abrasion resist.	Fair	Fair	Good	Good	Excel	Fair
Cut-through resist.	Fair	Fair	Fair	Excel	Excel	Good
Thermal						
Max operating temp. °C	260	250	250	150	135	150
Solder iron resist.	Excel	Poor	Poor	Poor	Poor	Poor
Electrical						
Dielectric K. @ 1 MHz	2.1	2.1	2.1	2.6	6.4	2.5
Volume resist. ohm-cm	$>10^{18}$	$>10^{18}$	10^{18}	10^{16}	10^{14}	$>10^{15}$
Dielectric, V/mil	1000	1000	1000	1000	950	-

Teflon TFE (tetrafluoroethylene), Teflon FEP (fluorinated ethylene propylene), and Teflon PFA (perfluoroalkoxy) all exhibit the following desirable properties:

- Outstanding electrical characteristics
- High temperature resistance

- Resistance to virtually all chemicals
- Excellent flame resistance
- Retention of strength, flexibility and dielectric properties at temperatures to 540 °C (1000 °F) for short periods

However, these fluorocarbon insulations lack:

- Good high-voltage characteristics
- Good resistance to nuclear radiation

Teflon TFE has a maximum operating temperature of 260 °C (500 °F). It is unaffected by molten solder and soldering-iron temperatures. So, TFE-insulated conductors can be spaced closer together than those insulated with other materials without the risk of damaging the insulation during terminal or connector soldering steps. The desirable characteristics of TFE insulation include:

- Low dielectric constant of 2.1 that does not change with temperature or frequency.
- Dissipation factor that is unaffected by temperature. It varies slightly between 60 and 10 MHz, remaining less than 0.0002 over this range.

These TFE properties made possible the manufacture of miniature coaxial cables.

The disadvantages of Teflon TFE include:

- Price is 8 to 10 times greater per pound than PVC.
- Lengths are limited to those practical with batch processing by hydraulic ram extrusion.
- Requires silver or nickel plating on all copper conductors to be insulated. Temperatures in excess of 600 °F are required to fuse the resin granules of TFE into a fluid mass that will flow over the conductor. This temperature would oxidize both bare copper and the tin on the tin-coated copper conductors.
- Poor cut-through resistance.
- Poor cold-flow properties.

Teflon FEP is a copolymer of tetrafluoroethylene and hexafluoropropylene. It was formulated as a thermoplastic to retain most of the properties of TFE, but make it is easier to extrude—because conventional extrusion processes can be employed. As a result, FEP insulated conductors can be produced in continuous lengths, reducing their cost. FEP will not even emit smoke when exposed to direct flame. It is suitable for use at temperatures of 200 °C (392 °F) and is chemically inert.

FEP and TFE both have the following properties:

- Specific gravity: ~ 2.15
- Dielectric constant: at 1 MHz: 2.1
- Volume resistivity: $> 10^{18}$ ohm-cm

FEP properties that nearly equal those of TFE are:

- Maximum operating temperature: for FEP it is 200 °C (392 °F), 60 °C lower than TFE's 260 °C.
- Dissipation factor @ 1 MHz: it is 0.0007 for FEP and 0.0002 for TFE.

Teflon PFA has the typical properties of other Teflon materials, but like FEP, it is a true thermoplastic. Because it can be extruded by conventional methods, PFA-insulated wire is available in long continuous lengths. PFA has an operating temperature of 250 °C (482 °F) and can withstand short-term exposure to temperatures in excess of 500 °F. However, PFA lacks TFE's resistance to direct soldering-iron temperatures. A benefit of PFA is that it can be applied to bare copper conductors, as well as those coated with tin, silver, and nickel.

Tefzel ETFE is a high-temperature fluorocarbon resin, a copolymer of ethylene and tetrafluoroethylene. Introduced by DuPont, it is 75 percent TFE by weight. It can withstand an unusual amount of physical abuse. Because it is extruded by conventional methods, it is available in long lengths. ETFE can be applied over all bare and plated conductors. It can also be cross-linked by radiation, transforming it into a thermoset material. Tefzel has a maximum operating temperature of 150 °C (302 °F), high enough to protect it from soldering-iron damage.

Halar ECTFE, introduced by the Ausimont Corp., has found limited use as a wire insulator. A copolymer of ethylene and monochlorotrifluoroethylene, it has a chemical structure similar to that of Tefzel, except that a chlorine atom has replaced one of Tefzel's four fluorine atoms. Halar's electrical, physical, and thermal properties are similar to those of Tefzel. The properties of Halar include:

- Maximum operating temperature of 150 °C (302 °F)
- Specific gravity of 1.68, lowest of any solid fluorocarbon
- Typical dielectric constant of 2.56 (at 1 MHz)
- Dissipation factor of 0.013 (at 1 MHz)

Kynar PVDF is a crystalline, high molecular-weight homopolymer of vinylidene fluoride introduced by Penwalt Corp. Its outstanding properties are:

- Maximum operating temperature of 150 °C (302 °F)
- Specific gravity of 1.76

- Typical dielectric constant of 6.4 (at 1 MHz)
- Great mechanical strength
- Superior resistance to abrasion and cut-through
- Self-extinguishing after flame removal and low-smoke emission
- Unaffected by long-term exposure to ultraviolet light
- High resistance to gamma radiation
- High resistance to corrosive chemicals
- Negligible moisture absorption
- Thermal stability

The disadvantages of Kynar are:

- Inherent stiffness
- High processing temperatures require the use of silver or nickel-coated copper conductors

Miscellaneous insulations

Polysulfone, introduced by Union Carbide, is a thermoplastic with satisfactory electrical and physical properties for most electronic wire and cable applications. It was first introduced as an insulation for wire wrapping computer backplanes because walls only 4 to 5 mils thick provided a tough protective coating. Polysulfone is a homopolymer of phenylene units linked by isopropylidene, ether, and sulfone groups. The sulfone group gives the polymer it thermal stability and oxidation resistance. The properties of polysulfone include:

- Maximum operating temperature of 130 °C (266 °F)
- Specific gravity 1.2
- Typical dielectric constant of 3.1 (at 1 MHz)
- Excellent resistance to cut-through and abrasion
- Nonflammable

The disadvantage of polysulfone is relatively poor resistance to solvents. It will swell or crack when cleaned with many of the solvents that are commonly used in the electronics industry.

Surlyn A is one of a family of thermoplastic resins, introduced by DuPont, that have many of the properties usually found in cross-linked polymers. The properties of Surlyn A include:

- Maximum operating temperature of 75 °C (167 °F)
- Specific gravity of 0.96
- Typical dielectric constant of 2.4 (at 1 MHz)
- Low-temperature flexibility

- High resistance to abrasion, cut-through, and stress fracture
- High resistance to oils, grease, and organic solvents

Silicone rubber, a thermosetting synthetic rubber, is used primarily as insulation. It is made from silicone polymers or gums, fillers, and a catalyst. This material offers better resistance to molecular degradation than organic plastics. Silicone rubber has the following properties:

- Maximum operating temperature of 200 °C (392 °F)
- Dielectric constant of 3.1 (at 1 MHz)
- Specific gravity of 1.3

The advantages of silicone rubber include:

- Low temperature range of − 80 °C (− 112 °F)
- Excellent low-temperature flexibility at − 90 °C (− 130 °F) compared to − 40 °C (− 40 °F) for most types of organic rubber
- Excellent resistance to soldering-iron heat, ozone, and corona
- Low moisture absorption
- Excellent radiation resistance
- Flame retardant, but burns to an insulating ash
- Resistant to ultraviolet light

The disadvantages of silicone rubber are:

- Low mechanical strength
- Poor resistance to abrasion
- Poor resistance to oils, solvents, and some strong acids
- Short shelf life in compound form
- Relatively high cost per pound compared to other thermosets

Polyester film is a tough, transparent material made from polyethylene terephthalate. It is used as a substrate in aluminized shield foil for electrical isolation and as a thermal barrier in cables. Polyester film is sold by DuPont under the trade name *Mylar* and by Celanese Corp. under the trade name *Celanar*. Its unusual characteristics include:

- Maximum operating temperature of 150 °C (302 °F)
- Tensile strength of 25,000 psi
- Dielectric strength of 7,500 volts per mil
- Excellent resistance to most chemicals and moisture

Kapton Type F is DuPont's trade name for *polyimide film*. When laminated with Teflon FEP resin, it forms a polyimide/fluorocarbon film, called Kapton

Type F. Tape made from the film can be used as insulation. It is very tough and can be heat sealed. Kapton Type F offers the following properties:

- Maximum operating temperature of 200 °C (392 °F)
- Specific gravity of 1.67
- Typical dielectric constant of 2.4 (at 1 MHz)
- Excellent resistance to abrasion, cut-through, and impact
- Very high resistance to degradation by oxidation, weathering, and all chemicals (except strong bases)
- High dielectric strength and insulation resistance
- Low dielectric constant and dissipation factors
- Excellent flame resistance
- High resistance to radiation

Jacket materials

Jackets or sheaths provide mechanical, thermal, chemical, and environmental protection for the insulated wires that they enclose. They aid installation when they enclose the components of a multiconductor cable. Most extrudable primary insulations can be used for jacketing. The selection of one jacketing material over another is dictated by the required operating characteristics and costs. TABLE 2-6 lists the typical properties of some jacket compounds. However, some materials (such as polyvinyl chloride, polyethylene, Kynar PVDF, Teflon FEP and Tefzel ETFE) are also used as jacketing materials.

Table 2-6. Typical Properties of Jacket Insulation Compounds.

Property	TPE Thermoplastic Elastomer	Nylon Polyamide	Neoprene	PU Polyurethane
Physical				
Specific gravity	1.20	1.13	1.45	1.20
Durometer hardness	A95	D85	A50	A82
Tensile strength, psi	2400	10,000	1800	4000
Elongation, % (min.)	700	300	450	500
Thermal				
Max operating temp. °C	125	105	90	75
Electrical				
Dielectric K. @ 1 MHz	2.2	4.0	—	—
Volume resist. ohm-cm	2×10^{16}	10^{12}	—	2×10^{11}
Dielectric, V/mil	500	400	—	400

The *rubber* and rubber-like materials that are suitable for jackets include natural rubber, neoprene, hypalon, ethylene propylene rubber, and silicone. Many formulations of natural rubber exist. Each formulation is used for a specific application. Some formulations are suitable for a −55 °C (−67 °F) minimum and others are suitable for +75 °C (167 °F) maximum.

The good to excellent properties of natural rubber include:

- Low temperature flexibility
- Abrasion resistance
- Electrical properties
- Water resistance
- Alcohol resistance
- Tensile strength
- Elasticity
- Tear strength
- Ability to rapidly recover from distortion.

Neoprene is the trade name for polychloroprene, a thermoset elastomer. It was the first synthetic rubber manufactured in the United States. Neoprene compounds suitable for cable jackets contain 40 to 60 percent polymer. The remainder consists of reinforcing fillers, plasticizers, vulcanizing agents, antioxidants, and other additives. Neoprene compares favorably to natural rubber and exhibits the following properties:

- Maximum operating temperature of 90 °C (194 °F)
- Specific gravity of 1.40
- Tensile strength of 1800 psi
- Elongation of 450 percent

Neoprene jackets, especially those that are reinforced, are tough and rugged. They are suitable for direct burial and aerial installation; they can be placed in conduit, trays, racks, or ducts. Neoprene is specified when a cable will be abused—frequently reeled and unreeled, kinked, twisted, and dragged. It is used in heater cords, sheathing for hi-voltage cables, and heavy-duty portable cords. The advantages of neoprene as jacketing include:

- Remains flexible at temperatures as low as −45 °C (−49 °F)
- Excellent resistance to flame (self-extinguishing)
- Superior resistance to gasoline, oil, solvents, oxidation, ozone, ultraviolet radiation, flexing, aging, and heat
- Lowest cost of the thermosetting rubber-like materials, but it costs more than PVC
- High abrasion resistance
- High tear strength
- Ability to rapidly recover from distortion

The disadvantages of neoprene include:

- Fair electrical properties
- Higher cost than thermoplastics
- Poor resistance to certain alcohols and benzols
- Difficult to color (other than black, brown, and gray)

Hypalon is DuPont's trade name for *chlorosulfonated polyethylene (CSPE, CPE)*, a rubbery polymer. It is made by adding chlorine and sulfonyl chloride to polyethylene. The polyethylene is then changed from a stiff plastic into an elastic substance. Hypalon has most of the properties of neoprene. It is used as a jacketing for automotive wire and cable. Many variations of the polymer can be produced and it can be formulated for composite extrusions. The advantages of Hypalon include:

- Maximum operating temperature of 90 °C (194 °F)
- Specific gravity of 1.4
- Better ozone, oxidation, and heat resistance than neoprene
- High tensile strength
- High resistance to abrasion and flex-fatigue
- Extremely good resistance to ultraviolet radiation, ozone, oil, and nuclear radiation oxidizing chemicals.
- Easily colored

The disadvantages of Hypalon include:

- Higher cost than PVC
- Stiffer than neoprene

Ethylene-propylene rubber (EPR, EPM) is a polyolefin made from the random copolymerization of ethylene and propylene. It has the best electrical characteristics of all polyolefins. The addition of fillers, antioxidants, flame retardants, cross-linking agents, and processing aids (in different amounts) also make EPR suitable as a primary insulating compound. EPR was designated as EPM for ethylene propylene monomer by the ASTM. It is also referred to as *ethylene-propylene copolymer*. The advantages of EPR/EPM also include:

- Outstanding resistance to weather, heat, and ozone
- Good resistance to compression, cutting, impact, tearing, and abrasion
- High resistance to acids, alkalies, organic solvents, and moisture; it is suitable for direct earth burial

The disadvantages of EPR/EPM are:

- Some formulations support combustion
- Poor resistance to certain hydrocarbons (such as gasoline, kerosene, and degreasing solvents)

Ethylene-propylene diene elastomer (EPDM) is a chemically cross-linked elastomer. The terpolymer was designated by ASTM as EPDM. The advantages of EPDM include:

- Maximum operating temperature of $+150\,°C$ ($+302\,°F$)
- Minimum temperature of $-55\,°C$ ($-67\,°F$)
- Good insulation resistance and dielectric strength
- Excellent abrasion resistance
- Better cut-through resistance than silicone rubber

The disadvantages of EPDM are similar to those of EPR/EPM.

The *polyurethanes* (see TABLE 2-6) include a broad range of materials in many forms. They are synthesized by reacting an aromatic di-isocyanate with a compound that contains hydroxyl groups. The properties of polyurethane can be varied by properly selecting the constituents. The polymers can take many forms: adhesives, potting compounds, varnishes, foams, elastomers, and thermoplastics. In the wire and cable industry, polyurethane is used primarily as a cable jacket material. As a class, they have relatively poor electrical properties. However, the thermoplastic and elastomer forms of polyurethane are tough and offer these excellent mechanical properties for jackets:

- Exceptional resistance to oil, radiation, fungus, oxidation, and ozone
- High tear strength
- Outstanding shock-absorption
- Water resistant
- Flame retardant
- Higher tensile strength and elongation than neoprene
- Better resistance to abrasion than neoprene
- Better low-temperature flexibility than neoprene
- Less expensive than neoprene

The major disadvantages of polyurethane jackets are:

- Poor resistance to acids, steam, and high temperatures
- More expensive than other jacketing materials.

Thermoplastic elastomer (TPE) offers the mechanical properties of vulcanized elastomers (thermoset rubbers) with the processing advantages of conventional thermoplastics (see TABLE 2-6). They do not require either compounding or vulcanization. In forming this elastomer, incompatible crystalline (polystyrene) and amorphous (polyethylene-butylene) regions are formed. Strong intermolecular forces cause the polystyrene segments to bond. The rigid polystyrene end segments are joined to the elastic polyethylene-butylene regions, which immobilizes them. This reinforced network structure behaves like a chemically cross-linked thermoplastic.

The advantages of TPE for jackets are:

- Good low-temperature flexibility at $-70\,°C$ ($-94\,°F$)
- Maximum operating temperature of $125\,°C$ ($252\,°F$)
- Excellent resistance to ozone and chemicals
- Dielectric constant of 2.2
- Good tensile strength and elongation
- Low water absorption

Nylon (polyamide) is the DuPont trade name for a family of polyamide resins (see TABLE 2-6). Because the formulations differ, family members have related, but not identical properties. Polyamides are formed either by the reaction of a diamine with a dibasic acid or by the polymerization of amino acids (or their derivatives). In the wire and cable industry, nylon is used primarily as a jacket on PVC-insulated wire—to improve the thermal properties. It is extruded in 2 to 6 mil wall thicknesses on typical conductors.

The advantages of nylon jackets on conductors include:

- High resistance to tensile forces, impact, flexing, abrasion, and cut-through because of its toughness
- Low friction coefficient
- Unaffected by most alkalies, coils, greases, and acids
- Inert to hydraulic fluid and aviation oil
- Burns slowly in direct flame, but is self-extinguishing

The disadvantages of nylon jackets include:

- Poor to fair electrical resistance
- Reduced cable flexibility
- Poor resistance to phenols, formaldehyde, hot benzyl alcohol, and hot nitrobenzine
- Tendency to absorb moisture
- High cost—approximately six times that of PVC

Polyvinyl chloride (PVC) jackets are specified for indoor and general-purpose use. PVC can be formulated for a wide range of applications. "Noncontaminating" jackets for coaxial cables are prepared so that the plasticizers will not migrate into the polyethylene core. The use of PVC eliminates temperature-related attenuation in long cable at 70 °C (158 °F) and higher. See *polyvinyl chloride* under *Extrudable Primary Insulations*.

Kynar or *polyvinylidene fluoride* has long been used as primary insulation on back panel wires. Kynar is tough and the qualities that make it suitable as primary insulation also make it useful for jacketing. *See Kynar* under *Extrudable Primary Insulations*.

Teflon FEP is used as jacketing on fire-alarm-system cables. It is suitable for jackets that will be exposed to temperatures up to 200 °C (392 °F). See *Teflon FEP* under *Extrudable Primary Insulations*.

Tefzel is also suitable for jacketing where the cable will be exposed to temperatures up to 150 °C (302 °F). Tefzel, with properties similar to Teflon FEP, is a fluorocarbon. See *Tefzel* under *Extrudable Primary Insulations*.

3

Conductor and
cable manufacture

The simplest insulated conductor consists of solid or stranded wire coated with primary insulation. Today, this insulation is usually a synthetic polymer such as solid-color PVC. Many conductors are used in this form as hook-up wire and backplane wire in wire wrapping. However, other forms of insulated wire undergo further processing steps:

- Color coding with stripes or spirals for identification.
- Imprinting with identifying legends.
- Direct jacketing over the primary insulation, thus improving the thermal or electrical characteristics and the mechanical protection.
- Shielding to prevent internal signal radiation or interference from external natural or man-made sources. The shield can also function as a second conductor as in coaxial cables.
- Cabling with similar or dissimilar insulated conductors for easier handling and installation.

The manufacture of simple insulated conductors, as well as the general procedures for the manufacture of cable (such as cabling, shielding, and jacketing), are covered in this chapter.

The primary insulation (or dielectric) that is applied to the uninsulated conductor is usually extruded. Today, textile braiding is rarely used as primary insulation for conductors in electronics applications. When used, it usually provides additional mechanical protection for extruded primary insulation on conductors.

Extrusion

Extrusion is the process of forcing molten plastic material through a die so that it adheres to an axially positioned conductor, which is moving through a container of molten plastic. The spacing between the external diameter of the conductor and the internal diameter of the die, in part, determines the wall thickness of the primary insulation.

In the most widely used process for extruding insulation uniformly on a single conductor (solid or stranded wire), a continuous conductor is pulled by a capstan through a chamber containing the molten plastic. The plastic adheres to the moving conductor, but it is applied uniformly to the conductor as it passes through the circular die. The soft extruded plastic solidifies on the wire after it passes through a water cooling bath.

The insulating plastic softens and eventually liquifies as it is forced down the length of the heated chamber by the rotating feed screw in the extrusion machine. Figure 3-1 shows the basic principle of insulation extrusion on a moving conductor as a continuous process. A wide selection of synthetic polymers can be applied using this method, including polyvinyl chloride (PVC), polyethylene (PE), polypropylene, and fluorocarbons (such as Teflon FEP). This method insulates wire at high speed with a controlled, uniform, homogeneous coating. It can also be used in the extrusion of jackets for single or multiconductor cables. The jacketing materials applied by extrusion include neoprene, thermoplastic elastomers, PVC, PE, and fluorocarbons.

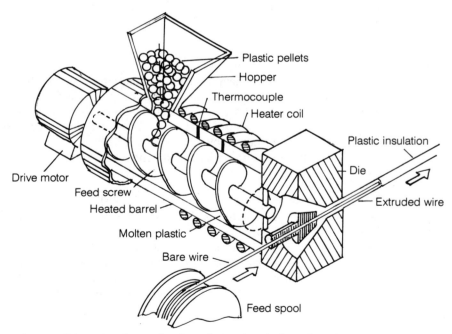

Fig. 3-1. Diagram of extruder for primary insulation of conductors.

Granulated thermoplastic and color chips (if the color of the thermoplastic is to be altered) are poured into the hopper of the extruder. The chips are then fed by gravity into the horizontal barrel of the machine. An axial motor drives the helical screw that forces the molten plastic to the end of the heated barrel. The action of the screw also blends the plastic pellets and pigment granules into a hot, homogeneous, viscous liquid.

The actual extrusion chamber is called the *crosshead* because it changes the direction of plastic flow by 90 degrees from the cylinder and screw. This chamber contains the conical tip and a funnel-shaped die—through which the wire is pulled. The tip positions the moving conductor concentrically, with respect to the die, as it is pulled through. The gap between the tip and the die is filled with molten plastic insulation. The alignment between the tip and the die affects the concentricity, shape, and final wall thickness of the extruded insulation. To achieve uniform wall thickness on the conductor, the following factors must be closely controlled:

- Speed of the capstan that pulls the wire through the crosshead and the cooling tank
- Speed of the extruder screw
- Inside diameter (ID) of the die
- Temperature of the uncoated conductor
- Temperature levels in each heating zone of the extruder barrel
- Concentricity of the wire within the die

Discontinuities, weak spots, and foreign materials in the insulation are detected with an in-line spark tester as the wire moves between reels. This test exposes the moving insulated wire to as much as 50 times its rated voltage for a specified amount of time. Defects in the coating are indicated by short-circuit burns. Visual and audible signals of these faults permit the extruder operator to take corrective action.

By pulling two conductors (in parallel) through a figure-8 shaped die, dual-conductor cable or cord (for portable appliances, television lead-in wires, etc.) can be formed. Similarly, by pulling multiple conductors in parallel through a shaped die, flat ribbon cable is formed. The die defines the webbing thickness and spacing between the parallel conductors, as well as the wall thickness around the individual conductors. Two or more insulated conductors can also be jacketed by extrusion methods.

Concentricity, minimum wall, and minimum average wall

The position of the conductor in its surrounding insulation is determined by measuring its concentricity or by determining its minimum- and maximum-wall thickness.

Concentricity

Military specifications for primary insulation typically state that, at any cross section, the minimum wall thickness must be:

- Not less than 41 percent of the difference between the diameter over the insulation and the diameter over the conductor.
- Not less than 70 percent of the wall thickness measured directly opposite to the minimum wall.

Minimum average wall thickness

The Underwriters Laboratories (UL) specifies both minimum average walls and minimum walls for its wire styles. The UL procedure for determining the minimum average wall is detailed in UL standards 62 and 758. Several micrometer readings must be taken along the length of the insulated wire and averaged (D). The conductor is then carefully removed from the sample length, similarly gauged, and an average (d) is obtained. The average wall (D-d/2) must equal or exceed the UL-required minimum.

Minimum wall thickness

This is not an average, but is the smallest individual wall thickness acceptable to UL. It is found by taking several readings with a pin-gauge micrometer around the circumference of a slit piece of insulation.

Cross-linking

When thermoplastic molecules are cross-linked, the material becomes a thermoset. This overcomes the characteristic of thermoplastics to soften with heat. There are many reasons why thermoplastics are easier to work with and cost less than thermosets, but heat softening is an undesirable insulation characteristic in many applications. Cross-linking is performed either by chemical methods or by irradiation.

Irradiation

In the irradiation process for cross-linking insulated wire, a high-voltage electron beam is scanned over the wire as it makes multiple passes under the scanner. Figure 3-2 is an isometric drawing that shows the most important equipment used in this process. Electrons, accumulating on the cathode of a power supply, are accelerated by an electromagnetic field and formed into a narrow electron beam. The beam is deflected periodically by an alternating field that sweeps over the area traversed by the moving wire.

The moving wire passes around multiple spools so that its entire circumference is exposed to the moving electron beam. The dosage is controlled by

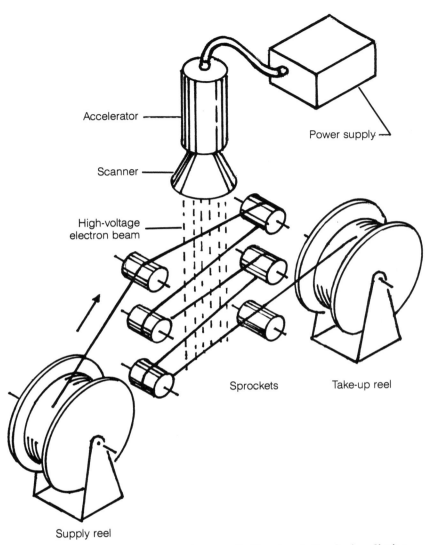

Fig. 3-2. Equipment arrangement for cross-linking insulation by irradiation.

varying the strength of the electron beam and the speed of the wire as it passes under the scanner. When high-energy electrons impinge on the long molecular chains of thermoplastics (such as polyethylene), some hydrogen atoms are displaced. Adjacent chains then cross-link at the locations of hydrogen deficiency and form permanent bonds. This new three-dimensional structural network is characteristic of thermoset plastics.

Polyvinyl chloride (PVC) must contain an additional chemical additive, called a *sensitizer*, to be cross-linked by irradiation. The cross-linking is done indirectly by a process, known as *grafting*. The additive, called a multi-functional monomer, creates highly active sites in the PVC chains when the PVC is exposed to high-energy electrons. These sites react with the monomer to form bridges between adjacent chains. This reaction gives PVC the characteristic three-dimensional structure of a thermoset.

Circuit identification

Visual conductor identification saves time and minimizes hook-up errors when terminating conductors in a multiconductor cable. If individual wires are coded by colors or labels, they can be readily identified during product or system assembly and testing. Coding also improves field equipment maintenance. Of the many possible methods for coding insulated wires, color coding predominates. Conductors are visually coded with a base insulation color, colored stripes, or with a legend printed on the insulation.

Color coding

Solid-color insulation can be color coded if there are generally 10 or less conductors. If 10 or more wires exist, the solid insulation can be striped with contrasting colors.

Solid colors   There are 10 standard color codes for both textile braid and plastic insulation (TABLE 3-1). In addition, a transparent "clear" and an unpigmented opaque "natural" color are available in some formulations for insulation. Some wire manufacturers offer variations of the 10 basic solid colors for customers who prefer not to use colored striping. However, these intermediate colors (lighter or darker shades of the base colors) could be confusing and difficult to read in dim light.

Table 3-1. Standard Color Code for Primary Insulation and Textile Braid.

Color	Designation
Black	0
Brown	1
Red	2
Orange	3
Yellow	4
Green	5
Blue	6
Purple (violet)	7
Gray (slate)	8
White	9

Striped combinations Most electronic cable specifications restrict solid color coding to the ten standard colors that are listed in TABLE 3-1. Therefore, contrasting stripes are generally used when more than 10 circuits are to be identified. Striped wires can even be specified for fewer than 10 circuits, because it might be more cost effective to specify two or more wires with the same base color.

In systems with more than 10 wires, striped wires can be specified by numerical designation that is based on TABLE 3-1. In this method, the first digit represents the base color of the insulation and subsequent digits represent the colors of the stripes. For example, 37 is a yellow wire with a violet stripe and 156 is a brown wire with green and blue stripes.

No standardized color code exists for electronic cables. As a result, many wire manufacturers have developed their own proprietary color code charts, which may be used by customers who have not developed in-house color-coding standards. Many of these color codes are based on the use of striped white insulated conductors for conductor position nine and higher.

Colored stripes on white insulation have the clearest color definition. Dark-colored stripes on dark-colored conductors are difficult to read in dim light and misreading could cause costly, time-consuming mistakes. However, industry-accepted color codes exist for process control cable. TABLE 3-2 is the Insulated Cable Engineers Association (ICEA) color code chart for ring band and spiral striping control cables.

Table 3-2. Color-Code Chart ICEA:
Insulated Cable Engineers Association for Ring Band and Spiral Striping.

Cond. No.	Color Code	Cond. No.	Color Code	Cond. No.	Color Code
1	Black	21	Orange-green	41	Green-white-blue
2	White	22	Black-white-red	42	Orange-red-green
3	Red	23	White-black-red	43	Blue-red-green
4	Green	24	Red-black-white	44	Black-white-blue
5	Orange	25	Green-black-white	45	White-black-blue
6	Blue	26	Orange-black-white	46	Red-white-blue
7	White-black	27	Blue-black-white	47	Green-orange-red
8	Red-black	28	Black-red-green	48	Orange-red-blue
9	Green-black	29	White-red-green	49	Blue-red-orange
10	Orange-black	30	Red-black-green	50	Black-orange-red
11	Blue-black	31	Green-black-orange	51	White-black-orange
12	Black-white	32	Orange-black-green	52	Red-orange-black
13	Red-white	33	Blue-white-orange	53	Green-red-blue
14	Green-white	34	Black-white-orange	54	Orange-black-blue
15	Blue-white	35	White-red-orange	55	Blue-black-orange
16	Black-red	36	Orange-white-blue	56	Black-orange-green
17	White-red	37	White-red-blue	57	White-orange-green
18	Orange-red	38	Black-white-green	58	Red-orange-green
19	Blue-red	39	White-black-green	59	Green-black-blue
20	Red-green	40	Red-white-green	60	Orange-green-blue

Braided stripes   Various stripes and patterns can be incorporated into textile braids: single-stripe, double-stripe, and even criss-cross patterns.

Inked stripes   Most stripes are printed directly on the plastic insulation with marking ink. Suitable insulated-wire marking inks must be:

- Firmly adherent to the plastic insulation
- Compatible with the plastic insulation
- Permanent
- Nonconductive
- Colorfast at high temperatures and in sunlight
- Resistant to most chemicals and solvents

Four patterns of inked stripes are used on insulated wires (FIG. 3-3):

- *Longitudinal*, with one or two lines printed along the entire length of the wire.
- *Spiral*, with up to three different colors spiraled around the insulation
- *Circumferential bands*, with contrasting color stripes placed at regular intervals around the wire.
- *Angular bands or hashmarks*, with contrasting colored stripes that span about half of the wire's circumference at regular intervals around the wire.

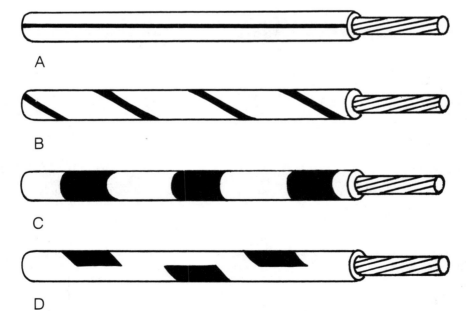

Fig. 3-3. Color-coded inked stripes: longitudinal stripe (A), spiral-stripe (B), band marking (C), and hash marking (D).

Alphanumerical printing

Wire and cable identification by letters and numbers is preferred in military applications. Two methods currently in use are:

- Surface printing
- Hot stamping

Surface printing   Wires and cables can be printed by type wheels turning in a bath of ink. Legends are imprinted on the rapidly moving wire as the insulation is applied. White or aluminum inks are generally used on black surfaces and black ink is used on other colors. The codes consist of numbers, letters, or combinations of these. Surface printing can be used to mark customer part numbers, temperatures, voltage ratings, and any required legends.

Hot stamping   *Hot stamping* is done by heating and pressing type against colored marking foil into the softened insulation surface. Hot stamping can be used to mark such information as wire number, circuit function, circuit designation, stock or part number, wire specification number, wire size and type, and assembly identification.

Braiding

Textile braid, used as primary insulation in pushback wire, has largely been replaced by extruded plastic that must be removed. However, textile braids are still used as mechanical and thermal protection of plastic insulation, as cable-segment separators in multiconductor cable, and as flame-retardant sleeving in cables.

A braid is woven by crossing a number of strands diagonally so that each strand passes alternatively over and under one or more of the others. By industry convention, the term *braid*, by itself, refers to a covering formed from textile yarn, and a *copper braid* is a shield that is formed from copper strands.

Braid patterns

A solid-colored braid is produced when all of the bobbins on the braiding machine have the same color. Stripes are formed by using different colored yarns on adjacent bobbins.

Definitions

Three terms, ply, ends, and pick apply to yarn and braiding. The *ply* is the number of strands or filaments that are twisted together to form a single thread. Two-ply yarns have two twisted strands, three-ply, three strands, etc. *Ends* are the number of parallel-wound threads on a bobbin of a braiding machine. The ends are payed off the bobbin together and are applied as parallel strips to the wire. A *pick* is the distance between two adjacent crossover points of braid filaments. Picks per inch is a measure of the degree of coverage.

Yarns

The most frequently used braiding yarns consist of cotton, rayon, nylon, Dacron, and fiberglass, but other materials (such as Orlon) are available.

- Cotton is the most commonly used braiding material. It provides good resistance to abrasion and deformation.

- Rayon replaces cotton where thinner braid coverings and brighter colors are important. Rayon braids offer better electrical properties than cotton—especially in high-humidity environments—but they are not as resistant to abrasion.

- Nylon resists abrasion and chemicals better than either cotton or rayon and it can be used at higher temperatures. Nylon braids add less to the diameter of unbraided wire than either cotton or rayon braids, but they are the most expensive.

- Fiberglass braids are specified where resistance to high heat and humidity are required. The Underwriters Laboratories approve fiberglass braiding for use at temperatures in excess of 105 °C (221 °F). Fiberglass is not as abrasion-resistant as cotton, but it can be protected with an extruded nylon jacket. Fiberglass braids add approximately the same thickness to the diameter of unbraided wire as rayon and nylon.

Color Yarns are colored to meet the requirements of MIL-STD-104, except that an exact match is more difficult with fiberglass. Ten standard colors are available (TABLE 3-1).

Serving

A *serve* or *binder* is a textile or plastic thread (or filament) that is wound spirally around a conductor or group of cabled conductors. Serves are used for two general purposes:

- Spacers in air-spaced (semi-solid core) coaxial cables. A filament, typically extruded from polyethylene, is wound around the uninsulated conductor and a plastic tube is then extruded over the spiral to permit air circulation.

- To hold together bundles of insulated conductors for further processing during assembly. They are applied as part of the cabling process by serving equipment that is attached to the cabler.

Shielding

A *shield* is an electrically conductive cover that encloses an insulated conductor, a group of insulated conductors, or a cable. Its purpose is to ensure that the surface of the insulated conductors are at ground potential or some predetermined potential (with respect to ground).

Shields perform both electrical and mechanical functions. For example, in electronic circuits shielding:

- Levels out surge impedance along the cable length.
- Confines signals within the cable to prevent them from interfering with nearby circuits (i.e., it prevents the cable from acting as a transmitting antenna).
- Screens signals within the shielded conductors from manmade or natural electromagnetic interference, (i.e., prevents the cable from acting as a receiving antenna).
- Protects telephone cables against shorts as a result of ground surges or lightning.
- Functions as a return wire in a coaxial cable.
- Protects the cable from termites and rodents.

Shield effectiveness Extraneous magnetic and electrostatic fields can degrade signal transmission in electronic circuits by inducing voltages that alter the transmitted signals. *Shield effectiveness* is a measure of a shield's ability to shield the internal conductors from induced voltages or suppress signals radiated from them.

The selection of the most cost-effective shielding depends on:

- A knowledge of the cable's electromagnetic environment.
- Compliance with all applicable specifications and standards for limiting electromagnetic radiation and interference.

Federal Communications Commission (FCC) Docket 20780 affects manufacturers and integrators of digital equipment that use radio-frequency energy at 10 kHz or higher in an incidental manner (i.e., not designed as a radio transmitter). In order to comply with this docket, the manufacturer must prevent the emission of pulses from the equipment that could interfere with other equipment in the vicinity.

The manufacturer must shield all enclosures and cables, which could leak or radiate these nuisance signals. In many cases, compliance requires that cables are effectively shielded and terminated with shielded connectors.

The optimum shielding method is one that performs its function and meets applicable environmental operating requirements at minimum cost. An undershielded cable fails to meet these requirements, but an overshielded cable wastes money and could make installation more difficult.

Magnetic shielding   Magnetic shielding is recommended for dc voltages, low frequencies, and radio frequencies. Ferrous material provides effective shielding against direct current and low-frequency magnetic fields. These materials short circuit the flux lines and prevent them from passing through the shield. Shield effectiveness is directly proportional to shield thickness. The reluctance (the opposition to the passage of the flux) of the shield is inversely proportional to shield thickness. Therefore, shields with high permeability (ease of establishing flux lines), such as permalloy or steel, are recommended—particularly at 60-Hz audio or power frequencies. Conductive shields, such as copper, must be excessively thick to be effective.

The most effective shields for magnetic flux at radio frequencies use materials with low electrical resistivity (high conductivity), such as copper or aluminum. In attempting to pass through this shield, magnetic flux induces voltages in the metal that generate eddy currents. These currents oppose the flux and prevent it from penetrating the shield.

Among the types of magnetic shields in general use are:

- Round wire in the form of braids or strands
- Metal tape
- Metallized conductive foil on a plastic backing
- Metal tubes

Electrostatic shielding   Shielding electrostatic fields is easier than shielding magnetic fields because neither shield thickness nor its conductivity are critical. The most important factor in electrostatic shield effectiveness is the percent of coverage. Braid made from any good electrical conductor can provide effective electrostatic shielding. A metal braid or tape shield with a ground wire is generally the most effective and least expensive protection from high-frequency electric fields.

Braided shields   *Braided shields* (FIG. 3-4) are woven from copper strands with the same technique as textile braid. Braided shields are widely used in electronic cables and it is most effective at frequencies between 1 kHz and 140 MHz. A woven braided shield retains its shape, even without a jacket, and yet remains flexible. Braided shields are used in all military specifications. Copper braids can be bare, tinned, or silver coated.

The effectiveness of a braided shield is proportional to the amount of underlying conductors that it covers. Coverage is expressed as a percentage of the underlying conductors that are covered by the metal. Because these shields are woven, it is not possible to achieve 100 percent electrical shielding; leakage can occur where shield strands cross. Nevertheless, 75 to 85 percent coverage is generally effective at the audio and low radio frequencies. At higher frequencies, 85 to 95 percent coverage is recommended.

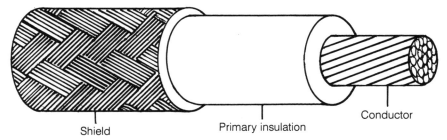

Fig. 3-4. Braided shield on a single conductor.

In applications where shielding must exceed 95 percent, use double-braided shielding; however, double braiding might attain only 97 percent coverage. If 100 percent coverage is required, use metallized foil or a combination of metallized foil and braided shield.

The coverage percentage of braided shields can be calculated from:

$$K = 100 (2F - F^2) \text{ Percent}$$

Where: $F = \dfrac{NPe}{\sin \beta}$ (2)

$\beta = \text{braid angle}$

$\text{Tan } \beta = \dfrac{2 \pi (D + 2e) P}{C}$ (3)

Definitions for the factors are given in FIG. 3-5.

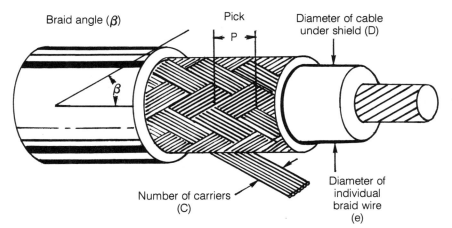

Fig. 3-5. Calculation of percentage coverage for braided shields.

C = number of carriers
e = diameter of individual braid wire (in inches)
D = diameter of the cable under the shield (in inches)
K = percent coverage
N = number of ends (wires) per carrier
P = picks per inch

Percent coverage is influenced by four factors:

1. *Number of ends per carrier* (N)   The typical number of ends per carrier range from four to seven. The number of ends affects attenuation, pushback characteristics, and, in combination with the number of picks per inch, the braid angle, and the coverage percentage.

2. *Picks per inch*   The number of picks per inch is typically between 10 and 30. The lower the number of picks, the faster the braiding machine can be run. From formula (3), the braid angle is directly related to the number of picks per inch (P) and inversely related to the number of carriers (C). The *braid angle* is the angle less than 90 degrees formed by the shield strand and the axis of the conductor. The angle will approach 0 degrees when the number of picks per inch is small and 90 degrees when the number as large.

    A large braid angle increases attenuation in a coaxial cable, but cables with high braid angles are more flexible and have longer flex lives. Shield design is a tradeoff influenced by cable application.

3. *Diameter of individual shield strand* (e)   Typical wire gauges are 34 or 36 AWG; however, the diameter could be as small as 40 AWG or as large as 28 AWG. Bare copper shields are widely specified for coaxial cable, and tinned or silver-coated copper shields are widely specified for electronic wires and cables. TABLE 3-3 lists diameter increases for braided shields with a range of shield strand gauges.

Table 3-3. Diameter Increases as a Result of Shields.

Shield Strand AWG	Braided Shield	Spiral Shield	Reverse Spiral Shield
40	0.014	0.006	0.013
28	0.018	0.008	0.016
36	0.022	0.010	0.020
34	0.028	0.013	0.025
32	0.034	0.016	0.032
30	0.044	0.020	0.041
18	0.056	0.025	0.051

4. *Number of carriers* (C)   Braiding machines with 16 and 24 carriers are
   typical in the industry.

Braided shield termination   The methods for terminating conventional braided shields include:

1. The shield is cut to the required length and a close-fitting metal ring is
   slipped over the wire insulation and under the shield. A grounding lead
   is then placed over the shield, followed by a second ring. Then, the two
   rings are crimped together.

2. The shield is pushed back and its strands are spread to form an opening through which the insulated wire is removed. The resulting shield
   pigtail is easily terminated.

3. If the shield covers a group of wires and method 2 is impractical, the
   shield can be unbraided and its strands pigtailed and solder dipped.

Spiral shields   Spiral shields (FIG. 3-6) are made by serving a group of
strands in one direction around the primary insulation of the conductor. There
are no braided stitches and all shield wires are parallel.

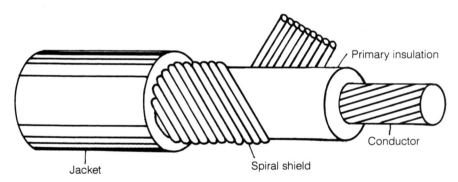

Fig. 3-6. Spiral shield on a single conductor.

Spiral shields are more flexible than braided shields. It is not necessary to
unbraid the conductor when the jacket is removed. The strands peel off and
they can be twisted together and solder-dipped—minimizing manual labor.

Spiral shields are not as effective as braided shields at high frequencies,
although more than 95 percent coverage can be obtained. Spiral shielding is
only recommended for audio frequencies because the coil effect of the strands

causes unwanted inductive reactance at higher frequencies. The coverage percentage (K) of spiral shields can be calculated from the following formula:

$$K = 100 \, F$$

Where: $F = \dfrac{NPe}{\mathrm{Sin}\ \beta}$

Reverse spiral shields   Reverse spiral shields (FIG. 3-7) are formed by placing one or more copper strands beneath a spiral shield. The two layers of wires are applied in opposite directions and are not interwoven.

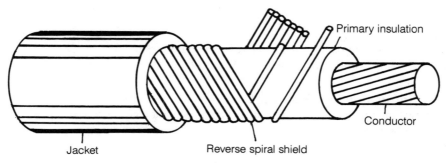

Fig. 3-7. Reverse spiral shield on a single conductor.

Reverse spiral shields reduce the inductive effects of spiral shields. The shielding percentage can be calculated from the formula listed for spiral shields. TABLE 3-3 shows the diameter increases of an insulated conductor from reverse spiral shields.

Flat-tape shields   Flat-tape shields for electronics are often a metallized sheet dielectric (typically aluminum-polyester). Spiral tape shields (FIG. 3-8) are frequently applied during the cabling of bundled wires. However, longitudinal tape shields (FIG. 3-9) are applied during the extrusion of the outer jacket.

The most commonly used tape shield in electronic cables is 0.00035-in. aluminum foil laminated to 0.001-in. polyester. The aluminum side can be toward or away from the wire when one wire, a pair, or a single group of wires is shielded. However, when several groups of wires are shielded, the tape is usually applied with the polyester (insulating) side out so that the possibility of random shield contacts is eliminated. This laminate is frequently made for wire and cable manufacturers and sold under a proprietary trade name.

Aluminum/polyester shields can provide 100 percent coverage and can save both weight and space. However, the fatigue life is only fair and the shielding does not add to the cable's strength. For these reasons, aluminum/

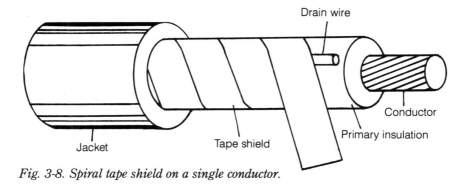

Fig. 3-8. Spiral tape shield on a single conductor.

Drain wire

Conductor

Primary insulation

Jacket

Tape shield

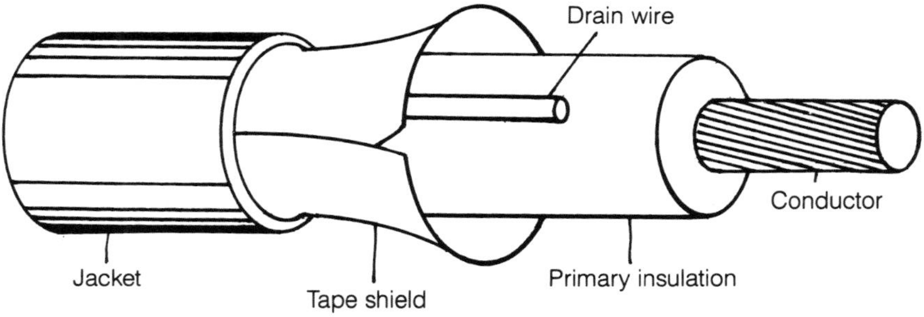

Fig. 3-9. Longitudinal tape shield on a single conductor.

polyester shields are generally confined to commercial and consumer applications in multiconductor cables. Tape shields are terminated with a drain wire that has been placed in contact with the shielding metal for its entire length.

Tape shields of copper, aluminum, and bimetals are used occasionally in electronic cables. Until recently, their use was largely confined to telephone cables. Corrugated metal shields improve the cable's flexibility, but if used, outside diameter must also increase.

Cabling

Cabling is the design and construction of multiconductor cable that ranges from a simple pair of conductors within a common jacket to a highly complex configuration. TABLE 3-4 lists the diameter and lay-up factors for cables with 2 to 20 identical conductors. The factor K, when multiplied by the outside diameter of an individual conductor, yields the overall cable diameter.

A simple rule applies to multiconductor cables: each additional layer can have six more conductors than the preceding layer. TABLE 3-4 shows that a cable with six conductors has a core of six conductors. However, a cable with seven conductors has a single conductor core that is surrounded by six conductors in the first layer.

A 19-conductor cable has a single-conductor core, a first layer with six conductors, and a second layer with 12 conductors. Also, a 20-conductor cable has a filler (f) as its core, the first layer has seven conductors, and the second layer has 12 conductors. A complete table of cabling diameter and lay-up factors can be found in the appendix.

The cabling of individual layers can be either concentric or bunched. A *concentric* or *planetary lay-up* consists of a central wire or filler surrounded by

Table 3-4. Concentric Cable Diameter and Layup.

Total Conds.	K Factor	Number of conductors per layer *		
		Core	1st	2nd
2	2.00	2		
3	2.15	3		
4	2.41	4		
5	2.70	5		
6	3.00	6		
7	3.00	1	6	
8	3.31	1 + f	7	
9	3.62	1 + f	8	
10	4.00	2	8	
11	4.00	2 + f	9	
12	4.15	3	9	
13	4.41	3 + f	10	
14	4.41	4	10	
15	4.70	4 + 2f	11	
16	4.70	5 + f	11	
17	5.00	5 + 2f	12	
18	5.00	6 + f	12	
19	5.00	1	6	12
20	5.31	f	7	13

*f = Filler   Note: fillers may be placed in layers other than those listed above

one or more layers of helically laid wires: the direction of lay is reversed for each successive layer and the length of lay is increased for each successive layer. The outer layer is generally left-hand lay. This construction technique ensures cable roundness and greater mechanical strength.

A bunched or unilay cable consists of many insulated wires cabled together in the same direction. This formation results in a cable with a smaller overall diameter, lighter weight, lower cost, and greater flexibility than one with a concentric lay-up.

Cable flexibility is directly related to the lay length of the individual layers—typically 8 to 16 times the pitch diameter of each layer. The smaller the lay length, the greater the flexibility of the cable. However, this technique results in a more expensive cable because more wire is required.

Fillers

Fillers are natural or man-made fiber materials that are used to round out a cable for symmetry. These materials are also used as the core in cables where a round cable cross section is required. For example, cables with 20, 22, 34, and 35 conductors have fibers as central cores. Electronic-cable fillers are typically polyethylene, vinyl, or nylon.

Tapes

Plastic tapes can be used in several different positions in the assembled cable. They can be placed under the outer jacket for added protection against mechanical abuse or between overall shields and underlying conductors to prevent insulation damage. The underlying contours of the individual conductors might show through the jackets of untaped cables.

Tapes are typically made from one mil of polyester that is spiraled with a 10 percent or greater overlap. Taped conductors reduce the flexibility of the cable, but ensure a smooth, round cable contour. Tape also acts as a separator to prevent the jacket from adhering to the conductors during cable jacket extrusion.

Jacketing

Extruded plastic jackets or sheaths are widely used over single conductors, pairs, and cabled conductors. Textile overbraids are no longer used in electronic cables as an outer covering. Jackets cover and protect the enclosed wires against mechanical damage (such as scuffs, cuts, and impacts). Jackets also protect the wires and the primary insulation against chemicals (such as oil, gasoline, solvents, salt solutions, and battery acid). Jacketing materials are discussed in chapter 2. Two types of jackets used in electronic cabling are:

- Jackets over primary insulation on a solid or stranded conductor for added thermal protection (typically nylon over polyvinyl chloride). Nylon jacket wall thicknesses are typically two to six mils,

- Jackets over insulated single and shielded conductors (as with the case of coaxial cables) or over insulated and shielded or unshielded conductors (as with multiconductor and multipair cables). Typical jacket materials include PVC, polyethylene, neoprene, and polyurethane. The wall thicknesses of cable sheaths are typically about 10 percent of the cable bundle diameter.

Jackets are applied with extruders that are similar, except for size, to those used to apply primary insulation on bare or clad wire (FIG. 3-1). Jackets are usually applied relatively loosely over the insulated wire bundle. Jackets are easier to strip than primary insulation and they generally show the outline of the cabled conductors they enclose. Neoprene jackets are pressure extruded to fill all voids and convolutions in the cable core. They are more difficult to strip unless the underlying conductors are:

- Insulated with a different plastic, which prevents fusion between the jacket and conductor insulation.
- Covered with a separator or other barrier material.

Shipping

Lengths   Electronics cable is typically sold by the manufacturer or distributor in multiples of 100-foot lengths: 100, 500, and 1000 ft. (30.4, 152.4 and 304.8 m). However, hook-up wire for engineers, service technicians, and hobbyists is available in 25 ft. spools (7.6 meters).

Dispensers   Some manufacturers offer cable in corrugated cardboard dispensers. This packaging and dispensing system saves time, eliminates labor, and cuts costs by avoiding unreeling equipment. The light weight rectangular carton dispensers save storage space and are stackable. Some cartons include indicators to show the user how much cable is left in the dispenser.

4

Codes and standards

Many different industrial and government organizations have prepared specifications, standards, and codes to design, manufacture, and test wire and cable products. Wire and cable can be considered an electrical/electronic component. The objectives of these standards, specifications, and codes include:

- Maintenance of minimum acceptable quality levels
- Assurance of compatibility and interchangeability of comparable products
- Reduction or elimination of electrical shock as a result of faults in wire and cable
- Reduction or elimination of fire hazards that are related to the wires and cables
- Reduction or elimination of EMI
- Guidance in the selection of appropriate wire and cable.

The organizations that have issued standards, specifications, and codes for wire and cable used in electronic applications include:

- American National Standards Institute (ANSI)
- American Society for Testing and Materials (ASTM)
- Canadian Standards Association (CSA)
- International Electrotechnical Commission (IEC)
- Institute of Electrical and Electronics Engineers (IEEE)
- Instrument Society of America (ISA)
- Insulated Cable Engineers Association (ICEA)
- National Fire Protection Association (NFPA)
- Underwriters Laboratories (UL)
- U.S. Department of Defense (DoD)

This chapter describes some of the principal standards, specifications, and codes that apply to the manufacture, compliance testing, and application of wire and cable products. Consult the latest edition of each document referenced for further details.

Underwriters Laboratories, Inc. (UL)

The Underwriters Laboratories, Inc. (UL) is an independent, not-for-profit product certification laboratory that establishes test programs, issues safety standards, tests, inspects, and lists acceptable products, including wire and cable. It also performs follow-up inspections at the manufacturer's facility to determine continued compliance with UL safety requirements. UL establishes test and inspection programs for new products or types as they are submitted for evaluation.

More than 60 percent of all UL activities are concerned with electrical and electronics products. Its emphasis is on safety and it does not evaluate product competence of the design or the efficiency of function unless a safety factor is involved. In some cases, UL investigates products for compliance with performance specifications of other organizations. Manufacturers accept the cost of inspection and certification of products by UL (or other standards organizations) because of the promotional value. But increasingly, these certifications are mandatory for the sale of a product or component. Thus, the cost of inspection is necessary when doing business in those product areas.

Wire and cable manufacturers submit their products to UL for examination and tests under applicable UL standards and requirements. A *standard* is a technical document that states the requirements for a product; it is used to compare and evaluate submitted products. If UL finds the product acceptable, it will be listed in its product directories. The UL maintains a recognized component directory and an electrical construction material directory for other types of wire and cable.

If no appropriate standard exists for a new type of wire or cable submitted, UL might develop one "under a procedure which provides for participation and comment from the affected public as well as industry."

The Underwriters Laboratories has two general classes of listings:

- *Type-R service.* A product that has been consistently manufactured for years undergoes periodic follow-up inspection and testing by UL field representatives.

- *Type-L service.* This service applies to products that are produced in high volumes where continuous quality control is required because of possible manufacturing variations. Under the UL Follow-up Program, UL field representatives visit wire and cable manufacturing plants frequently to verify compliance with applicable UL standards.

   ○ *Recognized components.* In 1975, UL introduced the Recognized Component Mark (a backward-reading *UR*) for use on recognized components to be included in end-use equipment. These components include power supplies, power relays, power switches, and appliance wiring materials (AWM). The items covered by this service are incomplete in construction features and are intended solely as factory-installed components. This symbol is printed on the surface of certain products or is included in the manufacturer's label on other products. Notice that a UL listing does not ensure product quality beyond the minimum acceptable levels for safe operation.

UL file number

All wire and cable manufacturers receive an individual file number from UL for each group of its products that are covered by a UL standard. The number identifies the manufacturer and it can be used interchangeably with the company name or symbol, where the UL requires surface printing on the product.

UL style numbers

UL has assigned a different style number for each appliance wiring material (AWM) construction. Each style states the general product use, as determined by UL evaluation. The style number description includes:

- Range of acceptable sizes
- Type of insulation and wall thickness
- Optional or required construction (braid, foil shields, and jackets)
- Assigned temperature and voltage ratings
- Usage

Canadian Standards Association (CSA)

The Canadian Standards Association (CSA), like UL, is an independent, non-profit organization that provides tests, examinations, and certification services for a wide range of products used in Canada. CSA uses the same general procedures as UL in developing its standards. However, it is important to remember that UL and CSA standards for wire and cable are not always identical. Nevertheless, CSA and UL standards are quite similar on:

- Size range
- Construction
- Marking and labeling requirements
- Assigned operating temperature and voltage ratings

Wire and cable manufacturers obtain CSA certification by following a procedure that is similar to that of the UL. Manufacturers are authorized to attach tags, which bear the CSA monogram, to certified wires and cables. However, in the case of flexible cords, the CSA label must be affixed to the tags.

Manufacturers are assigned individual CSA numbers for each type of certified wire and cable. The file number provides an optional method for identifying the manufacturer. Surface printing (the company name, trademark, or symbol) on the cable is also permitted.

Multi-listed wires and cables

Some wire and cable products are marketed in both the United States and Canada. For this reason, the manufacturer is likely to have the products both UL listed or recognized and CSA certified. As a result, the product can carry dual ratings and this information is listed in the manufacturer's standard product catalog. An example of dual rating is UL Style 1007 hook-up wire, which is rated for 80 °C 300-volt operation. This product is the nearest equivalent of CSA Type TR-64 hook-up wire, which has a 90 °C temperature rating.

Military specifications and standards

Military specifications and standards are issued by the Department of Defense. They govern the construction, composition, configuration, testing, and physical and electrical characteristics of wire and cable that is procured directly by agencies of the U.S. Government—primarily in defense-related activities. They also set standards for wire and cable installed in equipment that is procured by the U.S. Government. The appendix lists some of the more important military wire and cable specifications.

An important military specification is MIL-C-17, which covers radio-frequency coaxial cable. When referenced in military contracts, requests for quotation, and other documentation, the military specification number (such as MIL-C-17) will include a suffix letter (A, B, C, etc.) that indicates edition revisions. Other suffixes which are preceded by a slash (/) can be added. In addition, amendments, supplements, and their revisions can be added. All of these additions are important because they identify a specific wire or cable type and style. Earlier or later versions might not be acceptable substitutes because of changes in materials, dimensions, or electrical properties. In the case of MIL-C-17, revisions A, D, and F are all still referenced for government procurement.

Military standards and specifications exert a strong influence on the whole wire and cable industry. The standards even influence the design, manufacture, and tests of wire and cable that does not conform to the Qualified Products List (QPL) requirements, described later in this section. These standards and specifications are prepared as a cooperative effort between government and industry; the standards contain years of accumulated knowledge about the fabrication of quality wire and cable. Industrial and commercial wire and cable users are familiar with these specifications and have confidence in them as objective references.

The DOD has no single specification writing group, so groups within the Army, Navy, and Air Force all issue their own wire and cable specifications. However, these branches all generally accept and adopt specifications that are prepared by the other services (if appropriate for specific applications). Military wire and cable specifications can be divided into two categories: performance and qualification.

- *Performance specifications.* A manufacturer can supply wire and cable to meet performance specifications under a government procurement contract. This occurs when no specification or standard applies to that specific product. The manufacturer must accept responsibility for compliance with the performance specifications—the manufacturer must continuously perform acceptance tests on randomly selected samples from each wire and cable lot. The tests can be the same as those performed under a military specification for a comparable wire and cable product. When "source inspection" has been specified by the general contractor, the government inspector can request that any or all acceptance tests are performed under his direct supervision.

- *Qualification specifications.* Wire and cable that qualify under these specifications must pass comprehensive tests, which are listed in the applicable military specification for that product. The government may require that these tests be performed in a government or government-designated independent testing laboratory. Alternatively, the tests might be performed in the manufacturer's own test facilities, if found acceptable.

Manufacturers whose wire and cable products meet the qualification specifications have their names placed on a Qualified Products List (QPL). However, this listing does not relieve the supplier of the continuous quality testing. Acceptance testing must still be performed on each lot manufactured and complete inspection records must be kept.

Certification and inspection

If the supplier must certify that the wire and cable shipped against a purchase order meets the referenced military specification, certification is required. Any of the following forms might be required:

1. *Certificate of compliance* is a statement by the vendor that the wire or cable complies with all the requirements of the applicable specification. Although the test results are not required, the vendor must keep substantiating the records on file. This certificate is generally required for performance specifications.

2. *Certified test data* is a compilation of the required acceptance test data, which the manufacturer must keep on file. This certification is used with both performance and qualification specifications.

3. *Government source inspection* requires that the wire and cable is approved by a Government Quality Assurance Specialist (QAS), based on tests performed on the finished product at the designated manufacture stages.

4. *Customer source inspection* is when the wire and cable is examined by the contractor's inspector, who accepts it by signing off accompanying documentation.

Wire and cable manufacturers who offer QPL wire and cable for U.S. military procurement must comply with DOD-mandated provisions for plant and material inspection and they must complete all required lot-traceability documentation on these products. However, manufacturers can sell military specification products for commercial/industrial applications without this documentation.

Wire and cable manufacturers adopt sections of the military specifications and standards for their own internal standard manufacturing and test procedures. Designations on products as "RG-XX/U type," for example, indicate that the general design and manufacture of the product is based on a military specification. However, the manufacturer can alter materials or dimensions for one or more reasons:

- To adapt the product to an application that is not foreseen at the time the military specification was approved.

- To reduce cost by substituting low-cost materials or using less material than is necessary for military applications. Full compliance with the military specification might add unnecessary expense, which might not be required for the more-controlled industrial/commercial environment.

Commercial and industrial wire and cable companies can manufacture and test under certain provisions of military specifications and standards because these tests are better known to the public than internal factory specifications.

American Society for Testing and Materials (ASTM)

The American Society for Testing and Materials (ASTM) has prepared conductor specifications for copper (TABLE 4-1). ASTM has also prepared stan-

Table 4-1. ASTM Wire Specifications.

B-3	Soft or annealed copper wire
B-8	Concentric, lay, stranded copper conductors
B-33	Tinned soft or annealed copper wire for electrical purposes
B-172	Rope, lay stranded copper conductors, bunch stranded members
B-173	Rope lay stranded copper conductors, concentric stranded members
B-174	Bunch-stranded copper conductors
B-189	Lead coated and lead alloy coated soft copper wire
B-286	Copper conductors for use in hook-up wire for electronic equipment
B-298	Silver-coated soft or annealed copper wire
B-496	Compact round concentric lay stranded copper conductors

dardized test methods for materials. The tests that apply to insulation material tests are classified into three categories: physical, thermal, and electrical (see TABLE 4-2).

Table 4-2. ASTM Test Methods for Insulation.

Test Method	Property	Class
1. ASTM D-149	Dry dielectric, V/mil Wet dielectric, V/mil	Electrical
2. ASTM D-150	Dielectric constant @ 1 MHz Dissipation factor @ 1 MHz	Electrical
3. ASTM D-257	Volume resistivity, ohm-cm	Electrical
4. ASTM D-412	Tensile strength psi (min.) Elongation percent (min.)	Physical
5. ASTM D-476	Brittle temp. 50 percent non-failure, deg C.	Thermal
6. ASTM D-792	Specific gravity	Physical
7. ASTM D-1047	Heat distortion	Thermal
8. ASTM D-1505	Density	Physical
9. ASTM D-2240	Durometer hardness	Physical

Federal standards

The following federal standards apply to uninsulated copper wire:

- QQ-W-343 Electrical Uninsulated Copper Wire
- QQ-B-575 Braided Copper Wire

National Electrical Code (NEC)

The purpose of the National Electrical Code (NEC) is "the practical safeguarding of persons and property from hazards arising from the use of electricity.

This code contains provisions considered necessary for safety. Compliance therewith and proper maintenance will result in an installation essentially free from hazard, but not necessarily efficient, convenient, or adequate for good service or future expansion of electrical use." The NEC code covers:

1. Installation of electric conductors and equipment within or on public and private buildings, other structures (including mobile homes, recreational vehicles, and floating buildings), and other premises (such as yards, carnivals, parking on other lots, and industrial substations).
2. Installation of conductors that connect to the supply of electricity.
3. Installation of other outside conductors on the premises.
4. Installation of optical fiber cable.

The NEC, prepared by the National Fire Protection Association in Quincy, MA, is concerned with the spread of flame in certain kinds of circuits, as a result of a fault. The NEC text is contained in nine chapters and each chapter is divided into individual articles. The following NEC articles relate to electronic wire and cable:

- *Article 300 Wiring Methods* covers wiring methods for all wiring installations, with seven exceptions that are stated in the article. The provisions of this article are not intended to apply to conductors, which form an integral part of the equipment (such as motors, controllers, motor control centers, and factory-assembled control equipment).

- *Article 310 Conductors for General Wiring* covers general requirements for conductors and their type designations, insulations, markings, mechanical strengths, ampacity ratings, and uses. These requirements do not apply to conductors that form an integral part of the equipment (such as motors, motor controllers, and similar equipment, or to conductors that are specifically provided for elsewhere in the code).

- *Article 318 Cable Trays* covers cable tray systems (including ladders, troughs, channels, solid bottom trays, and other similar structures).

- *Article 340 Power and Control Tray Cable*

- *Article 510 Hazardous (Classified) Locations—Specific* covers occupancies or parts of occupancies that are or might be hazardous because of atmospheric concentrations of flammable liquids, gases, or vapors, or because of materials that might be readily ignitable.

- *Article 725 Class 1, Class 2, and Class 3 Remote-control, Signaling, and Power-limited Circuits* covers remote-control, signaling, and power-limited circuits that are not an integral part of a device or appliance.

- *Article 760 Fire Protective Signaling Systems* covers the installation of wire and fire protective signaling systems, which operate at 600 volts nominal, or less.

- *Article 770 Optical Fiber Cables* applies to the installation of optical fiber cables in certain circumstances. This article does not cover the construction of optical fiber cables. It distinguishes between three types of optical fiber cables: nonconductive, conductive, and hybrid.

- *Article 800 Communications Circuits* covers telephones, telegraphs (except radio), outside wiring for fire and burglar alarms, similar central station systems, and telephone systems that are not connected to a central station system, but which use similar types of equipment, methods of installation, and maintenance.

- *Article 810 Radio and Television Equipment* covers radio and television receiving equipment and amateur radio equipment, but not equipment and antennas that are used to couple carrier current to power-line conductors.

- *Article 820 Community Antenna Television and Radio Distribution Systems* covers coaxial cable distribution of radio frequency signals, typically employed in community antenna television (CATV) systems.

The 1987 NEC introduced guidelines that have greatly impacted the wire and cable industry (these guidelines were included in the 1990 revision). By January 1, 1987 and July 1, 1988, cable manufacturers were required to modify cable construction to pass one of four flame-test levels:

- Plenum applications: UL 910 (January 1, 1987). Test Method for Fire and Smoke Characteristics of Electrical and Optical Fiber Cables.

- Riser applications: UL 1666 (January 1, 1987). Standard Test for Flame Propagation Height of Electrical and Optical Fiber Cables Installed Vertically in Shaft.

- General-purpose applications: UL 1581 (July 1, 1988) Reference Standard for Electrical Wires, Cables, and Flexible Cords—UL Vertical Tray Flame Test.

- Restricted applications: UL 1581 (July 1, 1988) Reference Standard for Electrical Wires, Cables, and Flexible Cords and Other Standards Including UL 13, 44, 62, 83, 444, and 1424—UL Vertical Wire Flame Test VW-1 (replaced UL Flammability Rating FR-1).

An IEEE 383 70,000 BTU/hr Vertical Flame Test also exists and the Canadian Standards Association has Flame Tests CSA FT-1 and FT-4 for general-purpose applications.

To verify compliance, UL requires that approved cable must be listed and that it must carry necessary label markings and other appropriate information.

Four general designations and associated applications exist (TABLE 4-3). *Plenum* refers to the use of ducts, plenums, and other environmental air conditioning spaces used for cable placement. *Riser* refers to a vertical, floor-to-floor run of cables in a building shaft.

Table 4-3. Wire and Cable Application Areas.

Designation	Application Areas
Plenum	a. True plenum installations b. All applications below
Riser	a. Riser installations (vertical shaft) b. All applications below
General purpose (Commercial)	a. Concealed runs within building walls b. Non-plenum ceiling runs c. Conduit installations d. All applications below
Restricted (Residential)	a. Non-concealed spaces 10 ft. or less b. Fully enclosed in conduit or raceway c. Diameters less than 0.25 inch and a residential dwelling. d. Residential thermostat wire

Four important factors underlie each of the NEC articles:

- The application governs the cable requirement. For example, Article 760 covers fire protective signaling systems.

- The code of importance is the one that is currently approved and is used within the local municipality or state.

- The local inspector/fire marshall is the ultimate authority to approve or disapprove a cable for installation, in accordance with the code in effect.

- The substitute cable must meet the required electrical characteristics.

The most important cables in the NEC/UL listings have more than one application (TABLE 4-4). A descending hierarchy of application suitability exists. For example, Article 800, Communications Circuits, applies to communications circuits, as well as to power-limited circuits. Similarly, product designs cross applications lines: plenum products can be used in lower-ranking riser or even in general-purpose/residential applications.

A higher-grade cable than is required could be used to save inventory or storage costs. However, upgrading lower-ranking cable is not acceptable; general-purpose cable cannot be used in either riser or plenum applications.

Table 4-4. Areas of Cable Application.

NEC Article/type	Descrip.	Installation type Area of application Plenum	Riser	Gen. Purpose	Restricted
725 CL2	Class 2	CL2P	CL2R	CL2	CL2X @
725 CL3	Class 3	CL3P	CL3R	CL3	CL3X @
PLTC	Stand alone Power-limited Tray cable	(none)	(none)	PLTC	(none)
760 NPLF	Nonpower limited	NPLFP	NPLFR	NPLF	(none)
760 FPL	Power limited	FPLP	FPLR	FPL	(none)
770 OFC	Fiber cable/ metal conductors	OFCP	OFCR	OFC	(none)
770 OFN	Fiber cable	OFNP	OFNR	OFN	(none)
800 CM	Communications	CMP MPP	CMR MPR	CM MP	CMX @
820 CATV	Community antenna TV system	CATVP	CATVR	CATV	CATVX @@

@Cable diameter must be < 0.250 in.

@@ Cable diameter must be < 0.375 in.

The NEC has assigned designations to specific types of cable, listed in the appendix. The most significant change in 1990 was the introduction of a new multipurpose cable class. This cable satisifies the requirements for the communications cables of Article 800 and certain requisites of the fire protective cables of Article 860. The primary issue is fire resistance.

Additional changes in the 1990 code state:

- General-purpose cables cannot be used for multiple-floor penetration.

- CMX cables are limited for use in one or two family dwellings; but they can be used in multifamily dwellings if the diameter does not exceed 0.250 in. and if it is not in a concealed location.

- CL2X and CL3X can be used in any family dwelling, except in riser or plenum areas, and the cable diameter must not exceed 0.250 in.

- CMX, CL2X, and CL3X can be installed in conduit, but cannot be exposed beyond 10 feet.

TABLE 4-5 lists the NEC ranking of cables in terms of fire resistance, from most to least.

Table 4-5. NEC Ranking of Cable Fire Resistance, Most to Least.

Designation	Type
MPP	Multipurpose plenum cable
CMP	Communications plenum cable
MPR	Multipurpose riser cable
CMR	Communication riser cable
MP	Multipurpose general application cable
CM	Communication general application cable
CMX	Communication cable-limited use

The Insulated Cable Engineers Association (ICEA) is a professional engineering society whose standards are either used by or listed as reference documents in cable specifications that are written by individual electrical utilities or by the architect/engineering consultants who serve them. ICEA writes the standards, but it depends on the National Electrical Manufacturers Association (NEMA) to obtain acceptance and adoption.

Institute of Electrical and Electronic Engineers (IEEE) is a professional engineering society, which is organized into many specialized societies that have interests in specific applications or products. Some of these societies prepare standards that cover wire, cable, and connectors. These standards determine wire and cable configurations.

The Occupational Safety and Health Act (OSHA) requires that every place of employment must meet minimum safety and health standards. The wires and cables used by the process industry, for example, must comply with OSHA regulations. They must, therefore, be listed in the NEC and/or be recognized by UL or similar OSHA-accepted testing groups.

5

Single, paired,
and special wire

This chapter covers hook-up wire, backplane wire, twisted pairs, and other special-purpose single-conductor wires and leads in the following categories:

- Antenna wire
- Bus bar wire
- High-voltage leads
- Magnet wire
- Shielding and bonding wire
- Test prod wire

Hook-up wire

Hook-up wire is single-conductor insulated wire that is for use in consumer electronics and appliances as well as in a wide range of commercial, industrial, and military electric and electronic equipment. The discussion in this chapter is limited to hook-up wire that is suitable for business machines and electronics equipment.

Hook-up wire is made to meet UL, CSA, and military specifications. The characteristics of widely used hook-up wire that is suitable for electronics applications are listed in TABLE 5-1. The industry recognizes two groups of hook-up wire:

- Nonmilitary: UL Listed and/or CSA certified.
- Military: with qualification approval (QPL) or complying with performance requirements.

Table 5-1. Characteristics of Widely Used Hook-Up Wire.

UL Style	CSA Type	Volt. Rate (V)	Temp. Max (C)	AWG Size	Conduct. Matl.	Insul. Matl.	Nominal O.D. (in.)
1007	TR-64	300	80	28-16	TC	PVC	.047-.094
1015	TEW	600	105	24-10	TC	PVC	.086-.183
1028	TEW	600	105	8	TC	PVC	.253
1061	T2	300	80	30-16	TC	PVC	.030-.080
1180		300	200	24-16	SC	TFE	.054-.080
1213		300	105	30-20	SC	TFE	.032-.058
1371		300	105	32-22	SC	TFE	.022-.080
1569	RSR-64	300	105	28-16	TC	PVC	.047-.080
MIL-W-76B		1000	80	24-20	TC	PVC	.055-.066
MIL-W-16878D/E							
/1	Type B	600	105	32-14	TC	PVC	.029-.091
/2	Type C	1000	105	24-12	TC	PVC	.058-.124
/4	Type E	600	200	30-20	SC	TFE	.032-.080
/5	Type EE	1000	200	24-16	SC	PTFE	.054-.088
/6	Type ET	250	200	32-22	SC	TFE	.022-.042
/11	Type K	600	200	32-22	SC	FEP	.032-.054
/12	Type KK	1000	200	32-22	SC	FEP	.041-.064
/13	Type KT	250	200	32-22	SC	FEP	.022-.044
MIL-W-22759							
/11		600	200	26-18	SC	TFE	.038-.068
/16		600	150	24-18	TC	ETFE	.045-.071

TC = Tinned copper   SC = Silver-coated copper

As with other commercial wire and cable products, this classification encompasses a wide array of products that are available with different insulation materials in a variety of colors. The wire might also be manufactured to customer's specifications so that the desired product is not available as a catalog item. Hook-up wire is offered under one or more of the following categories:

- UL-listed style
- CSA type
- Military specifications MIL-W-76, MIL-W-16878, and MIL-W-22759

Conductors

Most hook-up wire used in electronic applications is fully annealed solid or stranded copper, 32 through 10 AWG. However, sizes 22 through 18 AWG are considered to be suitable for general-purpose use. The copper conductors are processed in accordance with ASTM B-3 or B-8. Hook-up wire is generally made in accordance with ASTM B-286, a specification for copper hook-up wire in electronic equipment.

Hook-up wire with bare copper conductors is available for temperatures up to 80 °C, but most of this wire (as well as wire for applications where temperatures will reach 105 °C) is tinned per ASTM B-33. The copper conductors can also be silver coated (per ASTM B-298) or nickel coated for use where temperatures will reach 200 °C. Copper-covered steel and high-strength copper alloys are used to manufacture hook-up wire.

Solid and stranded copper hook-up wire is not intended to be flexed, except during installation and infrequent maintenance. TABLE 5-2 lists the typical stranding configurations for true fixed service and moderate flexing.

Table 5-2. Stranding for AWG Hook-Up Wire Conductors.

AWG	Fixed Service	Moderate Flexing
32	7 × 40	7 × 40
30	7 × 38	7 × 38
28	7 × 36	7 × 36
26	Solid or 7 × 34	7 × 34
24	Solid or 7 × 32	7 × 32 or 10 × 34
22	Solid or 7 × 30	7 × 30 or 19 × 34
20	Solid or 7 × 28 or 10 × 30	7 × 28 or 19 × 32 10 × 30 or 42 × 36
18	Solid or 7 × 26 or 16 × 30	16 × 30 or 41 × 34
16	Solid or 19 × 29	19 × 29 or 26 × 30
14	Solid or 19 × 27	41 × 30
12	19 × 25	65 × 30

Insulation

Selecting a particular hook-up wire insulation is influenced by:

- Resistance to cut-through, flame, chemicals, and radiation
- Temperature requirements
- Voltage requirements
- Electrical properties
- Low-temperature flexibility
- Finished diameter and weight

Most hook-up wire is insulated with PVC or fluorocarbon thermoplastic insulation. PVC is flame and ozone resistant, and it is inert to most chemicals, oils, and solvents. It has a temperature range of $-40\,°C$ to $+80\,°C$ and a voltage rating of up to 600 volts. PVC can also be semi-rigid (SRPVC) or irradiated (XLPVC).

The UL and military specifications do not agree on all ratings for identical hook-up wire. For example, UL Style 1061 is the same as MIL-W-1878, Type B. As can be seen in TABLE 5-1, UL Style 1061 (CSA Type T2) is rated at $80\,°C$ for 300-volt operation. However, this same wire meets the requirements of MIL-W-16878 for $105\,°C$, 600-volt operation. The difference is caused by variations in test conditions and methods that are used by each agency. However, in the field no difference really exists. This difference suggests that the higher ratings are not always valid for all applications—that published characteristics should be used only as guides to determine the suitability of the wire for its intended use.

Fluorinated thermoplastics (such as Teflon, TFE, Teflon FEP, and Teflon ETFE) have outstanding thermal, physical, and electrical properties. They are resistant to oil, oxidation, heat, flame, sunlight, ozone, water, alcohol, gasoline, acids, alkalies, and solvents. Because of higher cost, these insulations are generally limited to applications where their high-temperature resistance is necessary.

Three UL Styles are insulated with Teflon TFE: 1180, 1213, and 1371. Two types of MIL-W-16878 hook-up wire have Teflon TFE insulation: E and ET; one has Teflon PTFE: EE; three have Teflon FEP: K, KK, and KT. MIL-W-22759 hook-up wire is insulated with Teflon TFE and Teflon ETFE.

Other insulation materials that are used on hook-up wire include polyethylene (PE), flame-retardant polyethylene (FRPE), and cross-linked polyethylene (XLPE). Semi-rigid PVC can be jacketed with nylon.

Stock hook-up wire is available in as many as 14 different solid colors. Special colors and stripes are available on a custom order.

Backplane wire

Wire wrapping was developed as an alternative to soldered wire interconnections on the backplanes of computers. The wiring technique is used on backplanes that are subject to field change or equipment that must be custom wired to dedicate it to a specific application.

Fine-insulated copper hook-up wire is stripped for a short distance at both ends, then each end is mechanically wrapped around rectangular terminal posts with controlled tension. Equipment is available to perform these interconnections manually or by automation at high speeds. With this technique, a secure gas-tight bond is formed between the conductor and the terminal, but the wire can be removed with relative ease.

Two mechanical systems were developed: Gardner Denver's *Wire Wrap*, which requires solid conductors, and AMP's *TermiPoint*, which can handle either solid or stranded wires. TABLE 5-3 lists typical characteristics of backplane wire. Tefzel and Kynar are favored as insulation because of the following properties:

- Physical toughness
- Resistance to cut-through and chemicals
- Ease of stripping
- Nonflammability
- Excellent high and low temperature range
- Absence of "set" when spooled
- Smaller outside diameter permits higher wiring density

Table 5-3. Typical Characteristics of Backplane Wire.

Conductors: Silver-plated solid or stranded copper
32 to 24 AWG
Insulation: Tefzel or Kynar
Ratings: 105°C, 300 volt
UL styles: 1422, 1423, 1426, 1427, 1508, 1516, 1517, 1523
Military specifications: MIL-W-81822

Twisted pairs

Twisted pairs are the least expensive signal-transmission conductors. They are available in a range of wire sizes with a variety of insulation materials. Twisted pairs are still widely used in signal and data transmission. However, in many systems the pairs have been replaced by coaxial cables and even optical fibers. Multiple-pair cables are discussed in chapter 7.

Twisted pairs are difficult to terminate and manual methods for terminating are slow. Electrically twisted pairs can be divided into three categories:

- Low-cost semi-rigid insulated PVC
- Higher cost irradiated PVC or low-dielectric insulations (e.g., Teflon FEP or polyethylene)
- Low-dielectric shielded insulation

Low-cost semi-rigid PVC-insulated twisted pairs are usually specified in systems where electrical properties are not critical. The conductors are typically stranded 30 to 20 AWG, rated at 80 °C 300 volts. At high frequencies where pairs are stacked, crosstalk might exist. The electrical properties of twisted pairs are improved with irradiated PVC and other low-dielectric insulations, but these materials cost more.

Attenuation (A) in paired conductors is expressed in decibels (dB) per unit length, which can be calculated from the formula:

$$A = 86.8 \sqrt{\frac{RGW}{2}}$$

Where:

R = Resistance (ac)
G = Conductance
W = 2 π f (f = test frequency in MHz)

Special-purpose wire and leads

Antenna wire typically consists of stranded bare copper-covered steel wire in 16 AWG (7 × 24) or 14 AWG (7 × 22). *Bus bar wire* is typically solid tinned copper wire that conforms to Federal Specification QQ-W-343; the wire gauge is generally between 30 and 12 AWG. *High-voltage leads* are designed to test high-voltage equipment and apparatus. High-voltage leads permit the detection of faults and other potentially dangerous conditions as part of final test and regular maintenance programs. This class of single-conductor wire is typically made from stranded and tinned 22 to 18 AWG conductors. Then, a conductive polyethylene coating is applied over the conductor and a second layer of nonconductive polyethylene dielectric material is applied.

This conductive/nonconductive layered construction distributes voltage stress more uniformly around the center conductor and reduces cable degradation that is caused by internal corona. Red PVC jacketing warns of potentially lethal voltages. The breakdown voltage ratings of 18 AWG high-voltage lead can be as high as 80 kVdc with suggested working voltages of 40 kVdc. This lead class is rated for 80 °C operation.

Magnet wire is solid copper 14 to 38 AWG wire that has been coated with insulating varnish. The coating might be a combination of polyester and polyimide, or polyurethane and nylon. This wire is used in the windings of coils, transformers, and solenoids.

Shielding and bonding leads are braided copper sleeves that conform to QQ-B-575 and are made in a range of tubular diameters for use as shielding or bonding leads. For example, a braid that consists of 576 34-AWG conductors forms a tube with a diameter of 25/32 inch. The braid can be tinned or silver coated.

Test prod wire is used to interconnect test probes with electronic test and measuring equipment. It is made as 24-to-18 AWG stranded and tinned copper with either rubber or PVC insulation in a range of colors. Fine stranding of 65×36 at 18 AWG or 45×40 at 24 AWG achieves the desired limpness. The suggested working voltage can be as high as 5000 Vdc on a product rated for 90 °C operation.

6

Flat cable and connectors

Flat cable, also known as *planar cable*, is an arrangement of parallel conductors bonded together by insulation. The most commonly used flat cable is made by simultaneously extruding insulation over as many as 64 parallel round-wire solid or stranded conductors.

Ribbon or *rainbow cable* is a form of flat cable made from conductors that have been pre-insulated in different colors. These cables can also be made by bonding the conductors in parallel on a common substrate. Alternatively, ribbon cable can be made by bonding pre-insulated twisted pairs with their ends in parallel on a common substrate.

The outstanding feature of flat cable is the uniform conductor-to-conductor spacing. This feature makes termination with mass termination insulation displacement (MTIDC) methods both feasible and economical. Figure 6-1 shows a length of extruded flat cable that is terminated at both ends with MTIDC connectors—for use in small computer systems. In addition, flat cable permits individual conductors or groups of conductors to be stripped for termination with more than one connector.

Flat cable was initially developed for aircraft use because many conductors had to be formed around sharp bends to fit in the restricted spaces of avionics cases. Conventional cables cannot be bent this way. The first military specification written to standardize flat cable was NAS-729. This document was later replaced by MIL-C-55543 and MIL-C-49059, which cover flat-conductor flat cables.

MIL-C-49055 is a general specification for round-wire flat cable—approved as a procurement document in 1977. It covers flexible, flat, unshielded electrical cable—with either solid or stranded inner round conductors—suitable for use in aerospace, ground, and shipboard applications.

Individual specification slash sheets or addenda cover cable with different AWG wire and pitch or spacing between the parallel wires. The first, MIL-C-49055/1, uses 16-AWG wire on a 0.200-inch (5.08 mm) pitch. Each successive

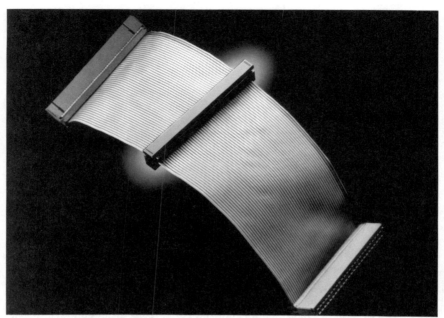

Fig. 6-1. Length of flat cable terminated with mass-termination insulation displacement connectors.

slash sheet goes to a smaller wire; finally, MIL-C-49055/8 uses 30-AWG wire on a 0.050-inch (1.27 mm) pitch. The first eight slash sheets all specify a 600-volt rating and either a 105 °C- (221 °F) or a 150 °C- (302 °F) temperature rating.

The ninth slash sheet, MIL-C-49055/9, was prepared to be compatible with existing commercial 28-AWG round-wire flat cable on a 0.050-inch pitch. The specification is essentially the same as that for commercial products that are rated for 300 volts and 105 °C. This slash sheet specifies 11 different widths in both stranded and solid wire. Conductor pitch is held to a tolerance of ± 0.002 inch (0.51 mm) to allow for mass termination with connectors, such as those specified in MIL-C-83503.

This slash sheet permits flat cable to be fabricated so that the conductors are insulated by mass extrusion. It also permits discrete pre-insulated wires to be joined together with any of the following methods:

- Melting or adhesive bonding
- Weaving together with filaments or threads
- Bonding to a film on one side
- Laminating between two films

Flat cables are now in use in computers that range in size from laptop and desktop models to mainframes. These cables are also found in computer printers and monitors, video terminals, business machines, test instruments and equipment, telecommunications systems, industrial controls, and military electronics. Flat cables offer many advantages over conventional multiconductor cables where both alternatives are acceptable:

- Space and weight savings.
- Ability to conform to the contours of the surfaces within cases or enclosures as allowed by their flexibility (extruded flat cable can be bent to small radiuses without damaging the insulation or conductors).
- Greater surface-to-volume ratio than bundled cable, providing better heat dissipation.
- Conductor positions within the cable are fixed with respect to each other, simplifying interconnections and reducing wiring errors.
- Uniform spacing of parallel conductors permits:
  ○ Uniform electrical properties: impedance, capacitance, inductance
  ○ Crosstalk reduction or elimination
  ○ Mass termination by insulation displacement (MTIDC)
- Mechanical loads are shared equally by all conductors, because they are bonded in a single plane.

Flat cable has encouraged the further miniaturization of electronics packaging. The flat form fits in otherwise unusable spaces—such as along the sides of a carrying case, or in an enclosure where standard wiring harnesses would be too stiff and bulky and could cause mechanical interference. Because flat cable can tolerate considerable flexing for many cycles, it is ideal to use it in electronic equipment drawers or between hinged covers and cases that are subject to opening and closing. This flexibility permits easier visual inspection and circuit maintenance.

The most widely used general-purpose commercial flat cable meets the requirements of MIL-C-49055/9 with 28-AWG stranded- or solid-round wire on a 0.050-inch pitch. Uniformly colored insulation is then mass extruded over the wires and edge-marked for orientation.

Flat cables are usually used within a protective case or enclosure, but shielded and jacketed flat cables are now available for use where the cable must pass outside the enclosure to connect two or more elements of a system. The shielding prevents the emission of high-frequency signals (in accordance with FCC Docket 20780) as well as shielding out unwanted signals or noise from the cable. The jacket provides the necessary mechanical protection from abuse. Cables with flat-to-round transitions are available wherever a flat external interconnection would be inconvenient or unwieldy.

The wide-range development of MTIDC connectors has also increased the popularity of flat ribbon cable. MTIDC connectors permit the simultaneous mass termination of up to 64 insulated wires in a single plane. Rows of movable contacts, which are mounted within the connectors, shear the insulation on the individual conductors. Thus, the mating wires form a gas-tight contact when uniform external pressure is applied to the connector. With MTIDC connectors, reliable contacts can be made economically and rapidly.

This chapter describes only a few of the many types of flat cables that are available as stock items from wire and cable manufacturers. If the ordered quantities cover the costs of special factory setup and tooling, many manufacturers will modify standard products or fabricate custom flat cables to meet unusual requirements for customers.

Testing flat cables

Two important factors that qualify flat cable for computer systems and instrumentation are attenuation and crosstalk.

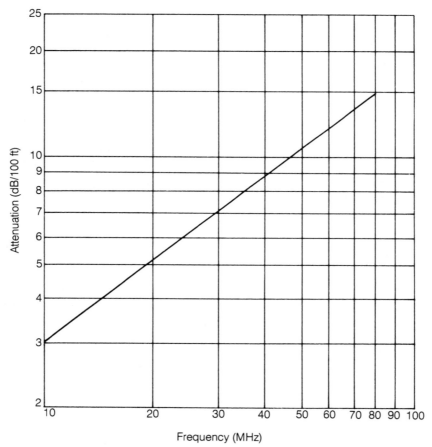

Fig. 6-2. Attenuation vs. frequency for a typical extruded flat cable.

Attenuation testing is performed to determine signal loss in decibels per 100 feet (dB/100 ft) as a function of frequency in megahertz (MHz). In general, flat cable attenuation is a linear function that increases directly with frequency in megahertz. Figure 6-2 is a typical attenuation graph for standard commercial-grade extruded flat cable—suitable for computer and instrumentation applications.

Crosstalk testing measures the interference caused by signals on a conductor, called the *drive line*, coupled into another conductor, called the *sample line*. Crosstalk measurements are made at two different locations on conductor pairs: at the near end and the far end.

Far-end crosstalk is measured by applying a signal on the drive pair at the near end and measuring the pick up on the sample pair at the far end. Near-end crosstalk is also measured by applying a signal on the drive pair at the near end, but the measurement is made on the sample pair at the near end.

Crosstalk can be measured with the unbalanced and the balanced methods. The user should determine which of these methods most closely approximates his cable application and use its results for cable comparisons.

The unbalanced crosstalk test is widely accepted in the flat-cable industry. It is a very good method to determine the pulse crosstalk of all types of cables that are connected in the ground-drive line-ground-sample-line-ground (GSG) mode. The apparatus for this test includes a signal generator that is capable of generating square-wave pulses with alterable leading-edge rise times and an oscilloscope.

Pulsed signals are applied to the drive line while measurements of disturbance are made on the sample line at the far end and the near end. Figure 6-3 is a normalized graph of crosstalk percentage, detected at the far end and the near end on the sample line as a function of the pulse rise time (in nanoseconds) using the unbalanced method. Crosstalk percentage can be determined with the formula:

$$\text{Crosstalk} = \frac{\text{Signal in sample line}}{\text{Signal in drive line}} \times 100\ \%$$

Flat cable descriptions

Round-wire flat cable with extruded insulation has been accepted as a standard product in the computer industry and is made to identical specifications by many manufacturers in the U.S., Europe, and Asia. It is the least expensive flat-cable style.

Figure 6-4 is a sectional view of standard extruded flat cable. It has a 0.050-inch (1.27 mm) pitch and stranded (7×36) 28-AWG tinned copper conductors. The insulation is gray extruded PVC. This type of flat cable was designed for mass termination, but individual conductors or groups of conductors can easily be broken out by slitting the webbing. TABLE 6-1 lists the basic

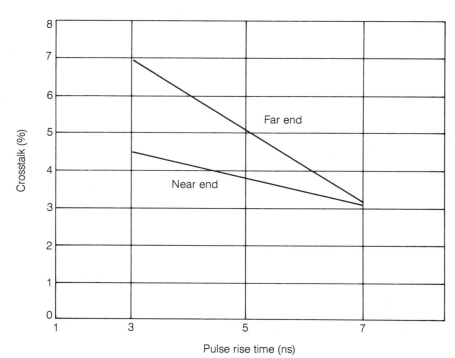

Fig. 6-3. Unbalanced crosstalk vs. pulse rise time for typical extruded flat cables.

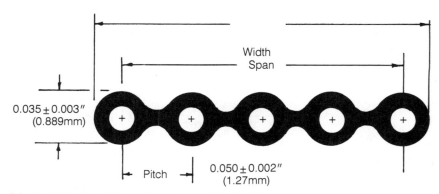

Fig. 6-4. Sectional view of an extruded flat cable.

specifications that are common to all standard 0.050-pitch flat cables. These specifications agree with those of MIL-C-49055/9.

Where greater cable flexibility is required, finer wire strands are used in the conductors. For example, 28-AWG (19 × 40) silver-plated copper wire can be substituted for the 28-AWG (7 × 36) tinned copper wire. All other mechanical and electrical properties of the cable are identical to those of the standard product.

Table 6-1. Specifications for 0.050-Pitch Flat Cable with 28-AWG Stranded Conductors.

Conductors.........................	28 AWG 7 × 36 stranded tinned copper
Number of conductors	9 to 64
Insulation	Fire retardant flexible PVC per VW-1
Insulation tensile strength	1,800 psi
Temperature rating..................	−20°C to +105°C
Voltage rating.....................	300 V rms (−20°C to +105°C)
Dielectric withstand voltage	2000 V rms
Propagation delay	1.4 ns/ft (4.6 ns/M) nom. GSG
Insulation resistance	10³ megohms /10 ft.
Characteristic impedance	150 ohms GS, 105 ohms GSG
Capacitance @ 1 MHz..............	10 pF/ft (33 pF/m) GS
	15 pF/ft (49 pF/m) GSG
Inductance @ 1 MHz...............	0.29 μH/ft (0.95 μH/m) GS
	0.20 μH/ft (0.66 μH/m) GSG
Standard lengths	100 ft. (30.4 m)
	300 ft. (91.4 m)

GS = Ground-Signal; GSG = Ground-Signal-Ground

Where higher temperature operation is desired, a fluorocarbon insulation (such as Teflon FEP) can be substituted for the PVC insulation. This insulation extends the temperature rating of the cable from 105° to 125°C.

For applications where heavier-gauge conductors are required, wider-pitch extruded cables are available. Flat cable with 0.100-inch pitch is made with 26-AWG, 24-AWG, or 22-AWG stranded and tinned copper conductors. Typical cable with 0.156-inch pitch is made with either 22-AWG or 20-AWG stranded and tinned copper conductors.

Shielded and jacketed 0.050-inch-pitch flat cable is interconnected to discrete system components where additional mechanical and EMI/RFI protection is required. The prefabricated flat cable is typically wrapped with aluminum-polyester foil to provide a flexible shield and a PVC jacket is applied. One or more stranded 28-AWG drain wires are included near the outer edges of the cable. Figure 6-5 is a sectional view of jacketed and shielded flat cable.

TABLE 6-2 summarizes the electrical data for jacketed and shielded 0.050-inch-pitch cable.

Data-link cable is another form of shielded and jacketed 0.050-inch-pitch cable. The conductors are 24-AWG (7 × 32) tinned copper and the shield is aluminum-polyester foil, metallized on both sides.

In many applications, color-coded conductors are more desirable than extruded monocolor wires. Multicolored flat cables are made by bonding discrete multicolored pre-insulated wires to each other or to a clear plastic-film substrate. Color coding is the standard ten-color repeat (brown, red, orange, yellow, green, blue, violet, gray, white, and black).

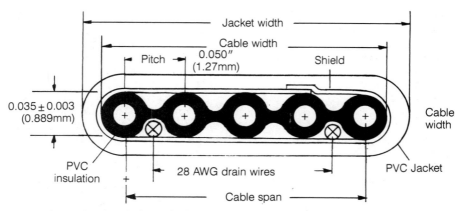

Fig. 6-5. Sectional view of a jacketed and shielded flat cable.

Table 6-2. Electrical Data on Jacketed and Shielded 0.050-Pitch Flat Cable.

Characteristic impedance	70 ohms GSG nominal
Capacitance	20 pF/ft nominal
Propagation delay	1.6 ns/ft, nominal
Resistance, direct current	67.5 ohms/100 ft

Crosstalk (nominal)	3.5 ns Rise time	7.0 ns Rise time
Near end:	5.5%	2.0%
Far end:	1.6%	0.5%

The electrical and mechanical characteristics of bonded flat cable are similar to those of extruded flat cable. Figure 6-6 is a sectional view of a multicolor flat cable. For applications where temperature ratings to 105 °C (221 °F) are specified, the conductor insulation and backing film is PVC. For higher, 150 °C (302 °F), ratings at lower voltages, silver-plated stranded-copper conductors are used and the insulation and backing is a thermoplastic fluorocarbon (such as Teflon FEP).

Pre-insulated twisted pairs of conductors in various colors are also used to manufacture multicolored flat cable. In one product for high-temperature applications, silver-plated stranded 28-AWG conductors with Teflon FEP insulation are laminated to a clear Teflon FEP substrate.

Figure 6-7A shows a sectional view through the twisted section. Figure 6-7B is a sectional view of a flat section, where the 0.050-inch pitch is maintained. Flat sections are formed at regular intervals along the length of the cable between twisted sections. Thus, if a cable is to be terminated with MTIDC connectors, its length must allow for flat sections at both ends of one or more twisted sections (FIG. 6-7C). For example, an 18-inch twisted section must be followed by a 2-inch flat.

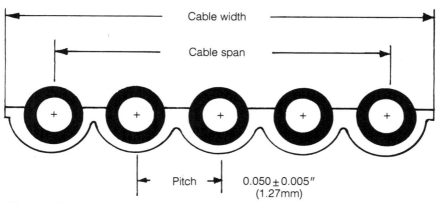

Cable width

Cable span

Pitch   0.050±0.005"
         (1.27mm)

Fig. 6-6. Sectional view of a rainbow flat cable.

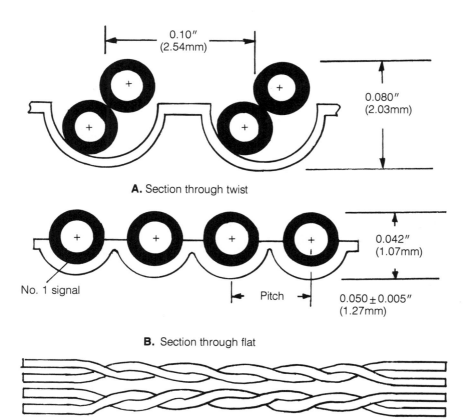

0.10"
(2.54mm)

0.080"
(2.03mm)

A. Section through twist

0.042"
(1.07mm)

No. 1 signal   Pitch   0.050±0.005"
                                (1.27mm)

B. Section through flat

C. Plan view of twisted section

Fig. 6-7. Sectional and plan views of twisted flat cable.

Each adjacent pair of color-coded pre-insulated wires is twisted in an opposite direction. In a commonly used color-coding scheme, each pair consists of a tan conductor paired with a different-colored conductor. The color sequence in each terminating section is: tan/brown, tan/red, tan/orange, tan/yellow, tan/green, tan/blue, tan/violet, tan/gray, tan/white, and tan/black. This sequence is repeated as many times as is necessary across the width of the cable. These cables contain as many as 32 twisted pairs, which might also be shielded and jacketed.

Ground plane flat cable is used where very low crosstalk is a requirement. Stranded tinned copper 28-AWG (7×36) conductors, drain wire, and an expanded copper-mesh ground plane are bonded together with extruded PVC. Figure 6-8 is a sectional view of this flat-cable style. Each cable can have as many as 60 conductors, but one will be designated as "ground."

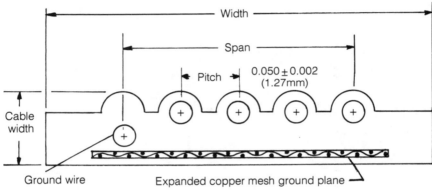

Fig. 6-8. Sectional view of a ground-plane flat cable.

Designers who need multiple coaxial cables would like to obtain the benefits of simple, low-cost termination that are inherent in flat cable. *Flat-ribbon coaxial cable* is a compromise between these two cable types and it contains the best features of each. Figure 6-9 is a sectional view of this type of cable, which shows its construction. The central conductors of each coaxial section are solid-copper 28- or 30-AWG conductors that are spaced 0.1 inch apart.

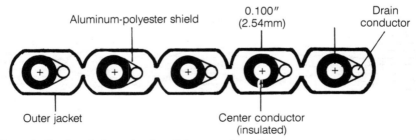

Fig. 6-9. Sectional view of a flat-ribbon coaxial cable.

Each conductor is covered with a solid or foamed polypropylene dielectric core and paired with a tinned-copper drain wire. An aluminum-polyester shield is wrapped around each coaxial element. The drain-wire pair and all of the shielded subassemblies are potted in a web of solid or foam polyethylene. The complete assembly is then given an outer protective jacket of PVC. The foamed polypropylene, which is used as the insulation and core dielectric, permits a higher signal-propagation velocity and a shorter propagation delay than solid polypropylene.

The termination requirements for this type of cable are more complex than for conventional flat cable. However, they can be terminated with insulation-displacement connectors. A short length of shield must be removed so that the connector can be attached. Drain or ground wires can be terminated at the same time as the signal conductors. Although they are in contact with the shield, ground wires are fixed to the core cable and remain in place when the shield is removed. As many as 25 signal conductors can be in these cables.

Many electronics package designers wish to take advantage of the ease of mass termination of flat cable, but prefer a conventional round-bundled conductor-cable format for external connections. *Round-to-flat cable* (FIG. 6-10) meets both requirements.

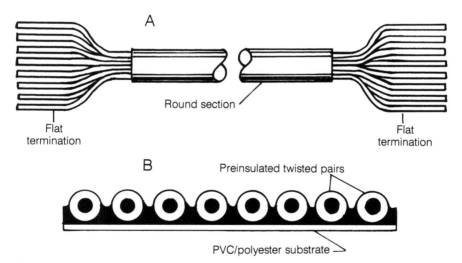

Fig. 6-10. Round cable with flat terminating sections that show plan view (A) and sectional view (B).

A variation of conventional 0.050-inch-pitch flat cable, round-to-flat cable is rolled to form a round central section with flat sections at each end for convenient, economical termination. The round section conserves space for external connections. This kind of cable is available with as many as 25 tinned copper 28-AWG (7×36) twisted conductor pairs. The primary insulation and jacketing is PVC. ·

Cable manufacturers have packaged ribbon cable with various combinations of conductors for specific applications: single-signal wires, twisted pairs, coaxial cables, and optical fiber cables. The cables might be color coded as an aid in various termination processes. Foamed dielectrics and aluminum-polyester shields conserve space and reduce weight.

Flat cable connector systems

A wide variety of connectors is now on the market to terminate flat cable. Many connector manufacturers furnish connectors designed for 0.050-inch-pitch flat cable. Some of these connectors are compatible with ribbon cable that has flat conductors. Connectors are available for 0.0025-inch pitch, but the selection is more limited. The most-common flat-cable connectors available and their applications are:

- *Socket connectors*: to repeatedly connect and disconnect a flat cable from printed-circuit cards.
- *Dual-in-line (DIP) plug connectors*: to plug into a DIP socket on a printed-circuit card.
- *Card-edge connectors*: to bus or connect one printed-circuit card to another card or to a card cage. Connector contacts grip the metallized fingers on the edge of the PC card.
- *Headers*: to receive the sockets for wire-wrapped or soldered connectors.
- *Low-profile headers*: to save space.
- *PC card solder transition connectors*: to permanently connect a cable to a PC card.
- *Subminiature "D" connectors*: to adapt plastic and metal standard subminiature "D" connectors for MTIDC.
- *Male plug connector*: to extend a flat cable that usually has a socket connector at the other end.

Interchangeability between similar products of various connector manufacturers is an important consideration when buying flat-cable connectors and cable. Compatibility reduces inventory costs and helps to avoid manufacturing mistakes. An alternate source for components is necessary to ensure a steady parts supply.

Mass termination by insulation displacement

The secret to fast economical flat-cable mass termination lies in the design of the tooth-shaped contacts (FIG. 6-11A). The contacts are lined up within the body of the connector—one for each conductor to be terminated. When the squared end of the cable is inserted and seated within the connector body, the conductors are aligned with their mating contacts. Uniform pressure is applied to a floating bar element on the connector above the contacts. The pressure forces each insulated conductor into a notch, which both pierces the adjacent webbing and shears away the insulation around the conductor (FIG. 6-11B). The conductor is flattened as the strands are forced into the narrow groove and a metal-to-metal gastight seal is formed (FIG. 6-11C).

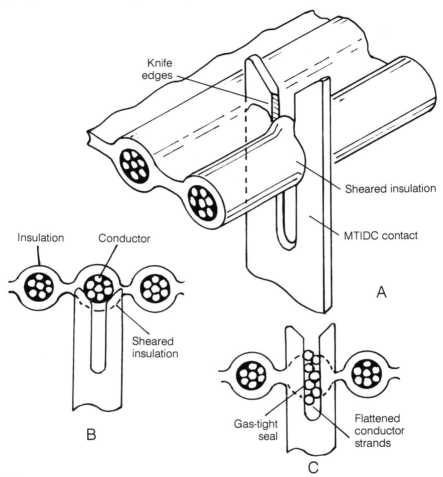

Fig. 6-11. Concept of mass-termination insulation displacement (MTIDC) of flat cable with general arrangement (A), insulation piercing and shearing (B), and seal formation (C).

Figure 6-12 shows two views of a D-type subminiature connector that is adapted for MTIDC. The illustration at the top shows the row of contacts within the connector body. The bar below it is the floating element that seats and seals the conductors in the contacts.

Several proprietary variations of the basic MTIDC contact design exist and some manufacturers claim their versions are superior to others. However,

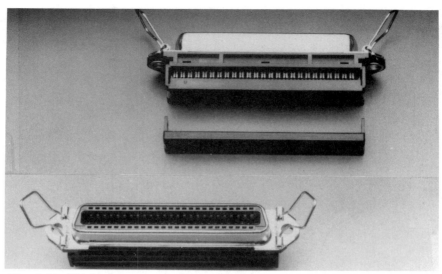

Fig. 6-12. Shielded D-type subminiature connectors adapted to mass termination IDC of flat cable.

all seem to work equally well if the manufacturers' directions are followed. The resulting terminations are satisfactory for most products that operate in a controlled environment. Also, the connector-cable assembly can be sealed or potted if it might be exposed to moisture, salt spray, or chemicals, which could cause conductor-to-contact seal corrosion.

Socket connectors from different manufacturers are usually interchangeable in any header, provided that orientation slots and tabs on the connector are compatible. If ejector latches are used, the overall height of the socket connector must be exactly the same for both products. Manufacturers might furnish strain-relief straps so that headers from more than one manufacturer are compatible. The manufacturer's recommended number of connect and disconnect cycles should be determined. These products typically have thermoplastic housings that pass the UL 94V-O flame-retardant test requirements.

The overall height of the *DIP connector* is critical. A retaining clip option can be used on the DIP socket to attach it firmly to the DIP connector.

The key dimensions on *card-edge connectors* are: overall height, tongue size, type of mounting style, and thickness of the PC card accepted.

Headers are made as full shrouded (4-wall), partially shrouded (3-wall) straight, and partially shrouded (3-wall) right-angle versions for 0.062-inch- and 0.125-inch-thick printed circuit boards. Also, wire-wrapped versions are available in straight and right-angle configurations for two- and three-level wrap. The tails are either square or rounded. The header must be compatible with the socket connectors when either the polarizing keys or the ejector latches are in place.

7

Multiconductor and multipair cables

A *multiconductor cable* is an assembly of three or more single-insulated conductors in a jacket and a *multipair cable* is an assembly of two or more insulated twisted-conductor pairs in a jacket. Both types of cable are used to interconnect computers to computer peripherals and connect computers in networks. They are also used in industrial control, intercom, and audio systems.

These cables are often named for their end-use applications: *communications* cables, *computer* cables, and *process-control* cables. The cables can be installed in conduits or trays, placed uncovered in air-conditioning plenums, or buried directly in the ground. The selection of materials for conductors, insulation, shieldings, and jackets determines the applications that are permitted under electrical codes and cable specifications. Specialized functions for multiconductor and multipair cables are discussed in chapter 11.

Cables with twisted conductor pairs allow balanced signal transmission, which results in lower crosstalk through common-mode rejection. The improved noise immunity of twisted pairs generally permits higher data speeds than those in conventional multiconductor cable.

Many cables have shielding requirements to prevent or reduce hum, noise, and crosstalk between conductors and eliminate the undesirable effects of EMI and RFI, both of which originate within the cable or are received from an external source. FCC Docket 20780 restricts signal emission from the cable; compliance is mandatory for signals or pulses that are 10 kHz or higher in frequency.

Shielding in both multiconductor and multipair cables can take the form of:

- Aluminum-polyester foil that is wrapped individually around a single conductor or around pairs and triads of conductors.

- Aluminum-polyester foil that is wrapped around insulated and cabled conductors for 100-percent cable coverage.

- Tinned or bare copper braid that surrounds insulated and cabled unshielded or shielded conductors to provide up to 90-percent coverage.

- Tinned spiral-wrapped copper that surrounds insulated and cabled unshielded or shielded conductors to provide up to 97-percent coverage.

- Combined overall shielding of all insulated and cabled unshielded or shielded conductors with both aluminum-polyester foil and copper braid to provide 100 percent coverage.

Multiconductor and multipair cables are manufactured to meet the requirements of many different codes and specifications including:

- UL covers insulated conductors, styles, and flammability ratings
- NEC covers temperature and voltage ratings for specified environments
- CSA covers styles and flammability ratings
- ASTM covers material standards and testing methods

These standards cover such subjects as the quality of the conductors and insulation materials, requirements for operation under specified environmental conditions, and environmentally appropriate flame tests. The NEC recognizes the following environments:

- Residential
- General purpose
- Riser
- Plenum
- Hazardous locations

Many options exist in the construction of multiconductor and multipair cable:

- Conductor gauge sizes range from 28 to 12 AWG (solid or stranded)
- Bare, tinned, or silver-coated copper conductors
- Conductor primary insulation typically is semi-rigid PVC, polyethylene, polypropylene, and Teflon FEP (both solid and foamed)
- Typically PVC or Teflon FEP jacketing materials
- Working voltages of 30, 150, 300, or 600 volts
- Temperature ratings of 60, 80, 105, and 200 °C

The discussion of multiconductor and multipair cables in this chapter is limited to those made as standard catalog products by American manufacturers. The intent is to show the possible combinations of materials and manufacturing methods, which are available when selecting cable to meet industry and military requirements. The products offered in the cable manufacturers' catalogs reflect customer demand and the preferences and manufacturing capabilities of each company.

Most American commercial cable manufacturers offer general-purpose cable that meets the requirements of NEC Article 725, Type CL2 (covering remote-control, signaling, and power-limited cables) and NEC Article 800, Type CM (covering communications wire and cable). Some of this cable might also qualify as Type MP multipurpose cable under NEC Article 800. These cables have from 3 to 50 identical insulated conductors. The largest volume orders are for cable with less than 10 conductors.

More flame-retardant, low-smoke producing heat-resistant materials are required for multiconductor and multipair cables that are used in riser and plenum applications. Plenum cables eliminate the need for expensive conduit and installation by permitting the cables to be run, unprotected, in the spaces that are used for air conditioning, heating, and ventilation. The NEC specifies that these cables must emit less smoke and be more flame resistant than those permitted for general-purpose or residential use. Some vendors also make what they call "high-temperature" cables, which are distinguished from riser and plenum cables. These cables use fluorocarbon resins for conductor insulation and cable jackets.

Customers with special cable requirements can request configurations that mix various conductor sizes and characteristics. For example, the gauge size of the conductors might differ or the cable might include coaxial cable or optical fibers. Certain cable styles have evolved for specific applications with different conductors (such as for LAN service) and these have become standardized.

The cable descriptions that follow are general and no attempt has been made to cover the limits in conductor gauge size, the materials, or the possible combinations permitted under the styles, codes, and standards referenced.

Unshielded multiconductor cable

Industry standards: NEC Article 725, Type CL2; NEC Article 800, Type CM; CSA FT-1 and FT-4; UL Styles 2464, 2576, 2589.

Application: Public address, audio and intercom systems, remote control interconnection, telephone and low-voltage relay control systems, EIA RS-232 and other computer uses.

Construction: (See FIG. 7-1) These cables can have solid or stranded, bare or tinned 22 to 12-AWG gauge copper conductors with color-coded PVC or polyethylene insulation. The conductors are cabled and the jacket is PVC. The voltage rating is 150 V and the temperature rating is 80 °C.

Unshielded plenum multiconductor cable

Industry standards: NEC Article 725, Type CL2P; NEC Article 800, Type CMP; CSA FT-4.

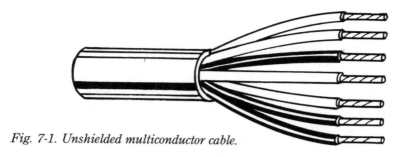

Fig. 7-1. Unshielded multiconductor cable.

Application: Public address, audio and intercom systems, remote control interconnection, telephone and low-voltage relay control systems, EIA RS-232 and other computer uses.

Construction: (See FIG. 7-2) Unshielded plenum cable is intended for use in air plenums without a conduit enclosure. Its construction is the same as CL2 and CM cables, except that conductors have fluorocarbon (typically Teflon FEP) insulation and can be tape wrapped. The jackets are also made of fluorocarbon resin, typically Teflon FEP. The voltage rating is 150 V and the temperature rating is 200 °C.

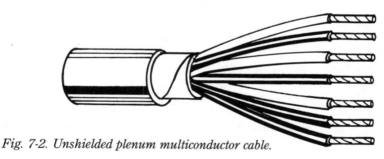

Fig. 7-2. Unshielded plenum multiconductor cable.

Foil-shielded multiconductor cable

Industry standards: NEC Article 725, Type CL2; NEC Article 800, Type CM; CSA T-2; UL Style 2464; UL 70,000 BTU Vertical Flame Test, CSA FT-1, FT-4 Flame Test.

Application: Overall foil-shielded multiconductor cable is used in computer networking, data transmission, industrial equipment control and computer interfacing including EIA RS-232 applications where an additional requirement for shielding exists.

Construction: (See FIG. 7-3) Stranded tinned-copper 24- to 20-AWG conductors have a primary insulation of color-coded semi-rigid PVC, per UL 1061. An overall aluminum-polyester foil shield provides 100-percent coverage and a stranded and tinned copper drain wire is included. The jacket is PVC. This cable can have a voltage rating of 300 V and a temperature rating of 80 °C.

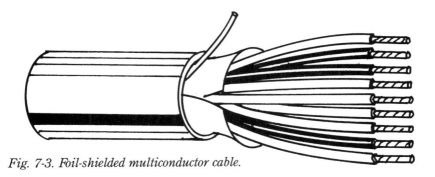

Fig. 7-3. Foil-shielded multiconductor cable.

Braid-shielded multiconductor cable

Industry standards: NEC Article 725, Type CL2; NEC Article 800, Type CM; CSA T-2; UL Style 2343; UL 70,000 BTU Vertical Flame Test, CSA FT-1 Flame Test.

Application: Braid-shielded multiconductor cable is used in computer networking, data transmission, industrial equipment-control circuits and computer interfacing—including EIA RS-232 applications where shielding must be more durable than foil, but where 100-percent shielding is not required.

Construction: (See FIG. 7-4) Stranded tinned-copper 24- to 20-AWG conductors have a primary insulation of color-coded, semi-rigid PVC, per UL 1061. An overall tinned-copper braid shield provides 70- to 85-percent shielding. The jacket is PVC. This cable can have a voltage rating of 300 V and a temperature rating of 80 °C.

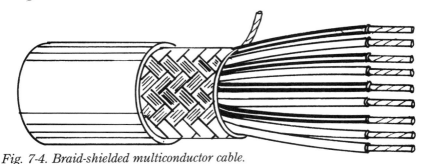

Fig. 7-4. Braid-shielded multiconductor cable.

Foil- and braid-shielded multiconductor cable

Industry standards: NEC Article 725, Type CL2; NEC Article 800, Type CM; CSA T-2; UL Style 2464; UL 70,000 BTU Vertical Flame Test, CSA FT-1 Flame Test.

Application: Foil- and braid-shielded multiconductor cable is used in computer networking, data transmission, industrial-equipment control circuits, and computer interfacing—including EIA RS-232 and CAD/CAM applications where the shielding must be more durable than foil. This class of cable helps the designers meet FCC Docket 20780 when used with shielded connectors.

Construction: (See FIG. 7-5) Stranded tinned-copper 28- to 20-AWG conductors have a primary insulation of color-coded semi-rigid PVC, per UL 1061. An overall aluminum-polyester foil shield provides 100-percent coverage and a tinned-copper drain wire is included. An additional stranded tinned-copper braid shield provides 65- to 90-percent coverage. The jacket is PVC. This cable can have a voltage rating of 300 V and a temperature rating of 80 °C.

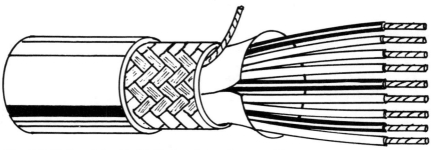

Fig. 7-5. Foil and braid-shielded multiconductor cable.

Foil- and braid-shielded plenum multiconductor cable

Industry standards: NEC Article 800, Type CMP; CSA FT-4; UL 910 Smoke and Flame Test, IEEE 383 70,000 BTU Flame Test.

Applications: Foil- and braid-shielded plenum multiconductor cable is used in computer networking, data transmission, industrial equipment-control circuits and computer interfacing—including EIA RS-232 and CAD/CAM applications where the shielding must be more durable than foil and the cable must withstand plenum temperatures. This class of cable helps the designers meet FCC Docket 20780 when used with shielded connectors.

Construction: (See FIG 7-5) Stranded tinned-copper 28- to 20-AWG conductors have a primary insulation of color-coded fluorocarbon resin, such as Teflon FEP. An overall aluminum-polyester foil shield provides 100-percent coverage and a tinned-copper drain wire is included. An additional stranded tinned-copper braid shield provides 65- to 90-percent coverage. The jacket is FEP. This cable can have a voltage rating of 300 V and a temperature rating of 200 °C.

Unshielded multipair cable

Industry standards: NEC Article 725, Type CL2; NEC Article 800, Type CM; CSA FT-1 and FT-4; UL Styles 2464, 2576, and 2589.

Application: Unshielded paired cables allow balanced signal transmission in public address audio systems, intercom systems, remote-control interconnecting cables, telephone and low-voltage relay control systems, and EIA RS-232 computer interfacing.

Construction: (See FIG. 7-6) These cables have solid- or stranded-tinned 24- to 12-AWG copper conductors with color-coded semi-rigid PVC primary insulation. The insulated conductor pairs are cabled and the jacket is PVC.

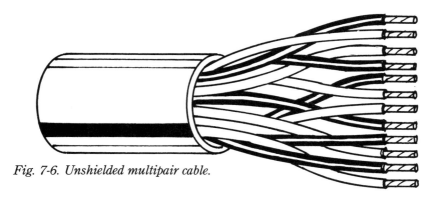

Fig. 7-6. Unshielded multipair cable.

Unshielded plenum multipair cable

Industry standards: NEC Article 725, Type CL2P; NEC Article 800, Type CMP; CSA FT-4; UL 910 Smoke and Flame Test, IEEE 383 70,000 BTU Flame Test.

Application: Unshielded paired plenum cables allow balanced signal transmission in public address audio systems, intercom systems, remote control interconnecting cables, telephone and low-voltage relay control systems, and EIA RS-232 computer interfacing. These cables are used in the more demanding plenum applications.

Construction: (See FIG. 7-6) These cables have solid- or stranded-tinned 24- to 12-AWG copper conductors with color-coded Teflon FEP or other fluorocarbon resin primary insulation. The insulated conductor pairs are cabled and the jacket is Teflon FEP.

Individually foil-shielded multipair cable

Industry standards: NEC Article 725, Type CL2; NEC Article 800, Type CM; CSA T-2; UL Styles 2919, 2094; UL 70,000 BTU Vertical Flame Test, CSA PCC FT-1.

Application: Individually foil-shielded multipair cable is recommended for audio, pulse, and radio-frequency systems where superior circuit isolation is required. These include computer networking, data transmission, industrial equipment control and instrumentation.

Construction: (See FIG. 7-7) Stranded-tinned copper 24- to 20-AWG conductor pairs have a primary insulation of color-coded polyethylene. Conductor pairs are individually shielded with aluminum-polyester foil that provides 100-

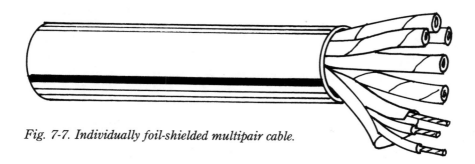

Fig. 7-7. Individually foil-shielded multipair cable.

percent shielding; also, a stranded- and tinned-copper drain wire is included with each pair. The jacket is PVC. This cable has a voltage rating of 300 V and a temperature rating of 80 °C.

Individually foil-shielded plenum multipair cable

Industry standards: NEC Article 725, Type CL2P; NEC Article 800, Type CMP; CSA FT-4; UL 910 Smoke and Flame Test, IEEE 383 70,000 BTU Flame Test.

Application: Individually foil-shielded plenum multipair cable is recommended for audio, pulse, and radio-frequency applications where superior circuit isolation is required in plenum placement. These applications include computer networking, data transmission, instrumentation and industrial equipment control.

Construction: (See FIG. 7-7) Stranded tinned-copper 24- to 20-AWG conductor pairs have a primary insulation of color-coded foamed Teflon FEP. The conductor pairs are individually shielded with aluminum-polyester foil that provides 100-percent shielding, also, a stranded and tinned-copper drain wire is included with each pair. The jacket is Teflon FEP. This cable can have a voltage rating of 300 V and a temperature rating of 200 °C.

Foil-shielded multipair cable

Industry standards: NEC Article 725, Type CL2; NEC Article 800, Type CM; CSA T-2; UL Style 2464; UL 70,000 BTU Vertical Flame Test, CSA Certified PCC FT-4.

Application: Overall foil-shielded multipair cable is used in computer networking, data transmission, industrial equipment control, sound, broadcast, and computer interfacing—including EIA RS-232.

Construction: (See FIG. 7-8) Stranded tinned-copper 24- to 20-AWG conductors have a primary insulation of color-coded semi-rigid PVC, per UL 1061. An overall aluminum-polyester foil shield provides 100-percent shielding and a stranded- and tinned-copper drain wire is included. The jacket is PVC. This cable can have a voltage rating of 300 V and a temperature rating of 80 °C.

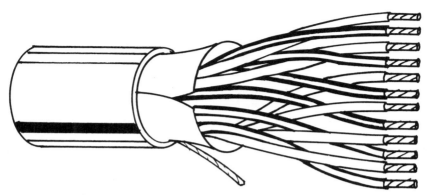

Fig. 7-8. Foil-shielded multipair cable.

Foil-shielded plenum multipair cable

Industry standards: NEC Article 725, Type CL2P; NEC Article 800, Type CMP; CSA Certified PCC FT-4; UL 910 Smoke and Flame Test, IEEE 383 70,000 BTU Flame Test.

Application: Overall foil-shielded plenum multipair cable is used in computer networking, data transmission, industrial equipment control, instrumentation, audio, broadcast, and computer interfacing—including EIA RS-232.

Construction: (See FIG. 7-8) Stranded tinned-copper 24- to 22-AWG conductors have a primary insulation of color-coded fluorocarbon resin, such as Teflon FEP. An overall aluminum-polyester foil shield provides 100-percent shielding and a stranded- and tinned-copper drain wire is included. The jacket is Teflon FEP. This cable can have a voltage rating of 300 V and a temperature rating of 200 °C.

Braid-shielded multipair cable

Industry standards: NEC Article 725, Type CL2; NEC Article 800, Type CM; CSA T-2; UL Style 2343 and 2344; UL 70,000 BTU Vertical Flame Test, CSA FT-1 Flame Test.

Application: Braid-shielded multipair cable is used in computer networking, data transmission, industrial equipment control circuits, and computer interfacing—including EIA RS-232 applications, where shielding must be more durable than foil, but where 100-percent shielding is not required. A tinned-copper braid shield with 85-percent coverage is used.

Construction: Stranded-tinned 24- to 20-AWG copper conductor pairs have a primary insulation of color-coded, semi-rigid PVC, per UL 1061. An overall tinned-copper braid shield provides 85-percent shielding. The jacket is PVC. This cable can have a voltage rating of 300 V and a temperature rating of 80 °C.

Foil and braid shielded multipair cable

Industry standards: NEC Article 725, Type CL2; NEC Article 800, Type CM; CSA T-2; UL Styles 2464, 2490, 2493, and 2919; UL 70,000 BTU Vertical Flame Test, CSA PCC FT-1 and PCC FT-4.

Application: Foil and braid-shielded multiconductor cable uses include computer networking, data transmission, industrial equipment control, CAD/CAM, and computer interfacing—including EIA RS-232 and EIA RS-485, where shielding must be more durable than foil and 100-percent shielding is required. Foil and braid-shielded cable with shielded connectors helps the designers meet the requirements of FCC Docket 20780.

Construction: (See FIG. 7-9) Stranded-tinned 28- to 20-AWG copper conductor pairs have a primary insulation of color-coded semi-rigid PVC or polyethylene. An aluminum-polyester foil shield, a 65-percent tinned-copper braid shield, and a tinned-copper drain wire provide 100-percent coverage. The jacket is PVC. This cable can have a voltage rating of 300 V and a temperature rating of 80 °C.

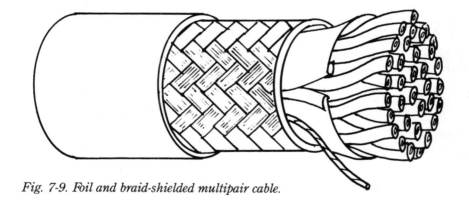

Fig. 7-9. Foil and braid-shielded multipair cable.

Foil- and braid-shielded plenum multipair cable

Industry standards: NEC Article 725, Type CL2P; NEC Article 800, Type CMP; CSA Certified PCC FT-4; UL 910 Smoke and Flame Test, IEEE 383 70,000 BTU Flame Test.

Application: Foil and braid-shielded plenum multiconductor cable is used in data transmission, industrial equipment control, CAD/CAM, and computer interfacing—including EIA RS-232 and EIA RS-485, where shielding must be more durable than foil and 100-percent shielding is required. Foil- and braid-shielded cable with shielded connectors helps designers meet the requirements of FCC Docket 20780.

Construction: (See FIG. 7-9) Stranded-tinned 28- to 20-AWG copper conductor pairs have a primary insulation of color-coded foamed Teflon FEP. An aluminum-polyester foil shield, a 65-percent tinned-copper braid shield, and a tinned-copper drain wire provide 100-percent coverage. The jacket is Teflon FEP. This cable can have a voltage rating of 300 V and a temperature rating of 200 °C.

Multiconductor and multipair cable connectors

Multiconductor and multipair cables can be terminated with many different kinds of connectors, including both rectangular and circular connectors (also called *cylindrical connectors*). Circular connectors have an efficient form factor and can withstand external forces and abuse better than rectangular connectors.

Figure 7-10 shows a widely used military specification circular connector, MIL-C-38999, Series IV with the plug at left and receptacle at right. The *plug* is the part of the connector that is attached to the free or moving end of the cable, and the *receptacle* is the part that is attached to the wall or side panel of a chassis or enclosure.

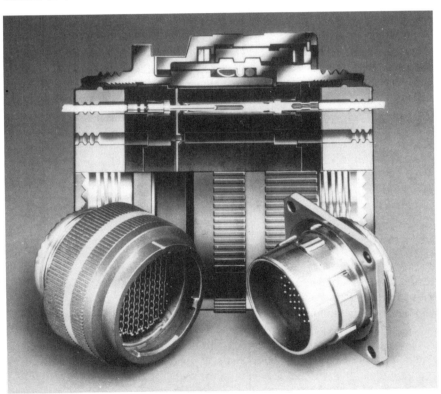

Fig. 7-10. MIL-C-38999, Series IV, circular connector with plug (left) and receptacle (right).

Originally developed more than 45 years ago for military applications, *cylindrical* or *circular connectors* can terminate cables with as many as 128 conductors. The first of these connectors was designed to externally couple separately enclosed military radio and radar systems. The U.S. armed forces are still major users of these connectors. TABLE 7-1 identifies an important group of military-style connectors that are still being procured.

*Table 7-1. Popular Military
Multiconductor Connectors.*

MIL-C-5015
MIL-C-22992
MIL-C-26482, Series I and II
MIL-C-26500
MIL-C-27599, Series I and II
MIL-C-38999, Series I, II, III and IV
MIL-C-81511
MIL-C-83723, Series III

MIL-STD-1353A lists the preferred connectors for military applications. There are three size classifications: *standard, miniature,* and *subminiature.* The construction and tests of all three size classifications are similar. Standard-size circular connectors are usually specified for large shipboard and ground-based systems, although the trend has been toward specifying miniature connectors in these applications. Subminiature connectors are favored for avionics because of their lighter weight and smaller size.

An important feature of all circular connectors is the rapidity with which they can be aligned, coupled, or uncoupled without the aid of tools. The metal shells of the receptacles and plugs protect against abrasion and external forces that would otherwise crush the connectors. The shells also protect the mating contacts from airborne contaminants, dust, moisture, and salt spray. Metal shells shield cable assemblies against both transmitted and received radio-frequency energy, if the mating cables are shielded.

The integral locking mechanisms, either complete or partially threaded shells (breech lock) or bayonet-style (pin and curved slot), provide a self-supporting interconnection. Neither internal nor external screws are required to secure the mating parts. Cylindrical connectors can also withstand the high shock and vibration forces that are encountered in aircraft, ships, and vehicles.

A knurled outer ring is twisted to unlock the mating shells. In addition, built-in keys ensure rapid and correct alignment or polarization for the mating contacts. Circular connectors are precision-made products, designed to ensure maximum conductivity between the connected circuits.

Bulkhead connectors serve as transitions between two cables located on opposite sides of a metal case or bulkhead in aircraft or ships. These connectors permit watertight or pressurized integrity to be maintained at the bulkhead.

Circular connectors are used in the avionics systems of both military and commercial aircraft for interconnecting parts of radio, radar, and navigational systems. These connectors are also used on military aircraft and missiles for interconnecting electronics warfare-, guidance-, and fire-control systems.

These connectors are also specified for many applications on military surface ships and submarines, tanks, and mobile weapons platforms. In addition, they are used in communications vans and portable aircraft ground control equipment shelters. Military and commercial aircraft ground-support and systems test equipment also use these connectors as do machine tool, robots, process-control systems, and radio and television broadcasting equipment.

Figure 7-11 is a cutaway view of an MIL-C-38999, Series IV circular connector. The other three versions of this connector have mechanical differences that represent modifications requested by the originating military service. Versions of each of these connectors can have from 4 to 128 contacts. Four sizes of contacts exist and some inserts permit intermixing two different sizes.

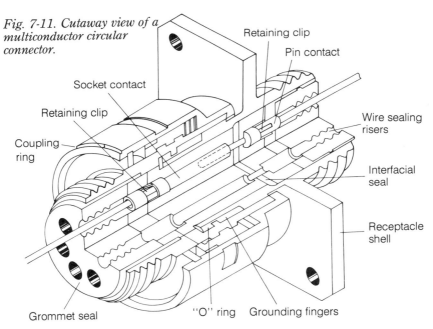

Fig. 7-11. Cutaway view of a multiconductor circular connector.

Retaining clip

Pin contact

Socket contact

Retaining clip

Wire sealing risers

Coupling ring

Interfacial seal

Receptacle shell

Grommet seal

"O" ring   Grounding fingers

Quick-release, breakaway versions of this and other military-style circular connectors that permit rapid disengagement as missiles are launched from aircraft, ships, submarines, ground silos, or vehicles. Braided metal lanyards are fastened to the outer shell. As the missile blasts-off, it applies tension to the lanyard, which pulls out threaded coupling segments for instant release.

Commercial versions of military-specification circular connector families are available. These versions do not require the same costly QPL testing and traceability documentation as the products that are procured for military use.

Military-specification circular connector pins are machined from brass or nickel-silver and sockets are formed from nonferrous materials (such as beryllium-copper, phosphor-bronze or nickel-silver). Sockets include flexible inner-leaf spring contact surfaces to grip the pins with sufficient force to obtain high-electrical conductivity—even after many engagements and disengagements.

Gold is preferred for plating mating contacts because it permits nondestructive sliding contacts and it resists corrosion, oxidation, and other contamination, which would block low-level "dry" signals. A minimum gold plating thickness of 50 microinches is specified for military-specification connectors, but 15 to 30 microinches is acceptable for many commercial avionics and industrial applications.

Pins and sockets are placed in aluminum or stainless-steel shells and inserted in multihole spacers, which establish contact distribution and spacing. The pins must be resilient to prevent damage to either pins or sockets from misalignment when the parts are coupled. Permissible center-to-center spacing of pins and sockets is determined by the voltage, current, and frequency of the transmitted signals.

The individual cable wires are crimped to the removable contacts in the military-style connectors. Wires with crimped, "poke-home" contacts are inserted into the shells of the connector with a special hand tool, which compresses the springs and locks the contacts into position within the shell. This design permits the pins and sockets to be removed easily for inspection. Field changes or repairs can be performed on individual wire terminations without disturbing adjacent wires.

Special coaxial cables with pins and sockets are available for cylindrical connectors. Fiber-optic cables have also been adapted to multipin circular connectors. Fiber-optic contacts have been designed to fit the space allowed by these connectors and they can be intermixed with lower frequency contacts.

Hermetically sealed connectors are made with contacts that are rigidly fixed within a spacer of glass or ceramic. Because the contacts are not removable, wires must be attached individually by welding or soldering. Care must be taken when using these connectors to avoid cracking the hermetic seals.

8

Coaxial, triaxial, and twinaxial cables and connectors

A *coaxial cable* is a shielded and jacketed single conductor with a central or inner conductor, core insulation, shield, and jacket. It is designed to transmit an electrical signal with minimum loss of strength (attenuation) and distortion. The cable's shield confines a transmitted signal to its electrical path and acts as a return conductor. To be effective, the core insulation, shield, and jacket materials must be carefully selected and precise dimensional control must be maintained throughout the manufacturing process. By contrast, little effort is made to control the signal quality in ordinary shielded and jacketed conductors.

Coaxial cables can transmit signals across the spectrum—from direct current (dc) well into the microwave frequency range. However, they are used most effectively from one kilohertz (kHz) to four gigahertz (GHz). The most important characteristics of coaxial cable are:

- Low signal loss
- Little or no signal distortion
- Minimum EMI radiated or received by the cable
- Wide bandwidth
- Minimal crosstalk

The wide bandwidth capability of coaxial cable permits up to 2,880 telephone channels to be handled on a single cable with low attenuation. It also permits telephone conversations and TV signals to be transmitted simultaneously over the same cable.

Description

Figure 8-1 shows the simplest type of coaxial cable, with a solid inner or axial conductor and solid dielectric. The outer conductor (shield or braid) is covered by an extruded insulating jacket. Figure 8-2 shows a variation of the basic design with a stranded inner conductor.

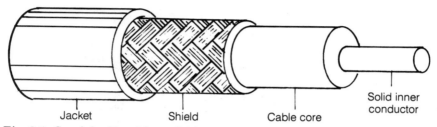

Jacket   Shield   Cable core   Solid inner conductor

Fig. 8-1. Coaxial cable with a solid inner conductor.

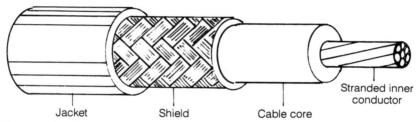

Jacket   Shield   Cable core   Stranded inner conductor

Fig. 8-2. Coaxial cable with a stranded inner conductor.

The central- or inner-signal conductor of a coaxial cable is positioned axially within an outer tubular "return-path" conductor, typically a woven metallic braid. This inner conductor can be made from either solid or stranded wire. It is separated from the outer conductor by a sleeve or core of solid or foamed plastic resin that acts as both a dielectric and as an insulating spacer.

Some coaxial cables use air as a dielectric within a suitable rigid plastic structure that holds the coaxial form of the cable. Whether the core is foamed, solid, or includes an air space, it must be rigid enough to maintain the correct separation between the inner and outer conductors despite bends or twists imposed on it.

Inner conductor

The center or inner conductor is typically solid or stranded annealed copper wire. Annealed copper is preferred over hard copper as an inner conductor for general-purpose coaxial cable. Certain applications might require the extra strength of copper-clad steel or high-strength copper-alloy conductors. A solid inner conductor causes less signal loss or attenuation than a stranded conductor, but a stranded conductor is more flexible than its solid equivalent. Military-specification coaxial cables, for example, might have 7, 19, or even 27 strands.

As in other cables, the coaxial-cable conductor material depends on both the intended temperature rating and the selected dielectric. Thus, the inner conductor can be bare copper (BC), silver-coated (SC) or tin-coated copper (TC). In the applications that require higher strength copper-clad steel (CCS), the copper cladding is usually silver-coated steel (SCS). Also, high-strength copper alloy is usually silver-coated alloy (SCA).

Outer conductor or shield

The outer conductor of coaxial cable typically consists of a single braid of small diameter bare, tinned, or silver-coated copper wires (BC, TC, or SC). Double braids are used where more effective shielding is required, and where crosstalk and noise must be minimized. The shield in a coaxial cable performs three functions:

- Confines the signal to its assigned electrical path and prevents the cable from acting as an antenna
- Serves as a "return" conductor
- Prevents or screens out EMI and RFI

The three methods to shield the dielectric core of a coaxial cable use:

- Bare, tinned, or silver-coated copper wire serving
- Bare, tinned, or silver-coated copper wire braid
- Aluminum braid
- Copper or aluminum braid and aluminum-polyester foil

Signal transmission through a shielded and jacketed coaxial cable should occur with minimum losses and little or no distortion. The higher the percentage of braid cover, the more complete is the shielding. Only copper braid shielding can be used on military specification cable. Copper braid typically provides 95-percent coverage, but ratings often extend from 88 percent to 97 percent. In some cases, two layers of braid are required to provide 95- to 97-percent coverage and adequate flexibility. High single-braid coverage reduces the flexibility of the cable and makes it difficult to install.

By contrast, nonmilitary coaxial cable uses any or more than one of the listed shielding methods. Aluminum-polyester foil will, by itself, provide 100-percent coverage. The braid on some of these cables might have relatively low coverage, perhaps only 20 percent, to save weight and cost. However, aluminum-polyester foil can be used to supplement the braid in one or more layers to provide 100-percent shielding. Nonmilitary coaxial cable might also have two layers of braid.

Dielectric core

The dielectric materials for coaxial cables are selected for their ability to:

- Minimize signal losses
- Withstand wide temperature range
- Provide excellent dielectric properties
- Permit cable miniaturization

The size and weight of the coaxial cable is related to the dielectric constant (K) of its core material. The core positions the inner conductor, with respect to the outer conductor, and establishes concentricity. If attenuation and impedance remain constant as K decreases, the radial separation between the conductors can be reduced. This reduction permits a lighter cable with a smaller diameter (miniaturization).

Solid dielectrics are more practical for most applications than air, which has a lower dielectric constant (approaching 1.0). An ideal core material, air permits high propagation velocities. However, its drawback is the size of the cable that is required for effective conductor separation. One solution is the air-spaced core coaxial cable, discussed further in this chapter.

Cable miniaturization has been obtained with cellular or foamed dielectrics, such as polyethylene and fluorocarbon resins. The lower dielectric constants of these materials have permitted substantially reduced cable size. Solid cores do not permit the same size reduction, but they reduce attenuation significantly and improve both capacitance and velocity of propagation, which is one of the many tradeoffs in cable design. TABLE 8-1 lists common core dielectric materials.

- Extruded or conventional polyethylene (PE) is most widely used. It is inexpensive, has very good electrical properties, and has a low dielectric constant. However, it is not generally specified in applications where the ambient temperature exceeds 80 °C (176 °F). Because polyethylene is flammable, it must be protected by an outer conductor and jacket.

- Cross-linked or irradiated PE has approximately the same electrical characteristics as conventional PE. Irradiation transforms it into a thermosetting material, improving its toughness, and resistance to cut-through, ozone, solvents, soldering temperature, and environmental stress cracking. Irradiated PE is rated for 125 °C (259 °F) operation and it has a higher dielectric constant.

- Cellular or foamed polyethylene (FPE) is specified when a requirement exists for a core material with a very low dielectric constant. By controlling the size and number of cells, effective dielectric constants as low as 1.4 are achieved.

- Flame-retardant polyethylene (FRPE) has additives to improve its flame retardance, but these give it the highest dielectric constant of any form of PE.

- Teflon FEP has excellent electrical properties and is rated for temperatures to 200 °C (392 °F). Its low dielectric constant is suitable for making miniature coaxial cables.

Table 8-1. Core Material Dielectric Constants.

Material	Dielectric Constant (K)
Polyethylene, solid	2.25
Polyethylene, cross-linked	2.45
Polyethylene, cellular (foamed)	1.4-1.7*
Polyethylene, flame retardant	2.5
Fluorocarbon, FEP	2.15
Fluorocarbon, FEP foamed	1.4-1.7*

*Varies with degree of foaming

Jacket

The jacket protects the conductors and the dielectric core from deterioration and mechanical abuse as a result of environmental stresses. Polyvinyl chloride (PVC) and polyethylene (PE) are the most widely used materials for coaxial-cable jackets. Teflon FEP is used if the cable will be subjected to high temperatures.

Coaxial-cable styles

Figure 8-3 shows a coaxial cable with a double-braided shield. This cable is used where from 97- to 100-percent shield coverage is required and the shield must be able to withstand severe mechanical stress. Figure 8-4 shows an alternate double-shielded cable with aluminum-polyester foil shielding, combined with copper braid. The braid shield might only have a coverage of 65 percent, but 100-percent coverage is achieved with the foil.

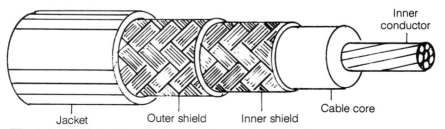

Inner conductor

Jacket   Outer shield   Inner shield   Cable core

Fig. 8-3. Coaxial cable with inner and outer braid shielding.

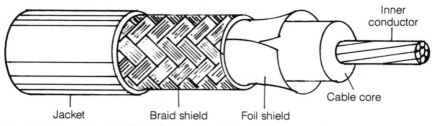

Fig. 8-4. Coaxial cable with foil and braid shielding.

Figure 8-5 shows an air-spaced coaxial cable and FIG. 8-6 shows an air-spaced coaxial cable with double-layer braid shielding for additional coverage. If air is the dielectric, some type of insulating spacers are needed to hold the shield (or outer conductor) concentric, with respect to the inner conductor. This can be done with dielectric beads "strung" on the inner conductor. However, the designs shown in the figures are more practical solutions that permit both mass production and improve cable integrity.

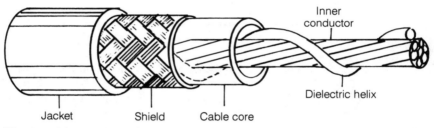

Fig. 8-5. Air-spaced coaxial cable.

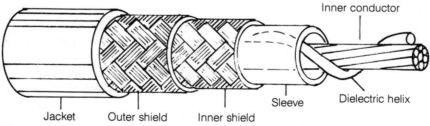

Fig. 8-6. Air-spaced coaxial cable with double-braid shielding.

A helix is formed from dielectric filament (such as polyethylene) that is wrapped around the inner conductor. Then, an insulating sleeve of the same material is extruded over the helix to act as a rigid form for the braid shield. A helical space is formed down the length of the cable for air circulation.

Cable core consists of air and solid dielectric helix and sleeve. The effective dielectric constant of this construction varies with the air-to-plastic ratio. The lowest value achieved is about 1.45.

Dual coaxial cable is essentially two separate but identical coaxial cables with a common extruded jacket (FIG. 8-7). This style permits twin cables to be conveniently pulled together during installation.

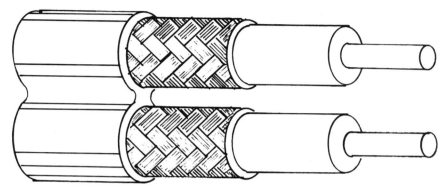

Fig. 8-7. Dual coaxial cable.

Twinaxial cable is a pair of coaxial cables that are packaged in a common shield and jacket (FIG. 8-8). Both parts might be identical or some distinguishing difference might exist, such as a tinned center strand in one of the inner conductors. Twinaxial cables are made with the same materials and construction techniques as coaxial cables.

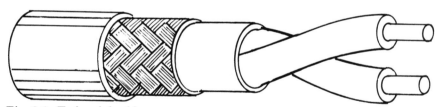

Fig. 8-8. Twinaxial cable.

Triaxial cable has three conductors. It is basically a coaxial cable with an additional dielectric layer and braided shield to form a third conductor as shown in FIG. 8-9. Triaxial cables are also made with the same materials and construction techniques as coaxial cables.

Origins of coaxial cable

Military radar R&D drove the early development of modern miniature coaxial cables more than 40 years ago. These cables were also used in military radio transmitters and receivers. Because of their origins in military and aerospace work, military specifications are still widely used for the design, manufacture, test, qualification, and selection of all coaxial cables—whether for military or nonmilitary applications.

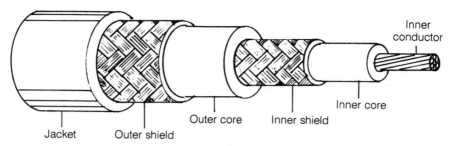

Fig. 8-9. Triaxial cable.

The designation *RG/U* indicates that a coaxial cable has been designed, tested, and qualified to DOD specifications—usually by one of the service branches (Air Force, Navy, or Army). *RG* stands for radio frequency guide and *U* stands for universal. TABLE 8-2 lists the characteristics of a selection of military spec RG/U cables.

The letters A, B, or C before the slash indicate a specification modification or revision. For example, RG-62A/U and RG-62B/U are modifications of the RG-62/U design. Qualified Products Listed (QPL) coaxial cables with the same RG/U designations are mechanically and electrically interchangeable, regardless of the manufacturer.

Military coaxial cables are identified by RG/U designations of MIL-C-17A through MIL-C-17F and also by MIL-C-17F M17 slash numbers. They can also be identified by the manufacturer's trade number, NEC type, or CSA certification. Cables identified only with a manufacturer's proprietary commercial trade number might only be interchangeable or compatible with similarly designated proprietary cable from the same manufacturer.

Newly developed or improved RG/U cables are regularly added to DOD's QPL list. Manufacturers of coaxial cable must manufacture and test these cables to all of the applicable military specifications and standards if they wish to sell this cable to the U.S. Government or to U.S. military contractors. They must also meet all requirements of their manufacturing facilities and cable-construction employees must be qualified. The companies must also be prepared to furnish all the required traceability documentation.

Nonmilitary coaxial cable

A nonmilitary or commercial user of coaxial cable can purchase military-qualified or QPL coaxial cable. Usually, the QPL testing and documentation is not necessary for commercial and industrial customers. Moreover, they do not normally need some of the qualities that are required for military applications (such as ability to withstand environmental extremes and rough treatment). The alternative is to purchase "RG-type" cable or cable that is made to company proprietary standards or to other commercial standards.

Table 8-2. Characteristics of Some RG/U Coaxial Cables.

MIL No. RG-	Nom. Imp. Ohms	Vel. of Prop %	Nom. Cap.	Diel.	Center Conductor Matl.	Center Conductor AWG/Strands	Shield	Jacket O.D. Matl.	Jacket in.
6A/U	75	66	20.5	PE	BCS	21 (Solid)	BC	2PE	.325
8/U	52	66	29.5	PE	BC	13 (7×21)	BC	PVC	.405
8A/U*	52	66	29.5	PE	BC	13 (7×21)	BC	PVC	.405
9/U	51	66	30.5	PE	SCC	13 (7×21)	BC	PVC	.420
11/U	75	66	20.5	PE	TC	18 (7×26)	BC	PVC	.405
11A/U*	75	66	20.5	PE	TC	18 (7×26)	BC	PVC	.405
22B/U*	95	66	16.0	PE	TC/BC	18 7×26)	TC	PVC	.432
58/U	53.5	66	28.5	PE	BC	20 (solid)	TC	PVC	.195
58A/U	50	66	30.8	PE	TC	20 (19×.0071)	TC	PVC	.195
58C/U#	50	66	30.8	PE	TC	20 (19×.0072)	TC	PVC	.195
59/U	73	66	21.0	PE	BCS	22 (Solid)	BC	PVC	.242
59/UD	75	66	17.3	PE	BCS	20 (Solid)	2BC	PE	.315
59B/U*	75	66	20.5	PE	BCS	23 (Solid)	BC	PVC	.242
62/U	93	84	13.5	PE	BCS	22 (Solid)	BC	PVC	.242
62A/U	93	84	13.5	PE	BCS	22 (Solid)	BC	PE	.242
62B/U*	93	84	13.5	PE	BCS	24 (7×32)	BC	PVC	.242
71/U	93	84	13.5	PE	BCS	22 (Solid)	BC	PE	.245
108A/U*	78	66	1.96	PE	TC	20 (7×28)	TC	PVC	.235
122/U*	50	66	30.8	PE	TC	22 (27×36)	TC	PVC	.160
141A/U*T	50	69.5	29.0	TFE	SCS	18 (Solid)	SCC	FBG	.190
142B/U#	50	69.5	29.0	TFE	SCS	18 (Solid)	2SCC	FEP	.195
174/U*	50	66	30.8	PE	BCS	26 (7×34)	TC	PVC	.101
178B/U#	50	69.5	29.0	TFE	SCS	30 (7×38)	SCC	FEP	.072
179B/U#	75	69.5	19.5	TFE	SCS	30 (7×38)	SCC	FEP	.100

Table 8-2. Continued.

MIL No. RG-	Nom. Imp. Ohms	Vel. of Prop %	Nom. Cap.	Diel.	Center Conductor Matl.	AWG/Strands	Shield	Jacket O.D. Matl.	in.
180B/U#	95	69.5	15.0	TFE	SCS	30 (7×38)	SCC	FEP	.140
187A/U*	75	69.5	19.5	TFE	SCS	30 (7×38)	SCC	TFET	.105
188A/U*	50	69.5	29.0	TFE	SCS	26 (7×.0067)	SCC	TFET	.106
195A/U*	95	69.5	15.0	TFE	SCS	30 (7×38)	SCC	TFE	.155
196A/U*	50	69.5	28.5	TFE	SCS	30 (7×38)	SCC	TFE	.080
213/U*	50	66.0	30.8	PE	BC	13 (7×21)	2SCC	PVC	.405
214/U#T	50	66.0	30.8	PE	BSC	13 (7×.0296)	2SCC	PVC	.425
233/U#	50	66.0	30.8	PE	SCC	19 (Solid)	2SCC	PVC	.212
316/U*	50	69.5	29.0	TFE	SCS	26 (7×.0067)	SCC	FEP	.098

* Per MIL-C-17D   # Per MIL-C-17F   T = Twinaxial

BC = Bare copper
BCS = Bare copper-clad steel
CCS = Copper-clad steel
SCC = Silver-clad copper
SCS = Silver-clad steel
TC = Tin-coated copper

PE = Polyethylene
PVC = Polyvinyl chloride
TFE = Tetrafluoroethylene (Teflon)
TFET = TFE tape
FEP = Fluorinated ethylene propylene (Teflon)
FBG = Fiberglass

Most coaxial-cable companies manufacture cable for nonmilitary applications that is generally similar in construction, dimensions, and even performance to QPL cable (called *RG/U type*). This cable is purchased for applications that are similar to military applications (such as data transmission and broadcasting). However, different materials can be substituted for those used in the QPL cable (such as insulation, jacketing, and shielding). Moreover, dimensions and electrical performance might differ from the QPL product.

In some cases, foil shielding, not permitted in the QPL cable, is used. These variations are permitted in situations where weight, size, and durability are less critical than in the military applications. The material selection is most often governed by cost-saving considerations. However, the elimination of QPL screening and documentation by itself significantly reduces the cost of coaxial cable.

Manufacturers also design and manufacture coaxial cable to meet commercial standards (such as those used in computer networking or video transmitting). When coaxial cable is used for nonmilitary communications, the NEC applies. This cable is fabricated to comply with the NEC requirements for general-purpose, riser, and plenum applications (such as CL2X, CL2, CL2R, and CL2P). Coaxial cable is classified under UL styles 1354, 1478, and 20121; dual cable is classified under UL style 20063; and twinaxial cable is classified under UL style 2498.

Cable selection

Coaxial cable is used when the distributed capacity must be held constant over the entire length of the transmission line. It is also used in applications where signal loss and attenuation must be minimized. The shielding of coaxial cables confines high-frequency signals to the cable and prevents the entry of unwanted EMI and RFI when used with shielded connectors.

The inner conductor must remain concentric with the outer conductor over the entire length of the cable or losses will reduce the efficiency of transmission. When bending a coaxial cable, care should be taken so that the minimum bend radius is never less than 10 times the outer diameter of the cable. Otherwise, the concentricity of the inner conductor could be altered, with respect to the outer conductor. Solid dielectrics can be permanently distorted by sharp bends.

Coaxial cables are selected according to rated impedance and attenuation at intended operating frequencies. The most widely specified coaxial cable has a solid dielectric, but low-capacity coaxial cable is air-spaced. The construction of air-dielectric coaxial cable results in lower effective capacitance. The RG-62/U, RG-62A/U, and RG-62B/U coaxial cables are examples of air-dielectric construction for broadcast and computer applications.

Applications

The military applications for coaxial cable include radar, radio, and satellite navigation systems, telecommunications, weapons fire control, sonar, and electronic warfare. The cables are widely used in electronic countermeasures (ECM) or jamming equipment, as well as electronic counter-countermeasures (ECCM) or anti-jamming equipment.

The nonmilitary applications for coaxial cable include telephone communications, radio and television broadcasting, community-antenna television (CATV), master-antenna television (MATV), and closed-circuit television (CCTV) systems. It is installed in homes, office buildings, factories, ships, aircraft, and vehicles. Some cables are specially made to be buried directly in the earth. These cables can withstand continuous immersion in water (flooded burial).

Nonmilitary standards and codes

Coaxial cable in nonmilitary applications is subject to the same codes and standards as other cables that are used in remote control and signaling—as communications cables and for CATV. These include:

- The National Electrical Code (NEC) Articles 725, 800, and 820
- Underwriters Laboratories (UL)
- Canadian Standards Association (CSA)

Catalog-standard coaxial cable is made to meet the requirements of NEC Article 725, Types CL2, and CM for general-purpose applications and CL2P and CMP for use in ducts, plenums, and other environmental air space.

Computer networking Within the past 10 years, coaxial cable has been used to form computer networks as an alternative to twisted pairs. However, many computer networks now include paired conductor cable and fiber-optic cable, as well as coaxial cable. Computer cables generally meet the requirements of IEEE 802.4 and are patterned after RG-6/U, RG-11/U, and RG62A/U cables, among others.

Figure 8-10 shows a trunk/transceiver coaxial cable for use in local-area networks. It meets the requirements of NEC Article 725, Type CL2P for

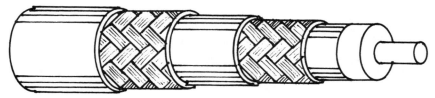

Fig. 8-10. Master television antenna (MATV) cable.

plenum use. The cable has a solid-tinned inner conductor, cellular Teflon FEP insulation, and a combination of aluminum-polyester and tinned-copper braid shielding. The jacket is Teflon FEP.

Radio and television broadcast   The selection of coaxial cables for broadcast applications generally depends on the broadcast frequency. They are specifically made for these applications and are patterned after the following cable types:

RG-8/U, RG-9/U, RG-11/U, RG-58/U, RG-59/U, RG-62/U, RG-174/U, RG-212/U, RG-214/U, and RG-223/U.

Many of these cables meet the requirements of NEC Article 725, Types CL2 and CL2X for general-purpose and residential applications. Some also meet the requirements of NEC Article 820, Type CATV. Others meet the requirements of NEC Article 725, Type CL2P and Article 820, Type CATVP for plenum use.

Master antenna television (MATV) includes community-antenna television (CATV) cables. Coaxial cables that are manufactured specifically for these applications are patterned on the following RG/U cables:

RG-6/U, RG-11/U, RG-59/U, and RG-62/U.

Many of these cables meet the requirements of NEC Article 725, Types CL2 and CL2X for general-purpose and residential applications. Some also meet the requirements of NEC Article 820, Type CATV. Others meet the requirements of NEC Article 725, Type CL2P and Article 820, Type CATVP for plenum use.

Electrical characteristics

The six variables that determine the operation of a coaxial cable are:

- Characteristic impedance (Z_o)
- Capacitance (C)
- Attenuation (A)
- Velocity of propagation (V_P)
- Time display (T_D)
- Inductance (L)

These variables are interrelated; they depend on cable dimensions and the choice of the core dielectric. The mathematical formulas presented here are intended to more clearly show the interrelationships between the variables—such as the inside diameter of the shield and the outside diameter of the center conductor.

The *characteristic impedance* can be defined in two ways:

- Total opposition to the current flow in a cable. It is directly related to the ratio of the diameters of the inner and outer conductors, and inversely related to the dielectric constant of the core material.

- Resistance that a cable, terminated in its own characteristic impedance, offers to a transmitter. A cable can transfer maximum power only when the characteristic impedances of the transmitter, the radio frequency line, and the receiver (or antenna) are equal to each other.

Matching a coaxial cable to the antenna or transmitter is important because:

- When an exact match exists, losses are attributable only to line resistances or attenuation
- When a mismatch exists, reflection losses will result

Characteristic impedance, unlike conductor resistance in a circuit, is not proportional to its length. Coaxial cables are designed to have impedances of 50, 75, and 95 ohms. However, coaxial cables can be designed and manufactured to match other impedances.

The characteristic impedance (Z_0) of a single coaxial line is measured in ohms and can be calculated with the formula:

$$Z_0 = \frac{138.2}{\sqrt{K}} \log_{10} \frac{D}{d}$$

Where:

D = Inside diameter of shield or braid (in inches)
d = Outside diameter of center conductor (in inches)
K = Dielectric constant (air is 1), as shown in TABLE 8-1

It can be seen from this equation that the ratio of the inside diameter of the outer conductor (D) to the outside diameter of the center conductor (d) relates directly to the impedance. Thus, a difference of only a few thousandths of an inch in the inside diameter (D) will significantly affect the impedance. Tolerance becomes even more important in the 50-ohm miniature coaxial cables.

Capacitance (C) is the property of conductors and dielectrics that permits electrical energy to be stored when the conductors are at different potentials. The cable capacitance is inversely dependent on the inner and outer conductor diameters and the dielectric constant of the core. In cables with the same dielectric constant, as the capacitance decreases, the impedance increases. TABLE 8-3 lists nominal capacitance values for standard coaxial cables.

Table 8-3. Nominal Capacitance Values for
Standard Coaxial Cables.

Resistance (ohms)	Dielectric	Capacitance (Pf/ft)
50	Polyethylene, solid	30.8
50	Polyethylene, foam	25.4
75	Polyethylene, solid	20.6
75	Polyethylene, foam	16.8
95	Polyethylene, solid	16.3
95	Polyethylene, air-space	14.4

Capacitance (C) in coaxial cables is expressed in picofarads per foot (pF/ft) and can be calculated with the formula:

$$C = \frac{MK}{\log_{10} \frac{D}{d}}$$

Where:

M = Cable construction constant
7.4 = single shielded solid conductor
7.0 = single shielded stranded conductor
K = Dielectric constant (TABLE 8-1)
D = Diameter over insulation (in inches)
d = Diameter of conductor (in inches)

Attenuation (A) is the loss of electrical power in a length of cable. These losses occur in the conductor and dielectric, as well as from cable radiation. As can be seen from the formula, an increase in conductor size reduces the attenuation because it decreases conductor electrical loss. Attenuation increases directly with frequency. Lowering the dielectric constant of the core material will lower the attenuation.

Coaxial-cable attenuation is measured in decibels per 100 feet (dB/100 ft) and it can be calculated with the formula:

$$A = 4.35 \frac{R_t}{Z_o} + 2.78 \, (pf) \; f \sqrt{K}$$

Where:

R_t = Measured line resistance (in ohms)
Z_o = Characteristic impedance (in ohms)
pf = Power factor of dielectric
d = Diameter of conductor (in inches)
D = Diameter over insulation (in inches)
K = Dielectric constant (TABLE 8-1)
f = test frequency (in MHz)

Figure 8-11 is a plot of attenuation vs. sinusoidal frequency for a typical coaxial cable.

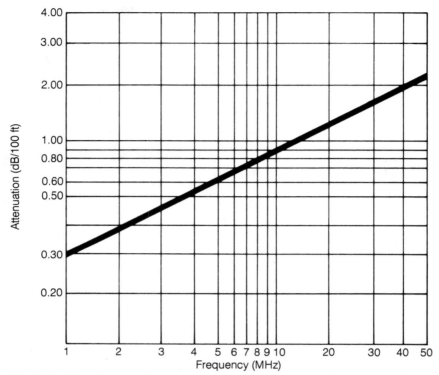

Fig. 8-11. Plot of attenuation vs. frequency for a typical RG/U-style coaxial cable.

Velocity of propagation (V_p) is the speed of signal transmission in a cable, as compared with its speed in air (considered to be 100 percent). Because velocity is inversely proportional to the dielectric constant, a decreased constant increases velocity. Velocity of propagation, V_p, is expressed as a percentage of the speed in air; it can be calculated with the formulas:

$$V_p = \frac{1}{\sqrt{K}} \times 100$$

Where: K = Dielectric constant (TABLE 8-1)

The velocities of propagation (in percentages) of typical dielectrics are:

Air	100.0
Polyethylene, solid	65.9
Polyethylene, foamed	80.0

Teflon TFE, solid	69.5
Polyvinyl chloride	45.0

Time delay (TD) is the interval between the initial signal transmission and its appearance at another point. It is the reciprocal of velocity of propagation and it is expressed in nanoseconds (10^{-9} sec) per foot (ns/ft). It can be calculated with the formula:

$$TD = \frac{1}{V_p}$$

Where:

V_p = Velocity of propagation (percent)

Inductance (L) is expressed microhenries per foot (μH/ft) and can be calculated with the formula:

$$L = Z_o^2 \, C \times 10^{-6}$$

Where:

Z_o = Characteristic impedance (in ohms)
C = Capacitance (in picofarads/ft)

Power rating

The power rating, as well as the other characteristics of coaxial cable, will be affected by such factors as flexing, bending (particularly if the bend radius is less than 20 times the cable's outside diameter), and variations in the atmospheric pressure (altitude).

The selection of cable size (as determined by dielectric diameter) will be influenced by the operating voltage requirements. The power rating is significantly influenced by the ratio of the inside diameter of the outer conductor (D) to the outside diameter of the inner conductor (d).

Frequency-vs.-power graphs for coaxial cables are normally based on an ambient temperature of 40 °C with matched transmission lines. Cables normally function with center conductor temperatures between 65 °C and 80 °C. Coaxial-cable operation with a polyethylene dielectric cable at a center-conductor temperature in excess of 80 °C is likely to cause permanent damage to the cable. If it is permissible for a cable with a center conductor temperature of

80 °C to accept maximum input power at an ambient temperature of 40 °C, it should typically be derated to:

- 75 percent of maximum rated power at an ambient temperature of 50 °C.
- 50 percent of maximum rated power at an ambient temperature of 60 °C.
- 25 percent of maximum rated power at an ambient temperature of 70 °C.

Cable selection should be based on limiting the temperature of the center conductor to a maximum of 65 °C in normal operation, particularly if it is subjected to continuous flexing.

Coaxial cable connectors

Coaxial cable connectors are circular radio-frequency connectors used to terminate coaxial cables. An example of a two-part connector with a bayonet-style locking mechanism is shown in FIG. 8-12. These connectors have axial contacts that are designed to mate with the inner conductors. Also, the braided shielding of flexible and semirigid coaxial cable can be clamped with plugs, jacks, receptacles, and adapters.

Plugs are the male connectors and jacks are the female connectors that are used primarily to terminate unsupported cable. Figure 8-13 is a section view of a mated plug and jack. *Panel jacks* are jacks that fit in panel cutouts and are fastened to panels with nuts and bolts. *Bulkhead jacks* are fastened through bulkheads with insulating bushings and lockwashers to act as transitions between cables that are terminated on opposite sides of the bulkheads in aircraft or ships. These connector elements permit watertight or pressurized integrity to be maintained at the bulkhead.

Right-angle plugs provide for a 90-degree turn between the cable and plug and right-angle jacks provide for a 90-degree turn between the cable and jack. Adapters match or adapt connector elements with different couplings, such as right-angle adapters, tee adapters, and bulkhead-jack adapters. Some connector series also include vertical and right-angle PC-board receptacles and front- and rear-mount receptacles.

Coaxial cable must be terminated in its characteristic impedance to avoid radio-frequency energy losses. This condition exists when the voltage is the same at all points on the line and no voltage standing waves exist. As a result of these requirements, the dimensions of coaxial connectors are highly standardized. The critical dimensions of coaxial connectors are determined by the diameters of the inner conductors and dielectric cores, the properties of the dielectric materials (of both cable and connector), and the transmission frequencies.

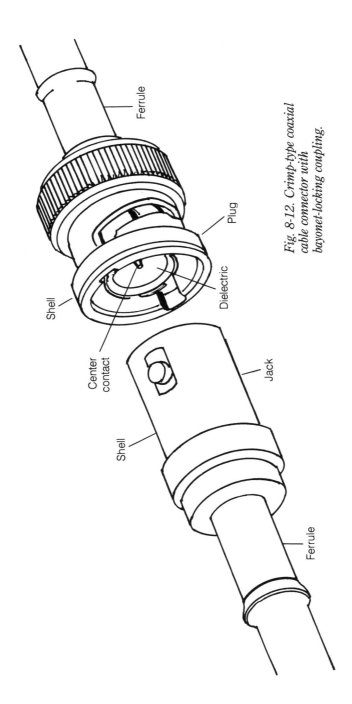

Ferrule

Plug

Shell

Dielectric

Center
contact

Jack

Shell

Ferrule

Fig. 8-12. Crimp-type coaxial cable connector with bayonet-locking coupling.

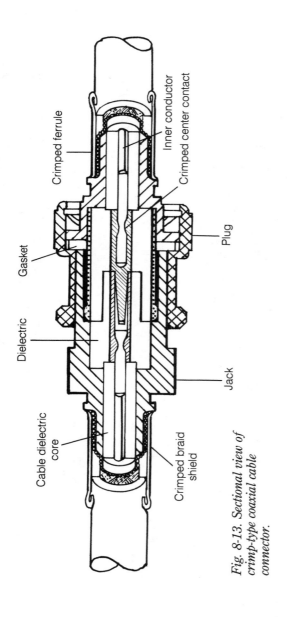

Fig. 8-13. Sectional view of crimp-type coaxial cable connector.

Coaxial connectors can be rapidly aligned, coupled, or decoupled without tools. Knurled or splined shells permit the connector elements to be secured or released with thumb and finger pressure. The cylindrical shells of the connector protect against abrasion and crushing forces. Shells seal against moisture, salt spray, dust, airborne contaminants, and emitted or received radio-frequency energy.

Coaxial connectors are also used to terminate dc and audio-frequency signal lines, where effective shielding is desired. The inner conductor carries the signal and the outer conductor is connected to a common ground. The external braid provides a continuous shield to prevent the radiation of high-frequency data-transmission signals when the connectors terminate data-transmission lines.

Federal Communications Commission (FCC) Docket 20780 requires that all pulsed emissions above 10 kHz in office equipment (including computers) must be suppressed. These requirements are met in part by shielded cables, shielded connectors, and filters. The FCC Docket features no requirements that concern the effects of externally produced interference on signals within the coaxial cable.

Coaxial connector construction The five basic groups of coaxial connectors are:

- Standard (C, N, twinax, triax, and UHF)
- Miniature (BNC and TNC)
- Subminiature (SMA, SMB, and SMC)
- Microminiature (SSMA, SSMB, and SSMC)
- Proprietary (APC-2.4, APC-3.5, and APC-7.0)

TABLE 8-4 lists the frequency ranges for these connectors.

The shells or bodies of standard and miniature coaxial connectors are typically made of half-hard brass, which is nickel or silver plated. The most commonly used dielectric in all coaxial connectors today is polytetrafluoroethylene (PTFE). Its quality is crucial to the proper functioning of the connector.

The bodies, coupling nuts, and other metal parts of subminiature SMA connectors are made of nonmagnetic stainless steel, insulators are made from PTFE, and all QPL versions have gold-plated beryllium-copper female contacts. By contrast, bodies of QPL SMBs and SMCs are made from half-hard brass that has been gold or silver-plated. The insulator and contact materials are the same as those of the SMA connector.

SMA connectors have threaded couplings and are about one-third larger than both SMB and SMC connectors. SMB connectors are spring mated with snap-fit couplings for quick-connect/disconnect applications. SMC connectors have screw-on couplings.

Low-cost coaxial connectors for terminating coaxial cable that is used in low-frequency data transmission are made from a die-cast zinc alloy. Neverthe-

Table 8-4. Frequency Range for Coaxial Connectors.

Size	Designation	Frequency Limit dc to	Band
Standard	C	10 GHz	X
	N	11 GHz	X
	Twinax	300 MHz	VHF
	Triax	300 MHz	VHF
	UHF	300 MHz	VHF
Miniature	BNC	11 GHz	X
	TNC	11 GHz	X
Subminiature	SMA	18 GHz	Ku
	SMB	10 GHz	X
	SMC	10 GHz	X
Microminiature	SSMA	40 GHz	Ka
	SSMB	18 GHz	Ku
	SSMC	18 GHz	Ku
Proprietary	APC-2.4	50 GHz	mm
	APC-3.5	24 GHz	Ka
	APC-7.0	18 GHz	K

less, all cast surfaces must be free of roughness or burrs that would cause RF losses and make coupling and decoupling difficult.

Connector quality control   MIL-C-39012 is the principal test specification for coaxial connectors made in the United States. The principal differences between military and aerospace QPL connectors and nonmilitary/commercial versions are the required markings and the DOD-specified traceability documentation. Each QPL connector is assigned a number (slash sheet), which relates it to MIL-C-39012.

The basic tests for all coaxial connectors are dimensional, typically performed on a sampling basis. The inner and outer dimensional ratios must be held to maintain the required characteristic impedance. Group A and B lot-by-lot inspections are required for QPL. Also, manufacturers of QPL coaxial connectors must be qualified by the DOD.

Commercial connectors can be tested with QPL methods, although the sampling would be less frequent. Most connector manufacturers do not perform permeability tests because they have confidence in the quality of the dielectric materials that are supplied by their vendors. Group A inspection can be conducted without the assembly of the connectors to a cable. The visual and mechanical inspection is done on an AQL basis; it includes inspecting material finish, construction marking, workmanship, and mating (visual indication). In addition, it also includes dielectric withstanding voltage testing and, if the connector is hermetically sealed, there is an AQL requirement for seal integrity. If the connectors are to be pressurized, but are not hermetic, leak testing must be done.

Group B inspections are set by a sampling plan in MIL-STD-105. The principal tests include: force to engage and disengage connectors, coupling-proof torque (for screw-type coupling nuts), and mating characteristics (interface dimensions). A permeability check is made to be sure that the connectors do not contain magnetic metals. In addition, insulation resistance is tested. The voltage standing-wave ratio (VSWR) or reflection coefficient is also measured.

Nondestructive plating thickness tests are performed with either beta backscatter or X-ray techniques. These tests are typically confined to the gold and silver-plated contact areas. Today, center contacts on QPL connectors must have a minimum of 100 microinches of gold plating (previously 50 microinches).

Voltage standing-wave ratio (VSWR), a function of frequency, describes the reflection characteristics of a mated pair of coaxial connectors related to the characteristic impedance of the measuring system. A VSWR of approximately 1:1 indicates that losses will be minimal. If the ratio is larger, the losses will increase.

Assembly of cable to connector

Coaxial connectors must be disassembled to be attached to the cable in a sequence of steps. The three most widely used methods for attaching coaxial connectors to flexible or semirigid cables are clamping, crimping, or soldering. *Crimping* both the outer and center conductors is replacing the *clamping* of metallic braid shields and the *soldering* of center contacts.

The standard clamp for flexible cable includes a threaded nut, a flat compression gasket, and a tapered braid clamp. The cable's center conductor is soldered to the connector's center contact. Solderless clamping requires a threaded cable clamp, a flat washer, and a threaded body clamp. The tip of the center contact screws over the cable's center conductor after assembly.

9

Fiber-optic cable and connectors

Fiber-optic cables transmit signals and data in the form of light-energy packets (photons) which have no electrical charge. Fiber-optic cables have advantages in safety, reliability, size, and security and they can transmit far more information than comparably sized conventional cables, because of their wider bandwidth. Some of the safety benefits of fiber-optic cable are:

- Elimination of electrical shock hazards to personnel
- Elimination of electrical arcing
- High isolation between electrical circuitry at the terminals

The advantages in transmission reliability, amount of information transferred, and security are:

- Noncorrosive fibers
- Immunity to EMI/RFI
- Wide signal bandwidth
- Inherent signal-transmission security
- Unaffected by high electric or magnetic fields

Jacketed fiber-optic cables have many advantages over jacketed copper cables of comparable size, because of:

- Superior signal- and data-transmission capability
- Resistance to greater mechanical abuse (crush, impact, flexure)
- Smaller size and lighter weight for amount of information transmitted
- Tolerance for weather extremes
- Tolerance to fluid immersion, including polluted water

The information that is transmitted within a jacketed fiber-optic cable is secure from external detection. The jacket is opaque and this prevents escaping light, which could be decoded. The opaque jacket also prevents light from interfering with adjacent fiber-optic cables. The most efficient method to obtain information from an optical fiber is to install a tap—a difficult task to perform in the field because of the high degree of skill and the special tools that are required. To install a tap, the jacket and buffer must be removed and the fiber must be broken. This act would terminate signal transmission and be detected immediately. However, even if a tap is installed surreptitiously, its presence can be detected by line monitors.

Aside from its wide bandwidth, fiber-optic cable should also be considered as a transmission media in situations where:

- Existing conduit is too small to permit additional copper cables
- Weight of additional copper wiring will become a structural problem for the host building

Fiber-optic cable should be considered if it is necessary to transmit signals or data reliably through rooms or spaces where any of the following hazards are present:

- Tanks or vats of corrosive chemicals
- Radioactive generators and radioactive materials, associated with nuclear power plants or experimental reactors
- Explosive, flammable, or toxic solids, liquids, or gasses
- Motors, generators, or other equipment that emits intense electromagnetic fields

Also, fiber-optic communication systems have drawbacks. Perhaps the most significant is the circuitry cost to transform electrical signals to modulated optical signals and back again to electrical signals. However, the cost of this circuitry has been declining steadily.

Other drawbacks relate to attenuation and losses. A system is limited by the ability of the optical transmitter to produce sufficient light energy to cover the required distance without the use of repeaters. Also, the optical receiver is limited by its ability to regenerate reliable signals and data from modulated light that is attenuated by transmission losses. The losses in a point-to-point fiber-optic system are:

- Insertion loss at the input and output
- Losses incurred through connectors
- Distance-related optical attenuation

Another problem is the difficulty in making low-loss splices and taps in the field. Although signals can be easily and effectively tapped from copper conductors, multiple taps on optical fibers are not presently economically practical.

Fiber-optic links are classed as short-haul and long-haul. *Short-haul links* are generally considered to be two kilometers or less and *long-haul links* are longer. Most private or nonutility fiber-optic networks employ short-haul links. The emitters for these systems are typically 820-nanometer (nm) planar light-emitting diodes (LEDs). Receivers are typically PIN photodiodes and the optical fibers have core diameters of 100 microns (μm) or less.

Fiber-optic principles

In all types of fiber-optic cable, individual optical fibers act as optical waveguides. The fibers have a dielectric structure that consists of a central circular transparent core, which propagates the optical signal, and an outer cladding, which completes the guiding structure.

Figure 9-1 shows a single-fiber fiber-optic cable. Light rays that enter the end of the fiber core axially pass easily down the length of the optical fiber with only attenuation losses. However, light rays that enter at an angle (with respect to the axis of the fiber) are either reflected at the boundary between the core and the cladding or are absorbed by the cladding. Thus, the entry angle (incidence) of the light ray is important in optical transmission.

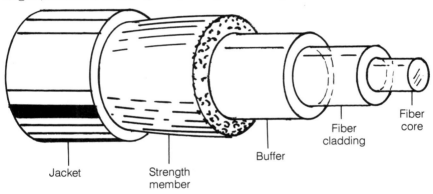

Jacket   Strength
              member

Buffer

Fiber
cladding

Fiber
core

Fig. 9-1. Construction of a simplex fiber-optic cable.

The solid-state transmitter and receiver must be closely matched to the fiber. Both the core and the cladding of communications-grade fibers are made of silica glass, but the cladding has different optical properties from the core.

Silicone coating is widely used to protect the cladding from becoming scuffed. A layer of plastic, called the *buffer*, is coated on the cladding. The buffer might be covered with high-tensile-strength fibers (such as Kevlar yarn), which strengthens the cable and permits it to be pulled through long conduits. The jacket protects the cable against crush and impact damage. A cable of this type tolerates more abuse than most copper-wire cable.

Optical fibers can also be made from plastic-clad glass (fused silica) or plastic-clad plastic. These fibers have lower performance characteristics than glass-clad glass fibers and are used only for short transmission distances.

Step-index fiber (FIG. 9-1) has a sharp optical boundary between the core and the cladding. Most optical fibers that are used in short-haul systems are step-index fibers: glass-clad glass, plastic-clad glass, and plastic-clad plastic.

Graded-index fiber was invented to minimize the transmission loss in step-index fibers. The Refraction index of the fiber changes gradually, with respect to radial distance from the axis of the fiber. As a result, the rays turn less sharply from core to cladding. Graded-index fiber has a higher coupling loss and generally costs more than step-index fiber.

Cable selection

The five principal variables to consider when selecting fiber-optic cable are:

- Core diameter (in microns)
- Cladding diameter (in microns)
- Numerical Aperture (NA)
- Cable attenuation (in decibels per kilometer dB/km)
- Cable bandwidth (in megahertz per kilometer MHz/km)

Table 9-1 is a summary of characteristics for typical step-index fibers.

The fiber core is the central region of an optical fiber with a refractive index that is higher than that of the fiber cladding. General-purpose commercial fiber-optic cable is made with core diameters from 50 to 100 microns (μm). These permit the most efficient coupling of light from available commercial light sources such as LEDs or laser diodes.

Table 9-1. Characteristics of Typical Optical Fibers.

Core dia. (microns)	50	62.5	85	100
Cladding dia. (microns)	125	125	125	140
Buffer dia. (microns)	900	900	900	900
Numerical aperture	.200	.275	.260	.290
Attenuation (dB/km)*	3.0 – 4.0	3.8 – 6.0	5.0	6.0
Bandwidth (MHz – km)*	600	100-160	200	100

* @ 850 nanometers

Cladding adds to the overall diameter of the fiber. In fibers with a 50-micron core, the diameter is typically 125 microns, which results in a cladding wall thickness of 62.5 microns. However, the cladding on a fiber that has a core of 100 microns is 140 microns in diameter, which provides a 20-micron cladding wall thickness.

Numerical aperture is a measure of the angular light acceptance for an optical fiber. Figure 9-2 is a sectional view of a step-index fiber that shows both the core and the cladding. Although both the core and the cladding are transparent, the cladding has different optical properties than the core.

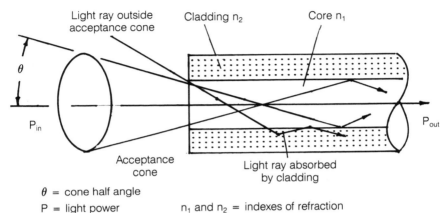

θ = cone half angle

P = light power n_1 and n_2 = indexes of refraction

Fig. 9-2. Diagram that illustrates the derivation of numerical aperture (NA).

As can be seen in the diagram, light rays that enter at shallow angles eventually reach the interface between the core and the cladding, where they are reflected back into the core. However, if the angle of incidence is too great, the light ray will cross the core/cladding boundary and be completely absorbed by the cladding, causing the light energy to totally dissipate.

Therefore, limits exist on the angle of incidence if the light ray is to contribute to signal transmission. *Total internal reflection (TIR)* of a light ray with the permitted angle of incidence is achieved by doping the cladding so that it has a lower refractive index than the core.

The *numerical aperture (*NA) is the sine of the largest incident ray angle that can be accepted by the fiber, and it is a dimensionless number. All incident light on the end of the fiber must be confined to the cone, which is defined by the numerical aperture if it is to be useful in signal transmission. Therefore, 100 percent of the optical output power is contained within this angle.

Most light energy that is coupled into an optical fiber core is prevented from escaping through the walls of the optical fiber because it is reflected back toward the axis of the fiber by the walls of the cladding. This reflection is caused by the index of refraction of the core (n_1), relative to that of the cladding, n_2.

The *index of refraction* is the ratio of the velocity of light in a medium to the velocity of light in a vacuum. As a ray of light passes from one medium into another with a different index of refraction, its direction changes according to Snell's Law:

$$n_1 \sin \theta_1 = n_2 \sin \theta_2$$

Where:

n_1 = index of refraction for the core (higher)
n_2 = index of refraction of the cladding (lower)

For rays that are incident from the high-index side (the core), a specific incidence angle exists for which the exit angle is 90 degrees, called the *critical angle*. Only a partial reflection exists at an incidence angle less than the critical angle. However, for angles greater than the critical angle, the ray is totally reflected, called *total internal reflection (TIR)*.

Rays within the core of an optical fiber can be incident at various angles, but TIR applies only to the rays that are incident at angles greater than the critical angle. TIR prevents these rays from leaving the core until they reach the far end of the fiber. The figure shows how the reflection angle at the core/cladding interface relates to the angle at which a ray enters the face of the fiber.

The acceptance angle θ is the maximum angle with respect to the fiber axis, at which an entering ray will experience TIR. The acceptance angle is related to the refraction indexes of the core and the cladding. When the external medium is air ($n\theta \sim 1$), the sine of the acceptance angle is called the *numerical aperture* (NA) of the fiber:

$$NA = \sin \theta = \sqrt{n_1^2 - n_2^2}$$

Optical attenuation is the amount of optical power lost as a result of absorbed and scattered optical radiation at a specific wavelength in a length of fiber. It is expressed in decibels of optical power per kilometer (dB/km). Attenuation is calculated as:

$$\text{Attenuation (dB)} = 10 \log \frac{P_{in}}{P_{out}}$$

Where:

P_{in} = Optical power in
P_{out} = Optical power out

The *bandwidth* at a specified optical radiation wavelength represents the highest sinusoidal light-modulation frequency that can be transmitted through a length of fiber with an optical signal loss that is equal to 50 percent (-3 dB) of the zero modulation frequency component. Bandwidth in an optical fiber is expressed in megahertz (MHz) over a kilometer length (MHz/km).

The *optical collection factor* is the added diameter of the fiber core and its numerical aperture to determine the light-gathering capability of commercial fibers. This factor is a measure of the fiber's ability to collect light. It is difficult to inject light into and remove it from a fine fiber core.

Cable construction

The two general methods for constructing optical-fiber cable are:

- Tight buffer
- Loose-buffer tube

Tight-buffer cable is fiber-optic cable that is made with a relatively thick buffer, applied directly to the optical fiber. The buffered fiber is then covered with a high-strength plastic fiber, such as Kevlar, for added strength and protection and an extruded outer jacket completes the cable. Figure 9-1 illustrates tight-buffer construction. This construction method usually results in the smallest, lightest-weight fiber-optic cable. It is more flexible and more crush-resistant than loose-buffer cable.

Loose-buffer tube cable is fiber-optic cable made by placing the optical fiber in a gel-filled plastic buffer tube whose inner diameter is larger than the external diameter of the fiber (FIG. 9-3). The gel isolates the fiber from exterior

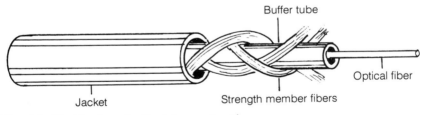

Buffer tube

Optical fiber

Jacket   Strength member fibers

Fig. 9-3. Simplex loose-buffer tube construction.

shearing, twisting, and compression forces, which are present on the cable. In single-fiber or simplex cables, the buffer tube is covered with a high-strength plastic-fiber braid, which provides load-bearing support for the cable. An outer jacket is extruded over the braid.

Duplex cable, as shown in FIG. 9-4, is made with the same technique as single-fiber cable, but a common outer jacket is used. The buffer tubes can be color coded. Multifiber cable (FIG. 9-5) is made by bundling a number of individual color-coded buffer tubes—each of which contains a single fiber. These tubes are reinforced with a longitudinal stress member.

Loose-buffer tube construction is used for general-purpose cables that are suitable for indoor installation in ducts, trays, or conduits. Single-fiber, duplex,

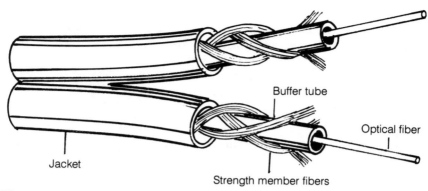

Fig. 9-4. Duplex loose-buffer tube construction.

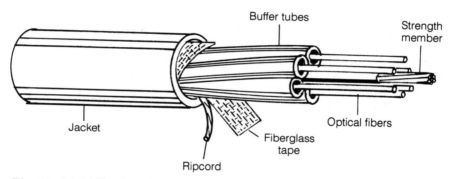

Fig. 9-5. Multifiber loose-buffer tube construction.

and multifiber general-purpose cables are available commercially. Similar construction is used to assemble heavy-duty cables, except that additional strength members and jackets with thicker walls permit the cable to withstand higher mechanical stress. Multiconductor fiber-optic cable is specifically made for telecommunications applications; it combines the features of both general-purpose and heavy-duty cables.

Special provisions must be made to seal the ends of the buffer tube to prevent gel leakage when a single fiber is broken out for termination. Some manufacturers offer special boots to seal the ends of the cable. Loose-buffer construction exhibits lower fiber attenuation than other construction methods. As a result, these cables are more stable under continuous mechanical stress.

Fiber-optic breakout cable is a modified form of tight-buffer construction (FIG. 9-6). A tightly buffered fiber is surrounded by high-strength plastic fibers and a jacket, typically made from PVC. These single-fiber subunit elements are then covered with a common sheath to form a breakout cable. This "cable within a cable" permits simple, direct termination and installation. The jacket is simply slit and the individual cables are used where needed.

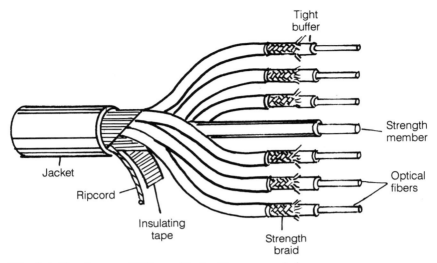

Fig. 9-6. Breakout multifiber cable for plenums and risers.

Strength members are added to bundles of fiber-optic cable that have been encased in buffer tubes. These members are added to both loose-buffer and tight-buffer tube cables prior to jacketing. They are also used in breakout cable for plenum and riser applications. Strength members isolate the fibers from longitudinal mechanical stress. They also minimize elongation and contraction and can provide temperature stabilization. Steel wire, fiberglass-epoxy rods, and high-strength plastic fibers (such as Kevlar) are used as strength members.

Fiber-optic cable jackets, like conventional cable jackets, protect the core from the external environment. Jacket materials must be selected with respect to the significantly greater thermal expansion coefficients for plastics than for glass fiber. Polyethylene, for example, has a thermal expansion coefficient that is at least 100 times greater than glass. Other factors to consider when selecting jacket materials are:

• Anticipated operating environment
• Possibility of exposure to destructive chemicals

Polyurethane-jacketed cables exhibit good optical performance over an extended operating temperature range of – 40 to 85 °C (– 40 to 185 °F). The recommended storage temperature range is approximately the same.

PVC-jacketed cables have a recommended operating temperature range of – 10 to 50 °C (14 to 122 °F) with a storage temperature range of – 40 to 80 °C (– 40 to 176 °F).

Optical fiber cables are covered by Article 770 of the NEC. The NEC distinguishes between nonconductive optical fiber cables (OFN) and conductive optical fiber cables (OFC). A conductive optical fiber cable contains noncurrent-carrying conductive members (such as metallic strength members and metallic vapor barriers). By contrast, a nonconductive optical fiber cable contains no metallic members and no other electrically conductive materials.

Stress and loads must be minimized on fiber-optic cables during installation and in the intended application so that no stress is transferred to the optical fiber. If the load and stress increase beyond the limit of the strength members and the optical fiber is placed under tensile stress, increased transmission losses (attenuation) could result. Where possible, the cables should be supported (even during installation) and kept free of loads in use.

Fiber-optic cable can be installed in the air (aerial), in the ground (direct burial), or in underground ducts, in plenums, and in cable raceways. Some optical fiber cables meet the specifications of NEC Article 770, Type OFN and OFC for general-purpose applications; Type OFNR and OFCR for riser applications; and Type OFNP and OFCP for ducts, plenums, and other space used for environmental air.

Catalog-standard fiber-optic cable

Fiber-optic cables are available in the manufacturer's catalog or they can be custom-ordered. Some important types of catalog-standard fiber-optic cable are:

- Simplex/duplex
- Breakout
- Plenum
- Distribution
- Steel-tape armored (to protect from rodents or damage in direct burial)
- Hybrid (both copper conductors and optical fiber in the same jacket)

Simplex/duplex fiber-optic cables are effective for:

- Interconnecting computers
- Sensing and process control
- Patching at splice panels

Simplex/duplex cable can be made in a general-purpose, heavy-duty loose-buffer style or in a tight-buffer style. All duplex cables consist of two simplex components that are extruded together in a common jacket.

Breakout cables are tight-buffer fiber-optic cables made primarily for connector-intensive applications (such as for data transmission within buildings or ships). They can be used to interconnect computers, security systems, process-control systems, PBXs, and LANs. Commercial breakout cables are available with 2 to 24 fibers. Because they consist of individually buffered and jacketed optical fibers, these cables can easily be broken out for individual connector attachment at the factory or in the field. These multiconductor cables have a central strength member.

Plenum cables are typically made with tight buffers for maximum flexibility and crush resistance. They can have simplex, duplex, or multiconductors with up to 12 cables. High-temperature fluorocopolymer jackets permit plenum-cable use at temperatures of -20 to $70\,°C$ (-4 to $158\,°F$). Typical applications include data processing, video, and process-control systems.

Distribution cables are primarily used where stable optical performance is critical. These cables are intended for use in LANs, telephone systems, computer interconnections, PBX installations, and process controls. Commercial distribution cable typically contains from 2 to 12 buffered fibers stranded around a steel or dielectric central strength member. This assembly is covered with a loose-fitting extruded polyethylene jacket. If direct-burial installation is required, the cable can be armored with steel tape or covered with a heavy-duty jacket.

Loose vs. tight   Special provisions must be made to terminate loose-buffer tube multifiber and multipurpose cables. Single-fiber cables with strength members must be sealed to separate the bundle so that it can be terminated with connectors. These preparations are not necessary with tight-buffered cables.

Fiber-optic applications

Fiber-optics are emerging as the preferred technology for LANs. A *LAN* is a privately owned network between two or more computers. LANs permit computer users to interchange and display information from each of the computers in the network.

LANs can interconnect computers up to about two kilometers (km) apart, about the size of a college campus or an industrial park. They can typically connect from 2 to 1000 users. A *metropolitan-area network (MAN)*, also privately owned, can cover an overall distance from 2 to 10 km (about the size of a city); it can be used to connect several thousand users. For network service beyond 10 km, *wide-area networks (WANs)* are used. However, these systems are usually operated by telecommunications utilities to connect many thousands of users. More complex LANs can serve hundreds of computer users simultaneously.

LANs are used to exchange electronic mail, monitor processes and control machines remotely, integrate data gathering, and teleconference. They can also share software for such functions as: computer-aided design and computer-aided manufacturing (CAD/CAM). Many LAN system architectures and protocols are in use. Some of them are proprietary:

- OSI (Open Systems Interconnection)
- Ethernet
- SONNET

- Token Ring
- FDDI (Fiber Distributed Data Interface)

The FDDI Token Ring architecture has a bandwidth capacity of 125 Mb/s on a 1300-nm carrier wavelength and it uses fibers with a core diameter of 62.5 μm.

LANs provide wider bandwidth with less crosstalk and EMI/RFI than twisted wire pairs or coaxial cable. At the present, the cost for fiber-optic interconnection is higher. However, under certain circumstances, the lower repeater-spacing requirements and wider bandwidth can result in lower overall system cost. Greater security, lower signal attenuation, lighter interconnection weight, and smaller size can also have economic benefits. LANs are defined by the way that information is passed around the network (FIG. 9-7).

- *Star-network topology*   Data is sent from a central computer or server to the intended smaller computer in a radiating, spoke-like network (e.g., a home telephone).

- *Bus-network topology*   Data is presented to all computers simultaneously and it appears as a parallel interconnection (e.g., Ethernet).

- *Ring-network topology*   Each computer in the network receives the data in turn and transmits it to the next station in a closed loop. Bidirectional capability permits the network to function if the loop is opened. It appears as a series connection (e.g., FDDI).

Low-speed networks that consist of personal computers and printers can be interconnected with twisted wire pairs, but the connecting backbone between systems might be coaxial or fiber-optic cable to obtain a higher data rate (bandwidth).

Connectors

No standard connectors exist for fiber-optic cables. Some connector manufacturers have produced their own proprietary designs. Methode Electronics, Inc. has made a fiber-optic connector system that is intermatable with AT&T's ST design (see FIG. 9-8) and with SMA-style connectors (such as Amphenol's Series 905/906).

Crimp-removable fiber-optic cable contacts have been developed for use in military-style multiconductor circular connectors. Figure 9-9 shows a size-16 crimp-removable fiber-optic cable contact. This Methode contact was designed for use in MIL-C-26500 cylindrical connectors, as well as in other interconnecting devices that are capable of accepting MIL-C-26636-style contacts. The contact can terminate multimode fiber-optic cables from 100/140 microns through 200/250 microns in diameter. The attenuation is said to be less than 2 dB.

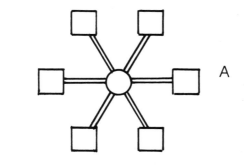

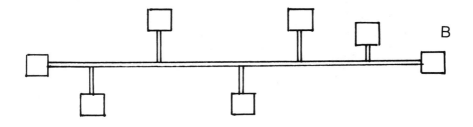

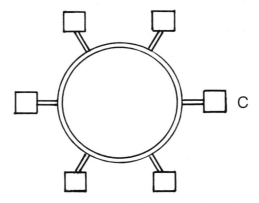

Fig. 9-7. Local-area networks (LAN) are star-network topology (A), bus-network topology (B), and ring-network topology (C).

Fig. 9-8. ST-type fiber-optic cable connectors.

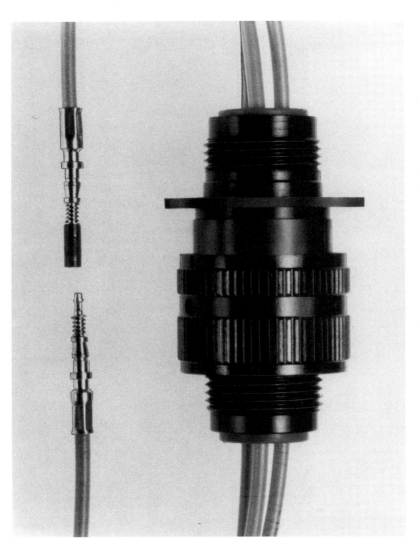

Fig. 9-9. Crimp-removable contacts for fiber-optic conductors in a circular multi-conductor connector.

10

Process-control cable

Process-control systems perform many different functions in industry including:

- Measurement of variables, such as liquid, vapor, and gas flow rate; temperature, pressure, weight, and pH factor from sensors.

- Analysis of chemical content and concentration of reagents.

- Indications and displays with indicator lamps, analog and digital panel meters, and computer screen and recording with strip and circular charts, and computer printouts.

- Regulate motor speed and direction, set and maintain temperature, pressure, weight, frequency, current, power, pH factor, and flow rate in open and closed loops; operate valves, relays, and switches; and direct robots.

These activities are carried out with the information and data from data-acquisition systems and the transmission of signals between sensors, controllers, or computers and process-controlling devices. Many different cables are available to perform these functions. The selection of a specific cable will depend on the volume, format, and frequency of the data transmitted, the operating environment, and the required reliability.

Conventional wiring

In a conventionally wired process-control system, many signal wires bring status information to or transmit control commands from a central control console, which might be computer based. Two fundamentally different wiring practices are now in use:

- Individual cables connect sensors and actuators directly to the control console or station.
- Multiconductor trunk cables transmit signals from a central control room or console to different zones in the plant.

Multiconductor cables offer savings in cable and installation costs by housing many individual cables in the same jacket. The disadvantage is the trunk cable's lack of flexibility and versatility.

Remote multiplexing

In conventional plant wiring, each signal, from a sensor to a control computer or process controller, is carried over its own dedicated wires. *Multiplexing* is an alternate method for transmitting signals; it allows many signals to be carried by a single twisted pair of wires or by a coaxial cable. These arrangements can serve many circuits because the signals are transmitted:

- Sequentially (time-division multiplexing, TDM)
- Modulated onto carrier frequencies (frequency-division multiplexing, FDM)

Process-control cables

Today, most continuous-process industrial plants are regulated by a system of electrical-control circuits, rather than pneumatic-control circuits, because of their compatibility with electronic circuits and computer control. Computer control has been decentralized, and in some cases, it might be under the direction of desktop personal computers.

The wire and cable in an electronic control circuit are referred to as *instrumentation cable*; those associated with electrical control circuits are called *control cable*. The subject of this chapter is instrumentation cable. The cables that are used in utilities for power distribution and nuclear plants (nuclear-grade products) are not covered here.

Industry standards for process control

The regulations, requirements, and standards that apply to process control are prepared by many different organizations. Most of these rules have been discussed in previous chapters. However, the wires and cables used in process control must comply with the OSHA regulations. OSHA is the Williams-Steiger Occupational Safety and Health Act, passed by Congress in 1970. It states that employers must meet minimum safety and health standards. They must, therefore, be listed in the NEC and/or recognized by UL or similar OSHA-accepted testing organizations. Many of these cables are also certified by the CSA.

Instrumentation cable

Power-limited tray cables

The general-reference document for instrumentation cable is NEC Article 725: Class 1, Class 2, and Class 3 for remote-control, signaling, and power-limited circuits. UL listings for these cables are issued under UL Standard 13—Power-Limited Circuit Cables. This chapter discusses Class 1, Class 2 (Type CL2), and Class 3 (Type CL3) power-limited circuit cable and power-limited tray cable (Type PLTC).

Class 1 power-limited circuits must be supplied from a source with a rated output of not more than 30 volts and 1000 volt-amperes. Power sources other than transformers must be protected by overcurrent devices.

Class 1 remote control and signaling circuits must not exceed 600 volts; however, the power output of the source is not limited.

As specified in the NEC, the ac and dc power for *Class 2 and Class 3 circuits* must be either inherently limited (requiring no overcurrent protection) or limited by a combination of power-source and overcurrent protection.

This chapter also discusses *power and control tray cables (TC)*, as defined in NEC Article 340.

Type TC power and control tray cable is a factory assembly of two or more insulated conductors, with or without associated bare or covered grounding conductors under a nonmetallic sheath. This cable is approved for installation in cable trays, in raceways, or where supported by a messenger wire.

General construction

Process-control cables consist of pairs, triads, or multiples of unshielded or shielded conductors. Twisted and nonshielded instrument pairs and triads are acceptable if static noise is not a problem and if they are located in a metal conduit.

Overall shielding with a separate stranded tinned-copper drain wire is recommended in instrumentation, computer, and control applications, where signals in excess of 100 millivolts are transmitted. Individual pairs or triads can be shielded for use in applications where optimum noise rejection is required. The fully isolated pairs or triads contain a separate stranded tinned-copper drain wire (for grounding) to provide maximum protection from crosstalk and common-mode interference. Cables with an overall shield provide additional electrostatic noise protection. A separate tinned-copper drain wire grounds the overall shield.

Commercial, stock catalog cables that are suitable for process control can have as many as 50 pairs or 24 triads of conductors. These cables can be generally classified as:

- 300 V, 105 °C power-limited tray cables
- 600 V, 90 °C tray cables

Power-limited tray cables with 300-volt ratings are UL/NEC listed as Type PLTC and can also be listed as CMR, CMP, CL3R, and CL3P, for use in accordance with NEC Article 725, Class 2 and Class 3 circuits. General-purpose cables can be installed in wet or dry locations where temperatures are as high as 105 °C. Their jackets, typically PVC, are flame retardant, sunlight and moisture resistant, and do not propagate flame (in accordance with UL Standard 13, UL 1581 Vertical-Tray Flame Test). They are approved for cable-tray use in Class 1, Division 2, hazardous and nonhazardous areas, cable trays, raceways, conduits, and supported by messenger wires.

Power-limited 300 V, 105 °C tray cables, for use in risers, have tinned-copper conductors that pass the UL 1666 Riser Flame Test (527,500 BTU) and the CSA FT-4 Flame Test. The conductors are bare soft-annealed copper, Class B concentric, per ASTM B-3 and ASTM B-8. Tinned-copper conductors are used to minimize oxidation and make soldering terminations easier.

Cables with bare copper conductors are color coded according to ICEA Method 1: pairs are black and white; triads are black, white, and red. Cables with tinned-copper conductors are color coded: pairs are black and white; triads are black, red, and white.

Tray cables with 600-volt ratings are UL/NEC listed as tray cable (TC) under UL Standard 1277 (NEC Articles 318, 340, 501, and 502) Class 1. These cables can be used in raceways and are supported by messenger wire. They can also be used in outdoor applications and can be approved for direct burial. Tray-cable jackets are flame-retardant PVC that is moisture and sunlight resistant. The 600-volt cables are approved for use as control, signal, and communications circuits in cable trays for Class 1, Division 2 areas—in accordance with NEC articles 340, 318, and 501, and for Class 1 circuits (as permitted in Article 725). They pass the UL Vertical Tray Flame Test that is comparable to the IEEE 383 (70,000 BTU) Flame Test.

Class 1, 600 V, 90 °C cables for use in risers have tinned-copper conductors, which pass the UL 1666 Riser Flame Test (527,500 BTU) and the CSA FT-4 Flame Test.

Cables with bare copper conductors are color coded according to ICEA Method 1: pairs are black and white; triads are black, white, and red. Cables with tinned copper conductors are color coded: pairs are black and white; triads are black, red, and white.

Cable descriptions

The cable descriptions listed in this chapter represent the construction requirements for specific types and classes of cable. The reader is urged to consult commercial catalogs for further details.

Unshielded power-limited tray cables

Industry standards Power-limited tray cable, Type PLTC; Class 3 remote-control, signaling and power-limited cable NEC Article 725, Type CL3.

Construction (FIG. 10-1) The conductors are bare stranded 22- to 12-AWG twisted pairs or triads with color-coded PVC primary insulation. The conductors are cabled and enclosed in a PVC jacket. These cables are rated for 300 V, 105 °C.

Fig. 10-1. Unshielded power-limited tray cable.

Overall-shielded power-limited tray cable

Industry standards Power-limited tray cable, Type PLTC; Class 3 remote-control, signaling and power-limited cable NEC Article 725, Type CL3.

Construction (See FIG. 10-2) The conductors are bare stranded 20- to 18-AWG copper pairs or triads with color-coded PVC primary insulation. Up to 50 pairs or 24 triads per cable are common. The conductors are cabled and shielded with aluminum-polyester foil and a stranded tinned-copper drain wire is enclosed. These cables might include a PVC-insulated, bare-stranded communications wire. The assembly is enclosed in a PVC jacket with a ripcord under the jacket to permit easy stripping. These cables are rated 300 V, 105 °C.

Individually and overall-shielded power-limited tray cable

Industry standards Power-limited tray cable, Type PLTC; Class 3 remote-control, signaling, and power-limited cable NEC Article 725, Type CL3.

Construction (FIG. 10-3) The conductors are bare stranded 20- to 18-AWG copper pairs or triads with color-coded PVC primary insulation. Up to 50 pairs or 24 triads are common per cable. The twisted pairs are shielded with aluminum-polyester foil and a tinned stranded-copper drain wire is included. The

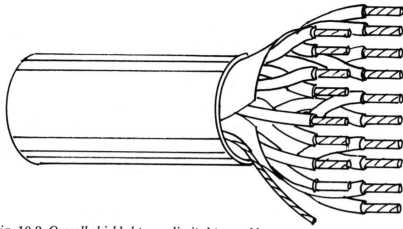

Fig. 10-2. Overall-shielded power-limited tray cable.

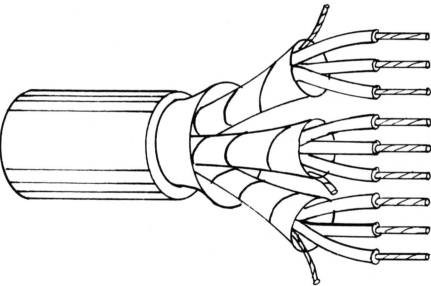

Fig. 10-3. Individually and overall-shielded power-limited tray cable.

triads are first cabled before the aluminum-polyester foil and tinned stranded-copper drain wire are applied. Then all individually shielded conductor groups are shielded overall with aluminum-polyester foil and another tinned stranded-copper drain wire.

These cables might also include a PVC-insulated, bare stranded communications wire. The assembly is enclosed in a PVC jacket with a ripcord under the jacket to facilitate stripping. These cables are rated for 300 V, 105 °C.

Overall shielded tray cable

Industry standards   Tray Cable, Type TC per NEC Articles 318, 340, 501, and 502. UL Standard 1277.

Construction   (FIG. 10-2) The conductors are twisted pairs or triads of bare stranded 18- and 16-AWG copper wire. They are insulated with PVC and a color-coded nylon overcoat. Up to 50 pairs or 24 triads are common per cable. The cable is shielded overall with aluminum-polyester foil and a tinned-copper drain wire is enclosed. The jacket is PVC. These cables are rated for 600 V, 90 °C.

Individually and overall shielded tray cable

Industry standards   Tray Cable, Type TC per NEC Articles 318, 340, 501, and 502. UL Subject 1277.

Construction   (FIG. 10-3) The conductors are twisted pairs or triads of bare stranded 18- and 16-AWG copper wire, PVC insulated with a color-coded nylon overcoat. Up to 50 pairs or 24 triads per cable are common. The twisted pairs are individually shielded with aluminum-polyester foil and a stranded tinned-copper drain wire is enclosed. The triads are cabled and also are individually shielded with aluminum-polyester foil and a stranded tinned-copper drain wire. The individually shielded groups are then shielded overall with more aluminum-polyester foil and another tinned-copper drain wire. The jacket is PVC. The cables are rated for 600 V, 90 °C.

Thermocouple wire and extension wire

A *thermocouple* is a temperature sensor that is formed by the junction of two dissimilar metal wires. The junctions are usually formed by butt-welding the two wire ends. The basic thermocouple circuit (FIG. 10-4) includes a thermocouple whose wire ends are terminated by a reference junction, which is maintained at a reference temperature. When a temperature difference exists

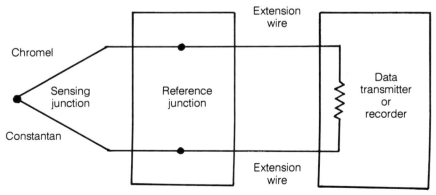

Fig. 10-4. Thermocouple circuit showing extension wires.

between the sensing junction and the reference junction, an *electomotive force (EMF)* is produced.

The magnitude of the produced thermocouple potential depends on the composition of the selected wires and of the temperature difference between the two junctions. TABLE 10-1 lists commonly used thermocouples and extension wire. The names Chromel, Constantan, and Alumel are proprietary trade names, which are registered by their developers. The polarities shown apply when the sensing junction temperature is higher than the reference junction temperature.

Table 10-1. Thermocouples and Extension Wire.

| Thermocouple | | Abbrev. | Couple | ISA Type |
Positive	Negative			Extension Wire
Chromel	Constantan	CR/AL	E	EX
Iron	Constantan	Fe/CN	J	JX
Chromel	Alumel	CR/AL	K	KX
Copper	Constantan	Cu/CN	T	TX

1. Chromel is 90 percent nickel, 10 percent chromium.

2. Constantan is 55 percent copper and 45 percent nickel.

3. Alumel is 95 percent nickel with traces of other metal.

The thermocouple wires, which form the sensing or measuring junction, are distinct from the extension wires, which are connected to them. The extension wires permit longer cable runs without introducing thermoelectric potentials at these connections. Because some characteristics of the extension wires are less critical than the coupling wires, the extension wires can be made less expensively. When the appropriate extension wires are properly connected to a thermocouple, the reference junction is transferred to the other end of the extension wires. The thermocouple wire gauges that are normally used for types J, K, and E are: 8, 14, 20, 24, and 28 AWG. For Type T the normal thermocouple wire gauges are: 14, 20, 24, and 28 AWG.

Extension wire gauges are usually limited to 14, 16, and 20 AWG. The wire can be solid or stranded, depending on the desired mechanical flexibility. ANSI color coding is widely used. TABLE 10-2 lists the insulation colors.

Extension wire that meets the NEC requirements for Types PLTC and CL3 for general-purpose applications can have solid conductors that are insulated with PVC or semirigid PVC. The conductors are shielded with aluminum-polyester foil and a stranded tinned-copper drain wire. The jacket is PVC. Optional thermoplastic insulation is PVC with nylon coating for increased physical and mechanical protection, as well as for increased moisture resistance. Other options include thermosetting cross-linked polyethylene and irradiated PVC.

Table 10-2. ANSI Thermocouple Wire Color Code.

ANSI Type	Positive wire		Negative wire		Jacket
	Material	Insul.	Material	Insul.	
EX	Chromel	Purple	Constantan	Red	Purple
JX	Iron	White	Constantan	Red	Black
KX	Chromel	Yellow	Alumel	Red	Yellow
TX	Copper	Blue	Constantan	Red	Blue

In applications where environmental temperatures can reach 200 °C (392 °F) and the extension cable must meet the requirements of NEC Type CL2P for use in plenums, either solid or stranded wires can be used. However, the recommended primary insulation and jacketing is Teflon FEP. The shielding can be aluminum-polyester foil with a drain wire, braided copper, or both.

11

Special cables

Many cables are designed for specific applications. However, they are purchased in large volumes to justify their manufacture as standard catalog products. This chapter provides brief descriptions of some of these application-specific special cables. Some special cables include:

Antenna rotor cable
Audio wire and cable
Camera cables for broadcast and TV
Communication and instrumentation cable (MIL-W-16878)
Computer cable
Direct burial multiconductor cable
Fire alarm and tray cable
Lead-in cable
LAN cable
Microphone cable
Flexible cord
Retractile cable
Flexible power supply cord and cord sets

The cable descriptions in this chapter are general in nature and intended only to provide background information on typical examples of each of the types. For more technical details and options in style and materials, consult manufacturers' catalogs. The NEC, UL, and the CSA have set standards on many of these products.

Antenna rotor cables typically consist of three to eight bare stranded 22- to 20-AWG copper conductors that are insulated with PVC. Two alternate constructions are:

- Extruded primary insulation to form a flat cable
- Color-coded insulated conductors in a PVC jacket

165

Audio wire and cable is specifically made for use as phono pick-up arm cables, low-capacitance cables for connecting stereos, and two-conductor speaker wire. In addition, communications and instrumentation cables are also designed for audio-frequency transmission.

- *Two-conductor speaker wire* is typically made as pairs of stranded parallel copper conductors, one bare and one tinned. Both conductors can be 24- to 16-AWG and the PVC insulation can either be clear or colored.

- *Audio communication and instrumentation cable* includes low-noise RG-58/U, RG-59/U, and RG-174U-type coaxial cables and multiconductor cable. The multiconductor cable for this application typically has stranded tinned-copper 25- to 16-AWG conductors with color-coded PVC, polyethylene, or polypropylene primary insulation that depends on user requirements. This cable classification includes both unshielded and shielded cable. The shielded cable has aluminum-polyester foil shielding that includes a stranded tinned-copper drain wire. PVC jackets are used for general-purpose applications. These cables are rated for 350-volt, 80 °C operation.

Camera cables for broadcast and closed-circuit TV are made for controlling, powering, and transmitting sound and picture information from monochrome and color TV cameras. These cables can be specified for remote control and monitoring systems that employ TV cameras. Camera cables typically meet the requirements of NEC Article 725 for remote control, signaling, and power-limited cables, Type CL2 for general-purpose cables, and Type CL2X for residential applications. These cables are expected to pass the VW-1 Vertical Wire Flame test. Included under this classification are:

- RG-59/U-type coaxial cable
- Multiconductor cables with shielded and unshielded single conductors and twisted pairs
- Coaxial and multiconductor cables in a common Siamese-type jacket (FIG. 11-1)

Communication and instrumentation cable, MIL-W-16878, is shielded and jacketed communication cable made to conform to military specification MIL-W-16878D (Type B). It is intended for demanding communication and instrumentation applications. This cable typically has from one to four stranded tinned-copper 22- to 16-AWG conductors. The primary insulation is color-coded PVC and this is covered with a sheath of clear nylon film. A tinned-copper braid shield with 90-percent coverage is applied over the cabled conductors. PVC jackets are used for cables that meet this specification. These cables are rated for 600-volt, 105 °C operation.

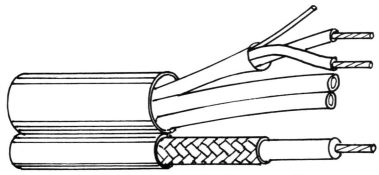

Fig. 11-1. Electronic news gathering (ENG) TV-camera cable.

Many types of cable are called *"computer" cable,* but some are made with a specified number of conductors for interface duties in accordance with a standard protocol. Many cables (including coaxial, fiber-optic, multiconductor and multipair cables) that are described in other chapters of this book are also suitable to interface or interconnect computers and peripherals.

Computer cables typically conform to NEC Article 725, Type CL2; and NEC Article 800, Type CM for general-purpose applications. Types CL2R and CMR are riser cables for use in a vertical shaft or from floor to floor, and Types CL2P and CMP are plenum cables for use in ducts, plenums, and other spaces that distribute environmental air. Two kinds of Type CM computer cables are:

- *Synchronous EIA interface cable* consists of 14 stranded tinned-copper 28-AWG conductor pairs with PVC primary insulation. Each conductor is individually shielded with aluminum-polyester foil (for isolation from adjacent conductors) and each foil shield has a stranded tinned-copper drain wire. The shielded conductors are then covered with an aluminum-polyester shield, which includes another stranded tinned-copper drain wire. The overall jacket is PVC. This cable is UL Type 2384, rated for 30-volt, 60 °C operation.

- *IEEE 488 interface cable* consists of 23 pairs of stranded tinned-copper conductors with color-coded semirigid PVC primary insulation. The cable is organized as six twisted 26-AWG pairs, ten 26-AWG single conductors, and a single 24-AWG conductor. The cabled conductors are shielded with a stranded tinned-copper braid that provides 91-percent shield coverage. A stranded tinned-copper drain wire is included. The jacket for this cable is PVC. This cable is UL type 2464, rated for 300-volt, 80 °C operation.

Direct-burial multiconductor cable is designed to withstand long-term burial in the earth and submersion in water without a conduit. A typical example of this cable features 20-AWG solid or stranded tinned-copper conductors with polypropylene or polyethylene color-coded primary insulation. These conductors are shielded with aluminum-polyester foil and have a stranded tinned-copper drain wire included. These cables are typically rated for 350-volt, 80 °C operation.

Fire alarm and tray cable is made for use in accordance with NEC Article 760, Fire Protective Signaling Systems. This cable is also suitable for Class 2 and Class 3 circuits, in accordance with NEC Article 725; Class 1, Class 2, and Class 3 Remote-Control, Signaling, and Power-Limited Circuits. Class 2 and Class 3 circuits are classified as *communications circuits.* Overcurrent protection is required when the power source is not inherently limited.

- Fire alarm and tray cables are power-limited for use as 300-volt fire-protection signaling-circuit cable, in accordance with NEC Article 725, Type CL2 or CL3, or NEC article 760, Types FPL, FPLR, and FPLP.

- *FPLR cable* is riser cable for use in a vertical shaft or from floor to floor. They are UL Style 2464 and are also certified to CSA FAS 105 and to the FT-4 flame test (FIG. 11-2A). It includes 2 to 12 solid tinned-copper 22- to 12-AWG conductors. The primary insulation is color-coded PVC. The conductors are cabled and jacketed with red PVC. The shielded version features an overall aluminum-polyester foil shield and a stranded tinned-copper drain wire (FIG. 11-2B).

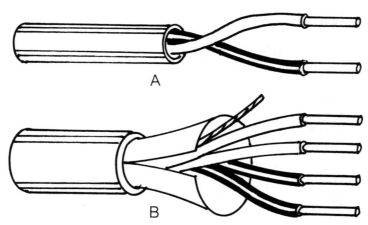

Fig. 11-2. Fire-protective signaling circuit cable: unshielded (A) and shielded (B).

- *FPLP cable* is plenum cable for use in ducts, plenums, and other space for environmental air distribution. It is made to conform to NEC Article 760, Type FPLP for 300-volt applications and to UL Standard 1424. A typical cable (FIG. 11-3) has stranded tinned-copper 14- and 12-AWG conductors and color-coded Teflon FEP insulation. The conductors are dual-shielded for 100-percent coverage with aluminum-polyester foil and a tinned-copper braid. The jacket is red Teflon FEP. FPLP cables are rated for 300-volt, 200 °C operation.

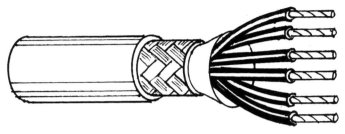

Fig. 11-3. Shielded power-limited fire-protective plenum cable.

Lead-in cable for FM and TV receivers is parallel-conductor cable designed to interconnect external antennas and receivers for FM radio and TV receivers. The conductors are typically copper-coated steel, rather than solid copper, for superior resistance to tension and twisting. This cable can be unshielded or shielded. Shielded lead-in cable is especially useful in urban areas, where EMI/RFI problems are greatest.

- *Unshielded TV lead-in cable* consists of two parallel bare stranded 22- to 20-AWG copper-coated steel conductors. Three different styles are available. Each offers a typical impedance of 300 ohms:

  ○ Polyethylene insulation jacket extruded over two conductors to form an oval cross section (FIG. 11-4A).
  ○ Polyethylene jacket with inert-gas-filled cellular-polyethylene core and a round cross section (FIG. 11-4B).
  ○ Polyethylene insulation web covered with a cellular polyethylene jacket in an oval cross section (FIG. 11-4C).

- *Shielded TV lead-in wire* (FIG. 11-5) also consists of two stranded parallel bare copper-covered steel 26-AWG conductors with a polyethylene insulation web. This primary insulation is covered with cellular polyethylene insulation. The cable is then shielded with aluminum-polyester foil and a stranded tinned-copper-covered steel drain wire included. A PVC jacket with an oval cross section is then extruded over the foil shield. This cable is rated at 185-ohms impedance and 80 °C operation.

LAN cables integrate computer and communications equipment to meet the demand for efficient information distribution, data processing, and collection. Today, the term applies to networks of personal computers, servers, printers, and terminals in offices, buildings, campuses, and industrial parks.

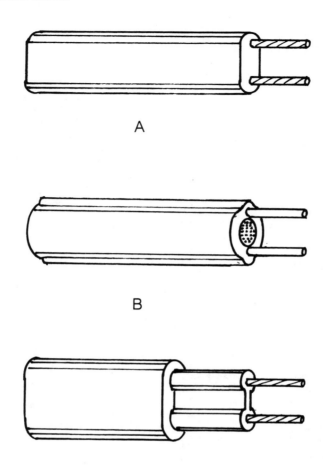

A

B

C

Fig. 11-4. Unshielded TV lead-in cable. Extruded insulation jacket (A), gas-filled cellular core (B), and cellular jacket (C).

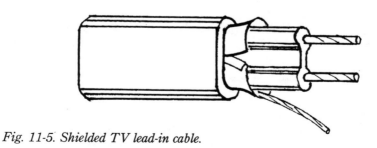

Fig. 11-5. Shielded TV lead-in cable.

LANs are formed with twisted pairs of insulated wire, coaxial cable, and fiber-optic cable in one of three different configurations: star-network topology, bus-network topology and ring-network topology. These cables are described in the chapters of this book on multiconductor and multipair, coaxial and fiber-optic cable. These cables should be chosen with a knowledge of the system data speed and electrical requirements. Electrical characteristics of concern are:

- Characteristic impedance
- Attenuation
- Velocity of propagation
- Shield transfer impedance

General-purpose *transceiver/drop cable* is typically made from stranded tinned-copper 20-AWG conductor pairs with polypropylene primary insulation. Each pair is individually shielded with aluminum-polyester foil, and a tinned-copper drain wire is included. An aluminum-polyester foil shield is applied over the shielded pairs and a stranded tinned-copper drain wire is included. This shield is covered with tinned-copper braid, which provides 94 to 95-percent coverage. The jacket is PVC. This cable is rated for 30-volt operation from −20 to 80 °C. LAN cables are also designed to conform to IEEE, Ethernet, IBM, and Apple computer specifications.

Microphone cable is designed for flexible interconnections between microphones, home-entertainment equipment, musical instruments, tape recorders, and amplifiers for reliable audio-frequency signal transmission. Shielded single-conductor cable is specified for use in high-impedance systems, but multiconductor cables are generally used in low-impedance applications.

Plastic-jacketed cables are recommended for low capacitance, low losses, ozone resistance, light weight, and small diameters. Rubber jackets are recommended where the cable is subject to abrasion and impact. The extra limpness of rubber is desirable because the cable will lie flat on studio floors or stages. Neoprene and other types of synthetic rubber are recommended for situations in which the cable will be used outside and in cold weather. Neoprene jackets are resistant to sunlight, oil, and ozone.

- *Single-conductor cable* is made from a conductor with mixed strands of copper and tinned copper-covered steel. For example, a 25-AWG conductor is wrapped with a rayon braid and is rubber insulated. A second rayon braid is applied and this is covered with a copper shield braid. Then, a wrap of cotton yarn is applied and the assembly is jacketed with rubber.

An alternate construction features a 20-AWG tinned-copper conductor that is insulated with rubber before a conductive textile shield is applied. Then, a tinned-copper spiral shield, paper tape, and a black neoprene jacket are applied.

- *Multiconductor cable* (FIG. 11-6) consists of from two to eight stranded, tinned-copper or cadmium-bronze 20- to 24-AWG conductors. Each conductor is then wrapped in cotton, insulated with rubber, and cabled together. This assembly is braided with a rayon or conductive textile wrap and covered with a tinned-copper braid shield, which has about 85-percent shield coverage. The shield is then wrapped in cotton and a suitable synthetic rubber jacket is applied. These cables are rated for use at 60 °C.

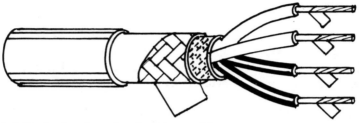

Fig. 11-6. Professional-grade microphone cable.

Flexible cord is used to connect electrical and electronic equipment to utility power lines. Flexible cord is typically classified as *lamp cord* or *power cord*. A power cord can be shielded or unshielded. A shielded power cord will minimize the disturbances caused by EMI and RFI. This benefit is particularly desirable for computers and instruments. UL Standard 62 applies to flexible cordage.

Flexible power cord is made with stranded conductors that are capable of withstanding considerable flexing and yet are limp enough to lie flat on a floor or bench. The most flexible cord is made of very fine wire strands to achieve the required wire gauge, typically from 18 to 14 AWG.

TABLE 11-1 lists typical flexible power cords for electronics use, identified by UL type. The trade names refer to the intended service (e.g., hard or junior), jackets (e.g., thermoset or thermoplastic), and, in some cases, the original intended use (e.g., vacuum cleaner cord).

- *Lamp cord* is typically a two-conductor parallel flexible electrical cord that is protected with an extruded insulation and jacket combination. Cord with a PVC or rubber insulation/jacket is rated for 300 volts at 60 °C. The use of a Hypalon insulation/jacket increases the rating to 300 volts at 90 °C. UL types SP and SPT are widely used for this application.

- *Portable power cords* can have two, three, or more insulated conductors and overall jackets. Most two-conductor power cords are made with 18-

Table 11-1. Stranding vs. Power Rating for Power Cord.

Trade Name	UL Type	Size AWG	No. of Conduct.	Insulation (Notes, 1,2 & 3)	Jacket (Notes 1, 2 & 3)
Hard service Cord	S	18-2	2 or more	Thermoset	Thermoset (rubber)
Junior hard service cord	SJ			Thermoset	Thermoset (rubber)
	SJE			Thermoplast Elastomer	Thermoplast Elastomer (TPE)
		18-10	2, 3, 4, or 5		
	SJO			Thermoset	Thermoset (neoprene)
	SJT (4)			Thermoplast	Thermoplast (PVC)
Hard service cord	SO	18-2	2 or more	Thermoset	Thermoset (neoprene)
Thermoset parallel cord	SP-1	18	2 or 3	Thermoset	Thermoset (rubber)
	SP-2	18-16		Thermoset	Thermoset (rubber)
All plastic parallel cord	SPT-1 SPT-2 SPT-3	18 18-16 18-16	2 or 3		Thermoplast (PVC)
Vacuum cleaner cord	SV (5)	18-17	2 or 3	Thermoset	Thermoset (rubber)
	SVT (4) (5)			Thermoplast	Thermoplast (PVC)

Notes:

(1) Thermoplst—Thermoplastic compound (PVC)

(2) Thermoplst Elastomer—Thermoplastic compound (TPE)

(3) Thermoset—Thermosetting compound (rubber or neoprene)

(4) May be shielded with aluminum polyester tape.

(5) Third conductor for grounding only.

to 14-AWG copper conductors. Paper-tape separators or cotton serve and filler can be used to shape the cord cross section. Shielding is typically aluminum-polyester tape. The third conductor is usually grounded; UL types SVT and SJT are commonly used for this application. The ratings are typically 300 volts at 60 °C.

Flexible power supply cords and cordsets are available in cut lengths that are terminated at both ends with a male plug and a female connector. UL Subjects 764 and 817 cover cordsets and power supply cords.

Cords and cordsets made from UL type SVT and SJT cords with PVC jackets permit ratings of 300 volts at 60 °C. Those made with UL types SJ with rubber jackets, SJO with neoprene jackets, and SJE with thermoplastic elastomer (TPE) jackets also have a rating of 300 volts at 60 °C.

Retractile cable prevents telephone and microphone cables from tangling. These are the familiar coiled cables used on telephones, amateur, CB and mobile transceiver microphones, hand and desktop public-speaker system microphones, musical instruments, and computer keyboards.

Retractile cables can be made many different ways. They can have from one to seven shielded or unshielded conductors or various combinations of shielded and unshielded conductors. The conductors of retractile cable can be made as:

- Solderable tinsel
- Stranded bare or tinned copper
- Combination stranded tinned copper and tinned steel
- Stranded tinned cadmium-bronze

Four alternate construction methods are:

- Stranded tinned-copper 28-AWG conductors are nylon insulated and covered with a spiral tinned-copper shield and jacketed with neoprene. These cables are rated for 30 volts at 90 °C.

- Bare stranded-copper 23-AWG conductors are PVC insulated and covered with a spiral-tinned copper shield, a paper-tape wrap, and a PVC jacket. These cables are rated for 90 volts at 75 °C.

- Combination stranded tinned-copper and tinned copper-covered steel 23-AWG conductors are rubber insulated, covered with a conductive textile wrap and an aluminum-polyester foil shield with a drain wire. The assembly is wrapped in paper tape and given a neoprene jacket. These cables are rated for 90 volts at 90 °C.

- Bare stranded-copper 18-AWG (41 × 34) conductors are rubber insulated and cabled with fillers. The fillers are wrapped in paper tape and jacketed in neoprene (FIG. 11-7). These cables are rated for 300 volts at 90 °C and are classified as UL Type SVO and SJO in UL Standard 62.

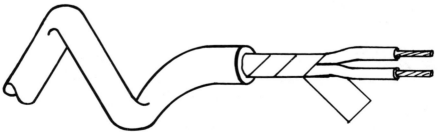

Fig. 11-7. Two-conductor retractile cable.

Appendix

Soft-, medium-, hard-drawn solid-copper conductor data

Size AWG	Dia.		Area		Weight	
	in.	mm.	cir. mil.	mm²	#/m'	kg/km
44	.0020	.051	4.00	.0020	.0121	.0180
43	.0022	.056	4.84	.0025	.0147	.0219
42	.0025	.064	6.25	.0032	.0189	.0281
41	.0028	.071	7.84	.0040	.0237	.0353
40	.0031	.079	9.61	.0049	.0291	.0433
39	.0035	.089	12.3	.0062	.0371	.0552
38	.0040	.102	16.0	.0081	.0484	.0720
37	.0045	.114	20.3	.0103	.0613	.0912
36	.0050	.127	25.0	.0127	.0757	.113
35	.0056	.142	31.4	.0159	.0949	.141
34	.0063	.160	39.7	.0201	.120	.179
33	.0071	.180	50.4	.0256	.153	.228
32	.0080	.203	64.0	.0324	.194	.289
31	.0089	.226	79.2	.0401	.240	.357
30	.0100	.254	100	.0507	.303	.451
29	.0113	.287	128	.0649	.387	.576
28	.0126	.320	159	.0806	.481	.716
27	.0142	.361	202	.102	.610	.908
26	.0159	.404	253	.128	.765	1.14
25	.0179	.455	320	.162	.970	1.44
24	.0201	.511	404	.205	1.22	1.82
23	.0226	.574	511	.259	1.55	2.31
22	.0253	.643	640	.324	1.94	2.89
21	.0285	.724	812	.411	2.46	3.66
20	.0320	.813	1,020	.519	3.10	4.61
19	.0359	.912	1,290	.653	3.90	5.80
18	.0403	1.02	1,620	.823	4.92	7.32
17	.0453	1.15	2,050	1.04	6.21	9.24
16	.0508	1.29	2,580	1.31	7.81	11.6
15	.0571	1.45	3,260	1.65	9.87	14.7
14	.0641	1.63	4,110	2.08	12.4	18.5
13	.0720	1.83	5,180	2.63	15.7	23.4
12	.0808	2.05	6,530	3.31	19.8	21.5
11	.0907	2.30	8,230	4.17	24.9	37.1
10	.1019	2.59	10,380	5.26	31.4	46.8
9	.1144	2.91	13,090	6.63	39.6	59.0
8	.1285	3.26	16,510	8.37	50.0	74.4
7	.1443	3.66	20,820	10.55	63.0	93.8
6	.1620	4.12	26,240	13.33	79.4	118.2
5	.1819	4.62	33,090	16.77	100.2	149.1
4	.2043	5.19	41,740	21.15	126.3	188.0
3	.2294	5.83	52,620	26.67	159.3	237.1
2	.2576	6.54	66,360	33.62	200.9	299.0
1	.2893	7.35	83,690	42.41	253.3	377.0
1/0	.3249	8.25	105,600	53.49	319.5	475.5
2/0	.3648	9.27	133,100	67.43	402.8	599.4
3/0	.4096	10.40	167,800	85.01	507.8	755.7
4/0	.4600	11.68	206,000	107.22	640.5	953.2

mm - Millimeters
cir. mil. - Circular Mils
kg/km - Kilogram Per Kilometer
#/m' - Pounds Per 1000 Feet
psi - Pounds Per Square Inch
mPa - Megapascals

		SOFT			
Tensile		Breaking Load		Max. DCR	
psi	mPa	pounds	n	ohm/m′	ohm/km
40,000	276	.1229	.034	2652.	8700
40,000	276	.1549	.043	2103.	6900
40,000	276	.1954	.054	1668.	5472
40,000	276	.2464	.068	1323.	4340
40,000	276	.3106	.086	1049.	3442
40,000	276	.3917	.109	831.8	2729
40,000	276	.4939	.137	659.6	2164
40,000	276	.6228	.173	523.1	1716
40,000	276	.7854	.218	414.8	1361
40,000	276	.9904	.275	329.0	1079
40,000	276	1.249	.347	260.9	855.9
40,000	276	1.575	.438	206.9	678.8
40,000	276	1.986	.552	164.1	538.4
40,000	276	2.504	.696	130.1	426.8
40,000	276	3.157	.878	103.2	338.6
40,000	276	3.981	1.11	81.84	268.5
40,000	276	5.020	1.40	64.90	212.9
40,000	276	6.331	1.76	51.47	169.9
40,000	276	7.983	2.22	40.81	133.9
40,000	276	10.07	2.80	32.37	106.2
40,000	276	12.69	3.53	25.67	84.22
40,000	276	15.41	4.28	20.36	66.80
40,000	276	19.43	5.40	16.14	52.96
40,000	276	24.50	6.81	12.80	41.99
40,000	276	30.89	8.59	10.15	33.30
40,000	276	38.95	10.83	8.051	26.41
40,000	276	49.12	13.66	6.385	20.95
40,000	276	61.93	17.22	5.064	16.61
40,000	276	78.10	21.71	4.016	13.18
40,000	276	98.48	27.38	3.184	10.45
40,000	276	124.2	34.53	2.525	8.284
40,000	276	156.6	43.53	2.003	6.571
40,000	276	197.5	54.91	1.558	5.111
40,000	276	249.0	69.22	1.260	4.134
40,000	276	314.0	87.29	0.9989	3.277
40,000	276	380.5	105.8	0.7921	2.599
40,000	276	479.8	133.4	0.6282	2.061
40,000	276	605.0	168.2	0.4982	1.635
40,000	276	762.9	212.1	0.3951	1.296
40,000	276	961.9	267.4	0.3133	1.028
40,000	276	1213	337.2	0.2485	0.8153
40,000	276	1530	425.3	0.1970	0.6463
40,000	276	1929	536.3	0.1563	0.5128
40,000	276	2432	676.1	0.1239	0.4065
40,000	276	2984	829.0	0.09827	0.3224
40,000	276	3763	1,046.0	0.07793	0.2557
40,000	276	4745	1,319.0	0.06180	0.2028
40,000	276	5983	1,663.0	0.04901	0.1608

(continued)

MEDIUM HARD							
Tensile Strength			Breaking Load			Max. DCR	
Maximum	Minimum	Maximum		Minimum			
psi mPa	psi mPa	pounds	n	pounds	n	ohm/m'	ohm/km
67,300 464	60,300 416	.2067	.0575	.1853	.0515	2,743	8,999
67,300 464	60,300 416	.2607	.0725	.2337	.0650	2,176	7,139
67,300 464	60,300 416	.3287	.0914	.2947	.0819	1,725	5,659
67,300 464	60,300 416	.4145	.1152	.3716	.0878	1,368	4,488
67,300 464	60,300 416	.5227	.1453	.4685	.1302	1,085	3,560
67,000 462	60,000 413	.6561	.1824	.5876	.1634	860.5	2,823
66,700 460	59,700 412	.8231	.2288	.7367	.2048	682.4	2,239
66,300 457	59,300 409	1.033	.2872	.9238	.2568	541.2	1,775
66,000 455	59,000 407	1.295	.3600	1.158	.3219	429.2	1,408
65,600 452	58,600 404	1.625	.4518	1.452	.4037	340.4	1,117
65,300 450	58,300 402	2.040	.5671	1.821	.5062	269.9	885
65,000 448	58,000 400	2.558	.7111	2.283	.6347	214.1	702
64,600 446	57,600 397	3.210	.8924	2.862	.7956	169.8	557
64,300 443	57,300 397	4.027	1.120	3.589	.9977	134.6	442
64,000 441	57,000 393	5.051	1.404	4.499	1.251	106.8	350
63,700 439	56,700 391	6.336	1.761	5.640	1.568	84.66	278
63,300 437	56,300 388	7.949	2.210	7.070	1.965	67.14	220
63,000 435	56,000 386	9.970	2.772	8.863	2.464	53.24	174.7
62,700 432	55,700 384	12.51	3.478	11.11	3.089	42.22	138.5
62,300 430	55,300 381	15.68	4.360	13.92	3.870	33.49	109.9
62,000 428	55,000 379	19.67	5.468	17.45	4.851	26.56	87.1
61,600 425	54,600 377	24.67	6.858	21.87	6.080	21.06	69.1
61,300 423	54,300 375	30.94	8.601	27.41	7.620	16.07	54.8
61,000 421	54,000 372	38.81	10.79	34.36	9.552	13.24	43.4
60,700 419	53,700 370	48.66	13.53	43.05	11.97	10.50	34.4
60,300 416	53,300 368	61.03	16.97	53.95	15.00	8.330	27.3
60,000 414	53,000 366	76.54	21.28	67.61	18.80	6.606	21.7
59,660 411	52,660 363	95.97	26.68	84.71	23.55	5.239	17.2
59,330 409	52,330 361	120.3	33.44	106.2	29.52	4.154	13.6
59,000 407	52,000 359	150.9	41.95	133.0	36.97	3.295	10.8
58,660 404	51,660 356	189.2	52.60	166.6	46.31	2.613	8.57
58,330 402	51,330 354	237.2	65.94	208.8	58.05	2.072	6.80
58,000 400	51,000 352	297.5	82.71	261.6	72.72	1.643	5.39
57,660 349	50,660 349	372.9	103.7	327.6	91.07	1.303	4.27
57,330 347	50,330	467.5	130.0	410.4	114.1	1.033	3.39
57,000 345	50,000	586.0	162.9	514.2	142.9	.8195	2.69
56,660 343	49,660	734.7	204.2	643.9	179.0	.6499	2.13
56,330 340	49,330	921.0	256.0	806.6	224.2	.5154	1.69
56,000 338	49,000	1,155	321.1	1,010	280.8	.4087	1.34
55,660 336	48,660	1,447	402.3	1,265	351.7	.3241	1.06
55,330 333	48,330	1,814	504.3	1,584	440.4	.2570	.843
55,000 331	48,000	2,274	632.2	1,984	551.5	.2038	.669
54,000 324	47,000	2,815	782.6	2,450	681.1	.1617	.531
53,000 317	46,000	3,484	968.6	3,024	840.7	.1282	.421
52,000 310	45,000	4,310	1,198	3,730	1,037	.1006	.330
51,000 303	44,000	5,330	1,482	4,599	1,278	.07980	.262
50,000 296	43,000	6,590	1,832	5,667	1,575	.06329	.208
49,000 290	42,000	8,143	2,264	6,980	1,940	.05019	.165

HARD DRAWN						
Tensile Strength		Breaking Load		Max. DCR		Size
Minimum		Minimum		ohm/m'	ohm/km	AWG
psi	mPa	pounds	n			
72,000	496	.2212	.0615	2,758	9,048	44
72,000	496	.2789	.0775	2,187	7,175	43
72,000	496	.3517	.0977	1,734	5,689	42
72,000	496	.4434	.1232	1,375	4,511	41
72,000	496	.5592	.1554	1,091	3,579	40
71,800	495	.7031	.1954	865.0	2,838	39
71,500	493	.8829	.2454	686.0	2,251	38
71,300	492	1.110	.3084	544.0	1,784	37
71,100	490	1.396	.3880	431.4	1,415	36
70,900	489	1.755	.4878	324.1	1,122	35
70,600	487	2.204	.6127	271.3	890	34
70,400	485	2.772	.7706	215.2	706	33
70,200	484	3.485	.9688	170.6	560	32
69,900	482	4.376	1.216	135.3	444	31
69,700	481	5.502	1.529	107.3	352	30
69,400	479	6.908	1.920	85.10	279	29
69,300	478	8.698	2.418	67.49	221	28
69,000	476	10.92	3.035	53.52	175.6	27
68,800	475	13.73	3.816	42.44	138.5	26
68,600	473	17.26	4.798	33.66	110.4	25
68,300	471	21.67	6.024	26.69	87.6	24
68,100	470	27.25	7.575	21.17	69.5	23
67,900	468	34.26	9.524	16.79	55.1	22
67,700	467	43.07	11.97	13.31	43.7	21
67,400	465	54.08	15.03	10.56	34.6	20
67,200	463	67.99	18.90	8.373	27.5	19
67,000	462	85.47	23.76	6.640	21.8	18
66,800	461	107.5	29.80	5.266	17.3	17
66,600	459	135.1	37.55	4.176	13.7	16
66,400	458	169.8	47.20	3.312	10.9	15
66,200	457	213.5	59.35	2.676	8.62	14
65,900	455	268.0	74.50	2.083	6.83	13
65,700	453	336.9	93.65	1.652	5.42	12
65,400	451	422.9	117.5	1.310	4.30	11
64,900	448	522.2	145.1	1.039	3.41	10
64,300	443	661.2	183.8	.8238	2.70	9
63,700	439	826.0	229.6	.6533	2.14	8
63,000	434	1,030	286.3	.5181	7.70	7
62,100	428	1,280	355.8	.4108	1.35	6
61,200	422	1,591	442.2	.3258	1.07	5
60,000	414	1,970	547.6	.2584	.848	4
59,000	407	2,439	678.0	.2049	.672	3
57,600	397	3,003	834.8	.1625	.533	2
56,100	387	3,688	1,025.0	.1289	.423	1
54,500	376	4,517	1,256.0	.1011	.332	1/0
52,800	364	5,519	1,534.0	.08021	.263	2/0
51,000	352	6,722	1,869.0	.06361	.209	3/0
49,000	338	8,143	2,264.0	.05045	.166	4/0

Solid copper conductor data

	Diameter			Cross Sect. Area		
AWG	inches	mils	mm	circ. mils	sq. mm.	
40	.0031	3.1	.079	9.61	.0049	
39	.0035	3.5	.089	12.3	.0062	
38	.0040	4.0	.102	16.0	.0081	
37	.0045	4.5	.114	20.3	.0103	
36	.0050	5.0	.127	25.0	.0127	
35	.0056	5.6	.142	31.4	.0159	
34	.0063	6.3	.160	39.7	.0201	
33	.0071	7.1	.180	50.4	.0255	
32	.0080	8.0	.203	64.0	.0324	
31	.0089	8.9	.226	79.2	.0401	
30	.0100	10.0	.254	100	.0507	
29	.0113	11.3	.287	128	.0649	
28	.0126	12.6	.320	159	.0806	
27	.0142	14.2	.361	202	.102	
26	.0159	15.9	.404	253	.128	
25	.0179	17.9	.455	320	.162	
24	.0201	20.1	.511	404	.205	
23	.0226	22.6	.574	511	.259	
22	.0253	25.3	.643	640	.324	
21	.0285	28.5	.724	812	.411	
20	.0320	32.0	.813	1,020	.519	
19	.0359	35.9	.912	1,290	.653	
18	.0403	40.3	1.02	1,620	.823	
17	.0453	45.3	1.15	2,050	1.04	
16	.0508	50.8	1.29	2,580	1.31	
15	.0571	57.1	1.45	3,260	1.65	
14	.0641	64.1	1.63	4,110	2.08	
13	.0720	72.0	1.83	5,180	2.63	
12	.0808	80.8	2.05	6,530	3.31	
11	.0907	90.7	2.30	8,230	4.17	
10	.1019	101.9	2.588	10,380	5.26	
9	.1144	114.4	2.906	13,090	6.63	
8	.1285	128.5	3.264	16,510	8.37	
7	.1443	144.3	3.655	20,820	10.55	
6	.1620	162.0	4.115	26,240	13.30	
5	.1819	181.9	4.620	33,090	16.77	
4	.2043	204.3	5.189	41,740	21.15	
3	.2294	229.4	5.827	52,620	26.67	
2	.2576	257.6	6.543	66,360	33.62	
1	.2893	289.3	7.348	83,690	42.41	
1/0	.3249	324.9	8.252	105,600	53.49	
2/0	.3648	364.8	9.266	133,100	67.43	
3/0	.4096	409.6	10.40	167,800	85.01	
4/0	.4600	460.0	11.68	211,600	107.22	

Weight		DCR @ 20°C		Break Strength	
lbs./M′	kg./km.	ohms/M′	ohms/km.	lbs. (max.)	kg. (max.)
.0291	.0433	1080	3540	.3106	.1409
.0371	.0552	847	2780	.3917	.1776
.0484	.0720	648	2130	.4939	.2240
.0613	.0912	512	1680	.6228	.2825
.0757	.113	415	1360	.7854	.3562
.0949	.141	331	1080	.9904	.4492
.120	.179	261	857	1.249	.5665
.153	.228	206	675	1.575	.7144
.194	.289	162	532	1.986	.9008
.240	.357	131	430	2.504	1.136
.303	.451	104	340	3.157	1.432
.387	.576	81.2	266	3.981	1.806
.481	.716	65.3	214	5.020	2.277
.610	.908	51.4	169	6.331	2.872
.765	1.14	41.0	135	7.983	3.621
.970	1.44	32.4	106	10.07	4.568
1.22	1.82	25.7	84.2	12.69	5.756
1.55	2.31	20.3	66.6	15.41	6.990
1.94	2.89	16.2	53.2	19.43	8.813
2.46	3.66	12.8	41.9	24.50	11.11
3.10	4.61	10.1	33.2	30.89	14.01
3.90	5.80	8.05	26.4	38.95	17.67
4.92	7.32	6.39	21.0	49.12	22.28
6.21	9.24	5.05	16.6	61.93	28.09
7.81	11.6	4.02	13.2	78.10	35.43
9.87	14.7	3.18	10.4	98.48	44.67
12.4	18.5	2.52	8.28	124.2	56.34
15.7	23.4	2.00	6.56	156.6	71.03
19.8	29.5	1.59	5.21	197.5	89.58
24.9	37.1	1.26	4.14	249.0	112.9
31.4	46.8	.9988	3.277	314.0	142.4
39.6	59.0	.7925	2.600	380.5	172.6
50.0	74.4	.6281	2.061	479.8	217.6
63.0	93.8	.4981	1.634	605.0	274.4
79.4	118	.3952	1.296	762.9	346.0
100	149	.3134	1.028	961.9	436.3
126	188	.2485	.8152	1213	550.2
159	237	.1971	.6466	1530	694.0
201	299	.1563	.5128	1929	875.0
253	377	.1239	.4065	2432	1103
319	476	.09825	.3223	2984	1354
403	599	.07793	.2557	3763	1707
508	756	06182	.2028	4745	2152
641	953	.04901	.1608	5983	2714

Solid and stranded copper and alloy conductor data

AWG	Stranding	Type Stranding[1]	Diameter[2] in.	mm.	Area circ. mils	sq. mm.	Weight lbs./M'	kg./km.	D.C. Resistance @20°C[3] Tin Coating[4] ohms/M'	ohms/km.	Bare or Silver Coating ohms/M'	ohms/km.	HSA[5] Silver Coating ohms/M'	ohms/km.
40	Solid[6]	—	.003	.080	9	.005	.029	.043	—	—	—	—	1440.0	4724.0
38	Solid[6]	—	.004	.102	16	.008	.048	.071	—	—	—	—	852.0	2789.0
36	Solid[6]	—	.005	.127	25	.013	.076	.113	—	—	—	—	540.0	1772.0
34	Solid[6]	—	.006	.160	36	.020	.120	.179	—	—	—	—	337.0	1106.0
32	Solid[6]	—	.008	.203	64	.032	.194	.289	—	—	—	—	208.0	682.0
32	7/40[6]	Co	.009	.234	81	.043	.210	.315	—	—	—	—	184.0	605.8
32	7/40	Co or BU	.010	.254	100	.051	.21	.31	176	577	—	—	—	—
32	Solid[6]	—	.008	.201	64	.032	.19	.28	—	—	—	—	208	682
30	Solid	—	.010	.254	100	.051	.30	.45	113	371	104	340	—	—
30	Solid[6]	—	.010	.254	100	.051	.30	.45	—	—	—	—	118	390
30	7/38	Bu	.012	.305	112	.057	.35	.52	106	348	92.6	303	—	—
29	Solid[6]	—	.011	.287	128	.065	.39	.58	—	—	—	—	92	302
28	Solid	—	.013	.320	169	.081	.48	.72	70.8	232	65.3	214	—	—
28	7/36	Co	.015	.381	175	.089	.55	.82	67.5	221	59.3	194	—	—
28	7/36[6]	Co	.015	.381	175	.089	.58	.86	—	—	—	—	69	228
28	Solid[6]	—	.013	.320	169	.080	.48	.72	—	—	—	—	74	244
27	Solid[6]	—	.014	.361	202	.102	.61	.91	55.6	182	51.4	169	58	192
27	Solid	—	.014	.361	202	.102	.61	.91	—	—	—	—	—	—

	65/44	Bu	.018	.455	260	.131	.70	1.05	—	—	42.0	138	—	—
26	Solid	—	.016	.404	253	.128	.77	1.14	44.5	—	41.0	135	—	—
	Solid[6]	—	.016	.404	253	.128	.77	1.14	—	146	41.0	135	46.2	152
	7/34	Co or Bu	.019	.483	278	.141	.87	1.29	42.5	139	37.3	122	—	—
	10/36	Bu	.019	.483	250	.127	.78	1.15	47.3	155	40.4	133	—	—
	19/38	Bu or Co	.021	.533	304	.154	.97	1.44	38.9	128	34.1	112	—	—
	19/38[6]	Co, Eq or Un	.021	.533	304	.154	.97	1.44	—	—	—	—	40.4	133
24	Solid	—	.020	.511	404	.205	1.22	1.82	27.2	89.2	25.7	84.2	—	—
	7/32	Co or Bu	.024	.610	448	.227	1.38	2.05	25.7	84.2	23.1	75.9	—	—
	16/36	Bu	.023	.609	400	.201	1.25	1.64	29.5	96.8	27.5	90.2	—	—
	19/36	Co or Bu	.025	.635	475	.241	1.48	2.20	24.9	81.7	21.8	71.6	—	—
22	Solid	—	.025	.643	643	.324	1.94	2.89	16.7	54.8	16.2	53.2	—	—
	7/30	Co or Bu	.031	.787	700	.355	2.19	3.26	16.6	54.4	14.8	48.6	—	—
	19/34	Bu or Eq	.032	.813	754	.382	2.35	3.50	15.5	50.8	13.8	45.1	—	—
20	Solid	—	.032	.813	1,020	.519	3.10	4.61	10.5	34.4	10.1	33.2	—	—
	7/28	Co or Bu	.038	.965	1,111	.562	3.49	5.19	10.3	33.8	9.33	30.6	—	—
	10/30	Bu	.036	.914	1,000	.507	3.14	4.67	11.4	37.4	10.4	34.0	—	—
	19/32	Co, Bu or Eq	.040	1.02	1,216	.616	3.84	5.71	9.48	31.1	8.53	28.0	—	—
	19/.0071[7]	Eq	.036	.914	957	.485	2.95	4.39	12.6	41.3	—	—	—	—
	26/34	Bu	.037	.940	1,032	.523	3.28	4.88	11.3	37.1	—	—	—	—
	42/36	Bu	.038	.965	1,050	.532	3.34	4.97	11.2	36.7	—	—	—	—
19	Solid	—	.036	.912	1,290	.653	3.90	5.80	—	—	8.05	26.4	—	—
18	Solid	—	.040	1.02	1,620	.823	4.92	7.32	6.77	22.2	6.39	21.0	—	—
	7/26	Co or Bu	.048	1.22	1,770	.897	5.55	8.26	6.45	21.2	5.86	19.2	—	—
	16/30	Bu	.046	1.17	1,600	.810	5.01	7.45	7.15	23.4	6.48	21.3	—	—
	19/30	Co, Bu or Eq	.050	1.27	1,900	.963	5.95	8.85	6.10	20.0	5.46	17.9	—	—
	19/.0092[7]	Bu	.046	1.17	1,608	.814	5.10	7.59	—	—	5.10	16.7	—	—
	41/34	Bu	.047	1.19	1,627	.824	5.09	7.08	7.08	23.2	6.60	21.6	—	—
16	Solid	—	.051	1.29	2,580	1.31	7.81	11.6	4.47	14.7	4.16	21.0	—	—
	7/.0192[7]	Bu	.058	1.47	2,581	1.31	7.90	11.8	—	—	4.16	19.2	—	—
	19/29[7]	Bu or Eq	.057	1.45	2,426	1.23	7.52	11.2	4.82	15.8	4.27	21.3	—	—
	19/.0117[7]	Bu	.059	1.50	2,601	1.32	8.02	11.9	4.39	14.4	4.13	17.9	—	—
	26/30	Bu	.060	1.52	2,600	1.32	8.15	12.1	4.39	14.4	3.99	16.7	—	—
	65/34	Bu	.060	1.52	2,580	1.31	7.98	11.9	4.47	14.7	4.16	21.6	—	—

(continued)

AWG	Stranding	Type Stranding[1]	Diameter[2] in.	Diameter[2] mm.	Area circ. mils	Area sq. mm.	Weight lbs./M'	Weight kg./km.	Tin Coating[4] ohms/M'	Tin Coating[4] ohms/km.	Bare or Silver Coating ohms/M'	Bare or Silver Coating ohms/km.	HSA[5] Silver Coating ohms/M'	HSA[5] Silver Coating ohms/km.
14	Solid	—	.064	1.63	4,110	2.08	12.4	18.5	2.68	8.79	2.52	8.28	—	—
	7/.0242	Bu	.073	1.85	4,100	2.08	12.7	18.9	—	—	2.61	8.56	—	—
	19/.27[7]	Co, Eq or Un	.071	1.80	3,831	1.94	12.1	18.0	3.05	10.00	2.71	8.88	—	—
	19/.0147	Bu	.074	1.88	4,106	2.08	12.7	18.9	—	—	2.61	8.56	—	—
	41/30	Bu	.069	1.75	4,100	2.08	12.9	19.2	2.81	9.22	2.53	8.30	—	—
12	Solid	—	.081	2.05	6,530	3.31	19.8	29.5	1.69	5.54	1.59	5.21	—	—
	7/.0305	Co	.092	2.34	6,512	3.30	20.2	30.1	—	—	1.64	5.38	—	—
	19/.25[7]	Co, Eq or Un	.090	2.29	6,088	3.08	19.4	28.9	1.87	6.13	1.70	5.59	—	—
	19/.0185	Bu	.093	2.36	6,503	3.30	20.2	30.1	—	—	1.60	5.23	—	—
	65/30	Bu	.091	2.31	6,500	3.29	20.8	31.1	1.82	5.97	1.60	5.23	—	—
10	Solid	—	.102	2.59	10,380	5.26	31.4	46.8	—	—	1.00	3.28	—	—
	7/.0385	Co	.116	2.95	10,376	5.25	32.0	47.6	—	—	1.00	3.28	—	—
	19/.0234	Bu	.117	2.97	10,404	5.27	32.0	47.6	—	—	.98	3.21	—	—
	37/.0169	Co	.112	2.84	9,361	4.74	29.2	43.4	—	—	1.25	4.10	—	—
	49/27[7]	Rp 7 × 7/27	.120	3.04	9,880	5.01	32.4	48.2	—	—	1.28	4.20	—	—
	105/30	Bu	.130	3.30	10,500	5.32	33.1	49.2	1.10	3.61	.99	3.24	—	—
9	7/.0432	Co	.130	3.30	13,064	6.61	43.0	64.0	—	—	.82	2.69	—	—
8	Solid	—	.129	3.26	16,510	8.37	49.9	74.3	—	—	.62	2.06	—	—
	7/.0486	Co	.146	3.71	16,534	8.38	50.1	74.5	—	—	.65	2.13	—	—
	19/.0295	Bu or Eq	.144	3.66	16,535	8.38	50.0	74.4	—	—	.65	2.13	—	—
	133/29	Rp 19 × 7/29	.167	4.24	16,983	8.61	54.0	80.4	.71	2.33	—	—	—	—
	168/30	Rp 7 × 24/30	.174	4.42	16,800	8.51	53.1	79.0	.70	2.30	—	—	—	—

6	Solid	—	.162	4.12	26,240	13.30	79.4	118	—	—	.40	1.30	—
	7/.0612	Co	.184	4.67	26,218	13.28	81.1	121	—	—	.41	1.34	—
	19/.0372	Bu	.186	4.72	26,293	13.33	81.1	121	—	—	.40	1.30	—
	133/27	Rp 19 × 7/27	.210	5.33	26,818	13.60	84.1	125	.43	1.41	—	—	—
	266/30	Rp 7 × 38/30	.204	5.18	26,600	13.49	83.2	124	.44	1.44	—	—	—
4	Solid	—	.204	5.19	41,740	21.15	126	188	—	—	.25	.82	—
	7/.0772	Co	.232	5.89	41,719	21.15	129	192	—	—	.26	.85	—
	19/.0469	Co	.235	5.97	41,793	21.19	129	192	.29	.95	.24	.79	—
	133/25	Rp 19 × 7/25	.257	6.53	42,615	21.61	135	201	.29	.95	—	—	—
	420/30	Rp 7 × 60/30	.257	6.53	42,000	21.29	140	208	.28	.92	—	—	—
2	19/.0591	Co	.292	7.42	66,407	33.67	205	305	—	—	.17	.56	—
	665/30	Rp 19 × 35/30	.338	8.59	66,500	33.72	213	317	.18	.59	—	—	—
1	19/.0664	Co	.332	8.43	83,771	42.47	266	396	—	—	.13	.43	—
1/0	19/.0745	Eq	.373	9.47	105,445	53.47	326	485	—	—	.11	.36	—
	37/.0534	Eq	.370	9.40	105,508	53.49	326	485	—	—	.10	.33	—
	259/24	Rp 7 × 37/24	.424	10.77	104,639	53.05	331	493	.11	.36	—	—	—
	1045/30[7]	Rp 19 × 55/30	.410	10.41	104,500	52.98	335	498	.12	.39	—	—	—
2/0	37/.0600	Co	.420	10.67	133,200	67.53	411	612	—	—	.08	.26	—
	259/.0227	Rp 7 × 37/.0227	.456	11.58	129,956	65.89	430	640	.09	.30	—	—	—
	1330/30	Rp 19 × 70/30	.496	12.60	133,300	67.58	430	640	.09	.30	—	—	—
3/0	37/.0673	Co	.470	11.94	167,584	84.97	518	771	—	—	.07	.23	—
4/0	37/.0756	Eq	.530	13.46	211,468	107.23	653	972	—	—	.05	.16	—
	427/.0223	Rp 61 × 7/.0223	.602	15.29	212,343	107.65	676	1,006	.06	.20	—	—	—
	2107/30	Rp 7 × 7 × 43/30	.608	15.44	210,700	106.82	674	1,003	.06	.20	—	—	—

1 BU—Bunched; Co—Concentric; Eq—Equilay; Rp—Rope; Un—Unilay
2 Actual nominal diameter for solid wires; average diameter for stranded wires by factoring.
3 Typical D.C. Resistance values for uninsulated wires. Multiply by 1.04 for typical values after insulation.
4 Values are for tinned, heavy tinned, prefused, overcoated or topcoated conductors
5 HSA High Strength Alloy
6 Alloy 135 (high strength cadmium chromium copper)
7 Does not meet UL conductor stranding requirements

High-strength copper-clad steel

Size	Dia.		Cross Sect. Area			Weight
AWG	in.	mm.	cir. mil.	sq. mm.	#/1000'	kg./km.
40	.0031	.078	9.89	.0049	.027	.0401
39	.0035	.0889	12.47	.0063	.035	.0520
38	.0040	.101	15.72	.0080	.044	.0654
37	.0045	.114	19.83	.0100	.055	.0818
36	.0050	.127	25.00	.0126	.069	.102
35	.0056	.142	31.52	.0160	.087	.130
34	.0063	.160	39.75	.0201	.110	.163
33	.0071	.180	50.13	.0254	.139	.206
32	.0080	.203	63.21	.0320	.175	.260
31	.0089	.226	79.70	.0403	.221	.328
30	.0100	.254	100.5	.0509	.279	.415
29	.0113	.287	126.7	.0642	.352	.523
28	.0126	.320	159.8	.0897	.443	.660
27	.0142	.360	201.5	.102	.559	.831
26	.0159	.403	254.1	.130	.705	1.05
25	.0179	.450	320.4	.162	.889	1.32
24	.0201	.510	404.0	.204	1.121	1.67
23	.0226	.574	509.5	.258	1.414	2.10
22	.0253	.642	647.5	.325	1.783	2.65
21	.0285	.723	810.1	.410	2.248	3.34
20	.0320	.812	1,022	.520	2.835	4.22
19	.0359	.911	1,288	.652	3.575	5.32
18	.0403	1.02	1,624	.820	4.507	6.70
17	.0453	1.15	2,048	1.03	5.684	8.46
16	.0508	1.29	2,583	1.30	7.167	10.66
15	.0571	1.45	3,257	1.65	9.038	13.44
14	.0641	1.63	4,107	2.08	11.40	16.96
13	.0720	1.83	5,178	2.63	14.37	21.38

mm - Millimeters
cir. mil - Circular Mils
kg/km - Kilograms Per Kilometer
m/kg - Meters Per Kilogram
psi - Pounds Per Square Inch
mPa - Megapascals

| Weight | | Resistance at 68° Fahr. | | | |
| | | 40% Cond. | | 30% Cond. | |
ft./#	m/kg.	ohms/1000'	ohms/km.	ohms/1000'	ohms/km.
36,440	24.48	2,675	8,776	3,566	11,699
28,900	19.42	2,121	6,958	2,828	9,278
22,920	15.40	1,682	5,518	2,243	7,358
18,180	12.21	1,334	4,376	1,778	5,833
14,410	9.68	1,058	3,471	1,410	4,625
11,430	7.68	839.0	2,752	1,119	3,671
9,065	6.09	665.4	2,183	887.0	2,910
7,189	4.83	527.7	1,724	703.4	2,307
5,701	3.83	418.5	1,373	557.8	1,830
4,521	3.03	331.9	1,088	442.4	1,451
3,586	2.40	263.2	863.5	350.8	1,150
2,843	1.91	208.7	684.7	278.2	912.7
2,255	1.51	165.5	542.9	220.6	723.7
1,788	1.20	131.3	430.7	175.0	574.1
1,418	.953	104.1	341.5	138.8	455.3
1,125	.756	82.55	270.8	110.0	360.8
891.9	.599	65.46	214.7	87.27	286.3
707.3	.475	51.92	170.3	69.21	227.0
560.9	.377	41.17	135.1	54.88	180.0
444.8	.299	32.65	107.1	43.52	142.7
352.8	.237	25.89	84.93	34.52	113.3
279.8	.188	20.53	67.35	27.37	89.80
221.9	.149	16.28	53.41	21.71	71.22
175.9	.118	12.91	42.35	17.22	56.49
139.5	.094	10.24	33.59	13.65	44.78
110.6	.074	8.12	26.64	10.83	35.53
87.75	.059	6.44	21.12	8.59	28.18
69.59	.047	5.11	16.76	6.81	22.34

(continued)

40% Conductivity			
Tensile Str.		Breaking Load	
psi	mPa	pounds	newtons
115,000	793	.893	.248
115,000	793	1.13	.314
115,000	793	1.42	.395
115,000	793	1.79	.498
115,000	793	2.26	.628
115,000	793	2.85	.792
115,000	793	3.59	.998
115,000	793	4.53	1.26
115,000	793	5.71	1.59
115,000	793	7.20	2.00
115,000	793	9.08	2.52
115,000	793	11.4	3.16
115,000	793	14.4	4.00
115,000	793	18.2	5.05
115,000	793	23.0	6.40
115,000	793	28.9	8.03
115,000	793	36.5	10.14
115,000	793	46.0	12.70
115,000	793	58.0	16.12
115,000	793	73.2	20.34
125,000	862	100.	27.80
121,000	834	122	33.91
120,000	827	153	42.53
115,000	793	185	51.40
123,000	848	250	69.50
117,000	806	300	83.4
124,000	855	400	111.2
120,000	827	490	136.2

30% Conductivity				
Tensile Str.		Breaking Load		Size
psi	mPa	pounds	newtons	AWG
127,000	876	.986	.27	40
127,000	876	1.24	.34	39
127,000	876	1.57	.44	38
127,000	876	1.98	.55	37
127,000	876	2.49	.69	36
127,000	876	3.14	.87	35
127,000	876	3.97	1.10	34
127,000	876	5.00	1.39	33
127,000	876	6.30	1.75	32
127,000	876	7.95	2.21	31
127,000	876	10.0	2.78	30
127,000	876	12.6	3.50	29
127,000	876	15.9	4.42	28
127,000	876	20.1	5.59	27
127,000	876	25.4	7.06	26
127,000	876	32.1	8.92	25
127,000	876	40.4	11.2	24
127,000	876	51.0	14.2	23
127,000	876	64.3	17.9	22
127,000	876	81.1	22.5	21
137,000	945	110.	30.6	20
133,000	917	135	37.5	19
157,000	1,083	200	55.6	18
149,000	1,028	240	66.7	17
133,000	917	270	75.1	16
129,000	890	330	91.7	15
136,000	938	440	122	14
130,000	896	530	147	13

Cabling lay-up and diameter factors

Total Conds	K Factor	Core	1st	2nd	3rd	Total Conds
			Number of conductors per Layer*			
2	2.00	2				51
3	2.15	3				52
4	2.41	4				53
5	2.70	5				54
						55
6	3.00	6				56
7	3.00	1	6			57
8	3.31	1 + f	7			58
9	3.62	1 + f	8			59
10	4.00	2	8			60
11	4.00	2 + f	9			61
12	4.15	3	9			62
13	4.41	3 + f	10			63
14	4.41	4	10			64
15	4.70	4 + 2f	11			65
16	4.70	5 + f	11			66
17	5.00	5 + 2f	12			67
18	5.00	6 + f	12			68
19	5.00	1	6	12		69
20	5.31	f	7	13		70
21	5.31	1 + f	7	13		71
22	5.62	f	8	14		72
23	5.62	1 + f	8	14		73
24	6.00	2	8	14		74
25	6.00	2	8	15		75
26	6.00	2 + f	9	15		76
27	6.15	3	9	15		77
28	6.41	3 + f	9 + f	16		78
29	6.41	3 + f	10	16		79
30	6.41	4	10	16		80
31	6.70	4 + 2f	10 + f	17		81
32	6.70	4 + 2f	11	17		82
33	6.70	5 + f	11	17		83
34	7.00	f	5 + f	11 + f	18	84
35	7.00	f	5 + f	12	18	85
36	7.00	f	6	12	18	86
37	7.00	1	6	12	18	87
38	7.31	f	6 + f	13	19	88
39	7.31	f	7	13	19	89
40	7.31	1 + f	7	13	19	90
41	7.62	f	7 + f	14	20	91
42	7.62	f	8	14	20	92
43	7.62	1 + f	8	14	20	93
44	8.00	1 + f	8 + f	14 + f	21	94
45	8.00	1 + f	8 + f	15	21	95
46	8.00	1 + f	9	15	21	96
47	8.00	2	9	15	21	97
48	8.15	3	9	15	21	98
49	8.15	3	9	15	22	99
50	8.41	3 + f	9 + f	16	22	100

* f = Filler

K Factor	Core	Number of conductors per Layer*				
		1st	2nd	3rd	4th	5th
8.41	3 + f	10	16	22		
8.41	4	10	16	22		
8.70	4 + 2f	10 + f	16 + f	23		
8.70	4 + 2f	10 + f	17	23		
8.70	4 + 2f	11	17	23		
8.70	5 + f	11	17	23		
9.00	f	5 + f	11 + f	17 + f	24	
9.00	f	5 + f	11 + f	18	24	
9.00	f	5 + f	12	18	24	
9.00	f	6	12	18	24	
9.00	1	6	12	18	24	
9.31	f	6 + f	12 + f	19	25	
9.31	f	6 + f	13	19	25	
9.31	f	7	13	19	25	
9.31	1 + f	7	13	19	25	
9.62	f	7 + f	13 + f	20	26	
9.62	f	7 + f	14	20	26	
9.62	f	8	14	20	26	
9.62	1 + f	8	14	20	26	
10.00	1 + f	8 + f	14 + f	20 + f	27	
10.00	1 + f	8 + f	14 + f	21	27	
10.00	1 + f	8 + f	15	21	27	
10.00	1 + f	9	15	21	27	
10.00	2	9	15	21	27	
10.20	2 + f	8 + f	15	22	28	
10.20	2 + f	9	15	22	28	
10.20	3	9	15	22	28	
10.41	3 + f	9 + f	15 + f	22 + f	29	
10.41	3 + f	9 + f	15 + f	23	29	
10.41	3 + f	9 + f	16	23	29	
10.41	3 + f	10	16	23	29	
10.41	4	10	16	23	29	
10.70	4 + f	10 + f	17	23	29	
10.70	4 + f	11	17	23	29	
10.70	5 + f	11	17	23	29	
11.00	f	5 + f	11 + f	17 + f	23 + f	30
11.00	f	5 + f	11 + f	17 + f	24	30
11.00	f	5 + f	11 + f	18	24	30
11.00	f	5 + f	12	18	24	30
11.00	f	6	12	18	24	30
11.00	1	6	12	18	24	30
11.31	f	6 + f	12 + f	19	25	30
11.31	f	6 + f	13	19	25	30
11.31	f	7	13	19	25	30 + f
11.31	1 + f	7	13	19	25	30 + f
11.62	f	7 + f	13 + f	20	26	30 + f
11.62	f	7 + f	14	20	26	30 + f
11.62	f	8	14	20	26	30 + f
11.62	1 + f	8	14	20	26	30 + f
12.00	1 + f	8 + f	14 + f	20 + f	27	30 + f

Insulation materials nominal temperature operating ranges

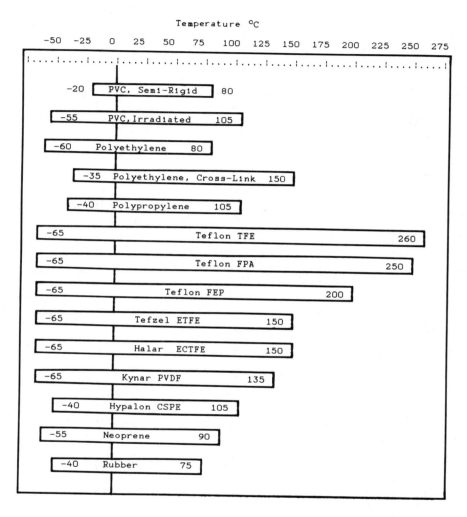

Temperature conversion table

Read known temperature in bold face type. Corresponding temperature in degrees Fahrenheit will be found in column to the right. Corresponding temperature in degrees Centigrade will be found in column to the left.

−5 to −100			0 to 100					100 to 500		
°C		°F	°C		°F	°C		°F	°C		°F
−73.3	−100	−148	−17.8	0	32.0	10.0	50	122.0	38	100	212
−70.5	−95	−139	−17.2	1	33.8	10.6	51	123.8	43	110	230
−67.8	−90	−130	−16.7	2	35.6	11.1	52	125.6	49	120	248
−65.0	−85	−121	−16.1	3	37.4	11.7	53	127.4	54	130	266
−62.2	−80	−112	−15.6	4	39.2	12.2	54	129.2	60	140	284
−59.5	−75	−103	−15.0	5	41.0	12.8	55	131.0	66	150	302
−56.7	−70	−94	−14.4	6	42.8	13.3	56	132.8	71	160	320
−53.9	−65	−85	−13.9	7	44.6	13.9	57	134.6	77	170	338
−51.1	−60	−76	−13.3	8	46.4	14.4	58	136.4	82	180	356
−48.3	−55	−67	−12.8	9	48.2	15.0	59	138.2	88	190	374
−45.6	−50	−58	−12.2	10	50.0	15.6	60	140.0	93	200	392
−42.8	−45	−49	−11.7	11	51.8	16.1	61	141.8	99	210	410
−40.0	−40	−40	−11.1	12	53.6	16.7	62	143.6	100	212	413
−37.2	−35	−31	−10.6	13	55.4	17.2	63	145.4	104	220	428
−34.4	−30	−22	−10.0	14	57.2	17.8	64	147.2	110	230	446
−31.6	−25	−13	−9.44	15	59.0	18.3	65	149.0	116	240	464
−28.9	−20	−4	−8.89	16	60.8	18.9	66	150.8	121	250	482
−26.1	−15	5	−8.33	17	62.6	19.4	67	152.6	127	260	500
−23.3	−10	14	−7.78	18	64.4	20.0	68	154.4	132	270	518
−20.5	−5	23	−7.22	19	66.2	20.6	69	156.2	138	280	536
			−6.67	20	68.0	21.1	70	158.0	143	290	554
			−6.11	21	69.8	21.7	71	159.8	149	300	572
			−5.56	22	71.6	22.2	72	161.6	154	310	590
			−5.00	23	73.4	22.8	73	163.4	160	320	608
			−4.44	24	75.2	23.2	74	165.2	166	330	626
			−3.89	25	77.0	23.9	75	167.0	171	340	644
			−3.33	26	78.8	24.4	76	168.8	177	350	662
			−2.78	27	80.6	25.0	77	170.6	182	360	680
			−2.22	28	82.4	25.6	78	172.4	188	370	698
			−1.67	29	84.2	26.1	79	174.2	193	380	716
			−1.11	30	86.0	26.7	80	176.0	199	390	734
			−0.56	31	87.8	27.2	81	177.8	204	400	752
			0.	32	89.6	27.8	82	179.6	210	410	770
			0.56	33	91.4	28.3	83	181.4	216	420	788
			1.11	34	93.2	28.9	84	183.2	221	430	806
			1.67	35	95.0	29.4	85	185.0	227	440	824
			2.22	36	96.8	30.0	86	186.8	232	450	842
			2.78	37	98.6	30.6	87	188.6	238	460	860
			3.33	38	100.4	31.1	88	190.4	243	470	878
			3.89	39	102.2	31.7	89	192.2	249	480	896
			4.44	40	104.0	32.2	90	194.0	254	490	914
			5.00	41	105.8	32.8	91	195.8	260	500	932
			5.56	42	107.6	33.3	92	197.6			
			6.11	43	109.4	33.9	93	199.4			
			6.67	44	111.2	34.4	94	201.2			
			7.22	45	113.0	35.0	95	203.0			
			7.78	46	114.8	35.6	96	204.8			
			8.33	47	116.6	36.1	97	206.6			
			8.89	48	118.4	36.7	98	208.4			
			9.44	49	120.2	37.2	99	210.2			
						37.8	100	212.0			

Interpolation Factors

°C		°F	°C		°F	°C		°F
0.56	1	1.8	2.22	4	7.2	3.89	7	12.6
1.11	2	3.6	2.78	5	9.0	4.44	8	14.4
1.67	3	5.4	3.33	6	10.8	5.00	9	16.2

Fraction, decimal, and millimeter equivalents

Inches		MM
Fractions	Decimals	
—	.0004	.01
—	.004	.10
—	.01	.25
1/64	.0156	.397
—	.0197	.50
—	.0295	.75
1/32	.03125	.794
—	.0394	1.
3/64	.0469	1.191
—	.059	1.5
1/16	.062	1.588
5/64	.0781	1.984
—	.0787	2.
3/32	.094	2.381
—	.0984	2.5
7/64	.109	2.778
—	.1181	3.
1/8	.125	3.175
—	.1378	3.5
9/64	.141	3.572
5/32	.156	3.969
—	.1575	4.
11/64	.172	4.366
—	.177	4.5

Inches		MM
Fractions	Decimals	
15/32	.469	11.906
—	.4724	12.
31/64	.484	12.303
—	.492	12.5
1/2	.500	12.700
—	.5118	13.
33/64	.5156	13.097
17/32	.531	13.494
35/64	.547	13.891
—	.5512	14.
9/16	.563	14.288
—	.571	14.5
37/64	.578	14.684
—	.5906	15.
19/32	.594	15.081
39/64	.609	15.478
5/8	.625	15.875
—	.6299	16.
41/64	.6406	16.272
—	.6496	16.5
21/32	.656	16.669
—	.6693	17.
43/64	.672	17.066
11/16	.6875	17.463

Inches		MM
Fractions	Decimals	
1 1/16	1.062	26.988
—	1.063	27.
1 3/32	1.094	27.781
—	1.1024	28.
1 1/8	1.125	28.575
—	1.1417	29.
1 5/32	1.156	29.369
—	1.1811	30.
1 3/16	1.1875	30.163
1 7/32	1.219	30.956
—	1.2205	31.
1 1/4	1.250	31.750
—	1.2598	32.
1 9/32	1.281	32.544
—	1.2992	33.
1 5/16	1.312	33.338
—	1.3386	34.
1 11/32	1.344	34.131
1 3/8	1.375	34.925
—	1.3779	35.
1 13/32	1.406	35.719
—	1.4173	36.
1 7/16	1.438	36.513
—	1.4567	37.

Fraction	Decimal	mm	Fraction	Decimal	mm	Fraction	Decimal	mm
3/16	.1875	4.763	45/64	.703	17.859	1 15/32	1.469	37.306
—	.1969	5.	—	.7087	18.	—	1.4961	38.
13/64	.203	5.159	23/32	.719	18.256	1 1/2	1.500	38.100
—	.2165	5.5	—	.7283	18.5	1 17/32	1.531	38.894
7/32	.219	5.556	47/64	.734	18.653	—	1.5354	39.
15/64	.234	5.953	—	.7480	19.	1 9/16	1.562	39.688
—	.2362	6.	3/4	.750	19.050	—	1.5748	40.
1/4	.250	6.350	49/64	.7656	19.447	1 19/32	1.594	40.481
—	.2559	6.5	25/32	.781	19.844	—	1.6142	41.
17/64	.2656	6.747	—	.7874	20.	1 5/8	1.625	41.275
—	.2756	7.	51/64	.797	20.241	—	1.6535	42.
9/32	.281	7.144	13/16	.8125	20.638	1 21/32	1.6562	42.069
—	.2953	7.5	—	.8268	21.	1 11/16	1.6875	42.863
19/64	.297	7.541	53/64	.828	21.034	—	1.6929	43.
5/16	.312	7.938	27/32	.844	21.431	1 23/32	1.719	43.656
—	.315	8.	55/64	.859	21.828	—	1.7323	44.
21/64	.328	8.334	—	.8661	22.	1 3/4	1.750	44.450
—	.335	8.5	7/8	.875	22.225	—	1.7717	45.
11/32	.344	8.731	57/64	.8906	22.622	1 25/32	1.781	45.244
—	.3543	9.	—	.9055	23.	—	1.8110	46.
23/64	.359	9.128	29/32	.9062	23.019	1 13/16	1.8125	46.038
—	.374	9.5	59/64	.922	23.416	1 27/32	1.844	46.831
3/8	.375	9.525	15/16	.9375	23.813	—	1.8504	47.
25/64	.391	9.922	—	.9449	24.	1 7/8	1.875	47.625
—	.3937	10.	61/64	.953	24.209	—	1.8898	48.
13/32	.406	10.319	31/32	.969	24.606	1 29/32	1.9062	48.419
—	.413	10.5	—	.9843	25.	—	1.9291	49.
27/64	.422	10.716	63/64	.9844	25.003	1 15/16	1.9375	49.213
—	.4331	11.	1	1.000	25.400	—	1.9685	50.
7/16	.438	11.113	—	1.0236	26.	1 31/32	1.969	50.006
29/64	.453	11.509	1 1/32	1.0312	26.194	2	2.000	50.800

Useful conversion factors

Centimeters	× 0.3937	= Inches
Circular Mils	× 0.7854	= Square Mils
	× 5.0671 × 10⁻⁴	= Square Millimeters
Cubic Centimeters	× 0.0610	= Cubic Inches
Cubic Inches	× 16.386	= Cubic Centimeters
Inches	× 2.54	= Centimeters
Kilograms	× 2.2046	= Pounds
Kilograms/Kilometer	× 0.6720	= Pounds/1000 Feet
Kilometers	× 0.6214	= Miles
	× 3280.8	= Feet
Meters	× 3.2808	= Feet
Mils	× 0.001	= Inches
	× 0.0254	= Millimeters
Miles	× 1.6093	= Kilometers
Millimeters	× 0.03937	= Inches
Ohms/Kilometer	× 0.3048	= Ohms/1000 Feet
Ohms/1000 Feet	× 3.2808	= Ohms/Kilometer
Pounds	× 0.4536	= Kilograms
Pounds/1000 Feet	× 1.4881	= Kilograms/Kilometer
Square Centimeters	× 1.55 × 10⁵	= Square Mils
	× 1.97 × 10⁵	= Circular Mils
Square Inches	× 1.2732 × 10⁶	= Circular Mils
	× 645.16	= Square Millimeters
Square Millimeter	× 0.1974	= Circular Mils

Exponential method of expressing numerals

$$
\begin{aligned}
10 &= 10^1 & 1.0 &= 10^{-1} \\
100 &= 10^2 & 0.01 &= 10^{-2} \\
1{,}000 &= 10^3 & 0.001 &= 10^{-3} \\
1{,}000{,}000 &= 10^6 & 0.000001 &= 10^{-6} \\
\text{etc.} & & \text{etc.} &
\end{aligned}
$$

Examples

$$
\begin{aligned}
123 &= 1.23 \times 10^2 & 0.123 &= 1.23 \times 10^{-1} \\
1{,}230 &= 1.23 \times 10^3 & 0.0123 &= 1.23 \times 10^{-2} \\
1{,}230{,}000 &= 1.23 \times 10^6 & 0.000123 &= 1.23 \times 10^{-4}
\end{aligned}
$$

To facilitate expressions of quantities, prefixes are frequently used. For example, 1/100 of a meter (1×10^{-2} meters) is called a *centi*meter (cm); 1000 grams is called a *kilo*gram (Kg). The prefixes and symbols used to designate the quantities are given below.

Quantity			Prefixes	Symbols
1 000 000 000 000	—	10^{12}	Tera	T
1 000 000 000	—	10^9	Giga	G
1 000 000	—	10^6	Mega	M
1 000	—	10^3	Kilo	K
100	—	10^2	Hecto	h
10	—	10	Deca	dk
0.1	—	10^{-1}	Deci	d
0.01	—	10^{-2}	Centi	c
0.001	—	10^{-3}	Milli	m
0.000 001	—	10^{-6}	Micro	μ
0.000 000 001	—	10^{-9}	Nano	n
0.000 000 000 001	—	10^{-12}	Pico	p

Military specifications related to wire and cable

The military specifications listed here are a selection of those widely referenced on drawings, contact documents and in manufacturers' catalogs and literature. The complete list of military specifications is subject to periodic change as new specifications are added. The text in brackets after the title provides additional information on the contents of the specification.

NOTE: Some of the specifications listed may no longer be referenced for U.S. Government procurement and not all have "electronic" end-use applications.

MIL-C-17 Cable, Radio Frequency Coaxial [polyethylene and Teflon TFE dielectric].

MIL-C-442 Cable, (Wire), Two Conductor, Parallel [rubber-jacketed, two-conductor rip cord cable].

MIL-C-915 Cable and Cord Electrical, for Shipboard.

MIL-C-3078 Cable, Electric, Insulated, Low Tension, Single Conductor 50 Volts.

MIL-C-3432 Cable and Wire, Electrical, Power and Control, Flexible and Extra Flexible, 300 and 600 Volts.

MIL-C-3885 Cable Assemblies and Cord Assemblies, Electrical, Electrical for use in Electronic communication and Associated Equipment.

MIL-C-5756 Cable and Wire, Power, Electric, Portable (ASG). [low-temperture, rubber-insulated, portable power cords].

MIL-C-7078 Cable, Electric, Aerospace Vehicle, General Specification for.

MIL-C-7974 Cable Assemblies and Attachable Plugs, External Electrical Power, Aircraft.

MIL-C-8721 Cable, Miniature Coaxial with Fluorocarbon Dielectric.

MIL-C-10065 Cables, Special Purpose, Electrical, Multipair, Audio Frequency.

MIL-C-10369 Cable, Telephone Field for Rapid Payout.

MIL-C-11060 Cable, Twisted Pair, Internal Hook-up, Unshielded and Shielded.

MIL-C-12064 Cable and Cords, Low Temperature Power for Arctic Service.

MIL-C-13777 Cable, Special Purpose, Electrical, Conductors, General Specification for.

MIL-C-13892 Cable, Telephone (Flexible) Cords and Cordage, Multipair.

MIL-C-19381 Cable, Special Purpose, Electrical (Nuclear Plant). [telephone switchboard cable and cable assemblies].

MIL-C-19547 Cables, Electrical, Special Purpose, Shore Use. [telephone and telegraph signal cables in shore communication stations and facilities].

MIL-C-19654 Cable, Telephone, Submarine.

MIL-C-21529 Cable Assemblies, Electrical.

MIL-C-21609 Cable, Electrical, Shielded, 600 Volt Non-Flexing Service. [multiconductor cable].

MIL-C-22731 Cable, Controlled Mine.

(continued)

MIL-C-22931	Cable, Radio Frequency, Semi-Rigid, Coaxial, Semi-Air Dielectric.
MIL-C-23020	Cable, Coaxial, for Submarine Use.
MIL-C-23086	Cable, Radio Frequency, Coaxial, Semi-Rigid, Foam Dielectric, General Specification for.
MIL-C-23437	Cable, Electrical, Shielded Pairs.
MIL-C-23553	Cable, Audio Signal, Shore Use.
MIL-C-27072	Cable, Special Purpose, Electrical Multiconductor. [non-portable multiconductor cables for electronics].
MIL-C-27500	Cable, Electrical, Shielded and Unshielded, Aerospace.
MIL-C-28661	Cable, Power, Electrical, High Voltage.
MIL-C-45820	Cable Assemblies, Electrical.
MIL-C-49055	Cable, Unshielded, Flat Flexible with Round Conductors.
MIL-C-49059	Cable, Unshielded, Flat Flexible with Flat Conductors.
MIL-C-52286	Cable Assembly, Power Electrical.
MIL-C-55021	Cable, Twisted Pair, Internal Hookup, Shielded and Jacketed, High Temperature.
MIL-C-55134	Cable, Telephone (Inside).
MIL-C-55357	Cable, Telephone, Shielded (Inside Wiring).
MIL-C-55442	Cable Assemblies and Cord Assemblies, Packaging of.
MIL-C-55446	Cable, Telephone, Switchboard, Plastic Insulated, Plastic Jacketed.
MIL-C-55543	Cable, Electrical, Flat Multiconductor, Flexible, Unshielded [Flat conductor].
MIL-C-82403	Cable, Submarine, Power, Control and Combination.
MIL-W-76	Wire and Cable, Electrical, Insulated, High Temperature [general purpose hookup wire for internal wiring of electronic equipment; temperature range −40 C to +80 C; vinyl-insulated types LW, MW, HW for use to 2500 V, polyethylene-insulated type HF for use to 1000 V].
MIL-W-583	Wire, Magnet, Electrical [for fabricating coils].
MIL-W-3318	Wire, Copper and Wire, Steel, Copperclad W154 and WS-24/U.
MIL-W-3795	Wire, Electrical (Tinsel).
MIL-W-3861	Conductors, Copper (Uninsulated) [solid, bunched, concentric, and rope constructions].
MIL-W-5086	Wire, Electric, Hookup and Interconnecting, Polyvinylchloride-Insulated, Copper or Copper Alloy Conductor [600-V rating for aircraft].
MIL-W-5845	Wire, Electrical, Iron and Constantan Thermocouple.
MIL-W-5646	Wire, Electrical, Chromel and Alumel, Thermocouple.
MIL-W-5908	Wire, Electrical, Copper and Constantan, Thermocouple.
MIL-W-7500	Wire, Antenna, WS-31/U.
MIL-W-8131	Wire, Copper and Copper Alloy, Polyimide Insulated.

(continued)

MIL-W-8259 Wire, Copper Cadmium Alloy.

MIL-W-13169 Wire, Electrical, for Instrument Test Leads.

MIL-W-16072 Wire, Electrical, High Temperature Magnet.

MIL-W-16400 General Specifications for Electronic Equipment, Naval Ship and Shore.

MIL-W-16878 Wire, Electrical, Insulated, High Temperature (Navy) [for internal wiring of electronic equipment; includes vinyl-types B, C, D, rated at 105 C; Teflon TFE-types E, EE, ET, rated up to 260 C; silicone rubber-types F, FF, FFW, rated at 200 C; polyethylene-type J rated at 75 C; Teflon FEP-types K, KK, KT rated at 200 C].

MIL-W-19150 Wire, Insulated, Hard Drawn Copper [polyethylene-isulated, nylon-jacketed].

MIL-W-22759 Wire, Electric, Fluorocarbon Insulated, Copper or Copper Alloy [Tefzel-insulated].

MIL-W-25038 Wire, Electrical, High Temperature and Fire Resistant, Aircraft [600-V asbestos-insulated].

MIL-W-27300 Wire, Electrical, Fluorocarbon Insulated, 600 Volts, Aircraft [Teflon TFE-insulated].

MIL-W-50557 Wire and Cable, Electrical, Insulated, High Temperature.

MIL-W-81044 Wire, Electric, Cross-Linked Polyalkene, Cross-Linked Alkane-Imide Polymer, or Polyarylene Insulated, Copper or Copper Alloy [for aircraft and hookup].

MIL-W-81381 Wire, Electric Polyimide-Insulated Copper and Copper Alloy.

MIL-W-81822 Wire, Electrical, Solderless Wrap, Insulated and Uninsulated.

Definitions of Cable Types Designated by the National Electrical Code (NEC) and Listed by Underwriters Laboratories Inc. (UL)

Location	Reference	Applicable UL Flame and Smoke Tests Document
Plenum	UL 910	Test Method for Fire and Smoke Characteristics of Optical Fiber Cables.
Riser	UL 1666	Standard Test for Flame Propagation Height of Electrical and Optical-Fiber Cables Installed Vertically in Shafts.
General Purpose	UL 1581	Vertical Tray Flame Test in Reference Standard for Electrical Wires, Cables, and Flexible Cords.
Restricted	UL 1581	Vertical Wire Flame Test, VW-1 in UL 1581.
Type CL2P		A Class-2 power-limited cable for use in plenums, in accordance with NEC Article 725, Sections 51(a) and 53(a), and it meets the requirements of UL 910.
Type CL2R		A Class-2 power-limited cable for use in riser shafts; in accordance with NEC Article 725, Sections 51(b) and 53(b), and it meets the requirements of the UL 1666.
Type CL2		A Class-2 power-limited cable for general applications within a building, in accordance with NEC Article 725, Sections 51(c) and 53(e), and it meets the requirements of the Vertical Tray Flame Test in UL 1581.
Type CL2X		A class-2 power-limited cable is suitable for restricted applications in any residence where the diameter does not exceed 0.25 in. and it is not concealed in raceways, as stated in NEC Article 725, Sections 51(d) and 53(e), Exceptions No. 1, 2, and 3. It can be installed in conduit if 10 feet or less is exposed. CL2X cable meets the requirements of VW-1 in UL 1581.

(continued)

Type CL3P
A Class-3 power-limited cable for use in plenums, in accordance with NEC Article 725, Sections 51(a) and 53(a), and it meets the requirements of UL 910.

Type CL3R
A Class-3 power-limited cable for use in risers, in accordance with NEC Article 725, Sections 51(b) and 53(b), and it meets the requirements of UL 1666.

Type CL3
A Class-3 power-limited cable for general applications within a building under NEC Article 725, Sections 51(c) and 53(e), and it meets the requirements of the Vertical Tray Flame Test in UL 1581.

Type CL3X
A Class-3 power-limited cable suitable for restricted applications in any residence where its diameter does not exceed 0.25 in. in nonconcealed locations (raceways) under NEC Article 725, Sections 51(d) and 53(e), Exceptions No. 1, 2 and 3. It can be installed in conduit if 10 feet or less is exposed. CL3X cable meets the requirements of VW-1 in UL 1581.

Type PLTC
A stand-alone power-limited tray cable that is qualified only for general-purpose applications, in accordance with NEC Article 725, Sections 51(e) and 53(c) and (d), and it meets the requirements of the Vertical Tray Flame Test in UL 1581.

Type NPLFP
A nonpower-limited fire-protective signaling-circuit cable for use in air-handling spaces, in accordance with NEC Article 760, Sections 17(c)(4) and 17(e)(2), and it meets the requirements of UL 910.

Type NPLFR
A nonpower-limited fire-protective signaling-circuit cable used in risers in accordance with NEC Article 760, Sections 17(c)(5) and 17(e)(3), and it meets the requirements of UL 1666.

Type NPLF
A nonpower-limited fire-protective signaling-circuit cable for general-purpose use, in accordance with NEC Article 760, Sections 17(c)(6) and 17(e)(4), and it meets the requirements of the Vertical Tray Flame Test in UL 1581.

Type FPLP
A power-limited fire-alarm cable for use in plenums, in accordance with NEC Article 760, Sections 51(d) and 53(a), and it meets the requirements of UL 910.

Type FPLR
A power-limited fire-alarm cable for use in risers, in accordance with NEC Article 760, Sections 51(e) and 53(b), and it meets the requirements of UL 1666.

Type FPL
A power-limited fire-alarm cable suitable for general-purpose use, in accordance with NEC Article 760, Sections 51(f) and 53(c). FPL cable meets the requirements of the Vertical Tray Flame Test in UL 1581.

Type OFCP A conductive optical-fiber cable for use in plenums in accordance with NEC Article 770, Sections 51(a) and 53(a), and it meets the requirements of the UL 910.

Type OFCR A conductive optical-fiber cable for use in risers, in accordance with NEC Article 770, Sections 51(b) and 53(b), and it meets the requirements of the UL 1666.

Type OFC A conductive optical-fiber cable for general-purpose use, in accordance with NEC Article 770, Sections 51(c) and 53(c), and it meets the requirements of the Vertical Tray Flame Test in UL 1581.

Type OFNP A nonconductive optical-fiber cable for use in plenums, in accordance with NEC Article 770, Sections 51(a) and 53(a), and it meets the requirements of UL 910.

Type OFNR A nonconductive optical-fiber cable for use in risers, in accordance with NEC Article 770, Sections 51(b) and 53(b), and it meets the requirements of the UL 1666.

Type OFN A nonconductive optical-fiber cable for general-purpose use, in accordance with NEC Article 770, Sections 51(c) and 53(c), and it meets the requirements of the Vertical Tray Flame Test in UL 1581.

Type CMP A communications cable for use in plenums, in accordance with NEC Article 800, Sections 51(a) and 53(a), and it meets the requirements of UL 910.

Type CMR A communications cable for use in risers, in accordance with NEC Article 800, Sections 51(b) and 53(b), and it meets the requirements of UL 1666.

Type CM A communications cable for general-purpose applications, in accordance with NEC Article 800, Sections 51(c) and 53(c), and it meets the requirements of the Vertical Tray Flame Test in UL 1581.

Type CMX A communications cable for use in restricted applications in one or two-family residences and in multi-family dwellings—if its diameter does not exceed 0.25 in. and it is in nonconcealed locations (raceways) under NEC Article 800, Sections 51(d) and 53(c), Exceptions 1, 2, 3, and 4. CMX cable can be installed in conduit if 10 feet or less is exposed. It meets the requirements of the Vertical Wire Flame Test VW-1 in UL 1581.

Type CMUC A communications cable for undercarpet applications, in accordance with NEC Article 800, Sections 51(e) and 53(c), exception No. 5, and it meets the requirements of the UL Vertical Wire Flame Test VW-1 in UL 1581.

(continued)

Type MPP A multipurpose cable for use in plenums, in accordance with NEC Article 800, Sections 51(f) and 53(e), and it meets the requirements of UL 910.

Type MPR A multipurpose cable for use in risers, in accordance with NEC Article 725, Sections 51(f) and 53(e), and it meets the requirements of the UL 1666.

Type MP A multipurpose cable for general-purpose use, which can be employed interchangeably in either communications (Article 800, Section 51(f) and 53(e), power-limited (Article 725) or fire protective (Article 760) applications, and it meets the requirements of the Vertical Tray Flame Test in UL 1581.

Type CATVP A community-antenna television cable for use in plenums, in accordance with NEC Article 820, Sections 51(a) and 53(a), and it meets the requirements of the UL 910.

Type CATVR A community-antenna television cable for use in risers in accordance with NEC Article 820, Sections 51(b) and 53(b), and it meets the requirements of the UL 1666.

Type CATV A community-antenna television cable for general-purpose use, in accordance with NEC Article 820, Sections 51(c) and 53(c). CATV cable meets the requirements of the Vertical Tray Flame Test in UL 1581.

Type CATVX A community-antenna television cable for limited use, in accordance with NEC Article 820, Sections 51(d) and 53(c), and it meets the requirements of the Vertical Wire Flame Test VW-1 in UL 1581.

Glossary

abrasion resistance Ability of material, such as a cable jacket, to resist surface wear and scuffing.

accelerated aging A test procedure that simulates long-term exposure to environmental stresses in relatively short time by accelerating or exaggerating the stresses of the environment. Variables such as voltage, temperature, ultraviolet light, and ozone are increased above normal levels to obtain observable deterioration in a short time. The test results are used to estimate expected service life under normal conditions.

accelerator A chemical additive that hastens a chemical reaction under specific conditions.

admittance The measure of the ease with which an alternating current flows in a circuit. It is the reciprocal of impedance.

aging The change in properties of a material with time under specified environmental conditions. *See* accelerated aging.

air-core cable A cable with air spaces formed between the conductor and jacket by dielectric helixes and an overall dielectric sleeve. It offers the benefits of having air as a dielectric.

air-spaced coaxial cable A coaxial cable with an air-filled space formed by a helically wound dielectric rod, which is enclosed in a dielectric sleeve between the inner conductor and the shield. Air is the primary dielectric material.

alloy A metal formed by combining two or more different metals to obtain properties that are not available from the constituents.

alternating current (ac) Electric current that periodically reverses its direction at a frequency measured in cycles per second, and expressed in hertz (Hz).

ambient Conditions that surround a circuit, component, or system prior to energizing it (e.g., ambient temperature).

American National Standards Institute (ANSI)   An organization for setting technical standards.

American Society for Testing and Materials (ASTM)   A nonprofit, industry-wide organization that publishes standards, test methods, recommended industrial and commercial practices and definitions.

American Standard Code for Information Interchange (ASCII)   An 8-bit code for data transmission with seven bits for information and one for error checking. There are 128 characters in the ASCII code; 64 represent the letters of the alphabet, numbers, and punctuation that are found in on a standard typewriter keyboard. The other characters represent control functions.

American Wire Gauge (AWG)   The standard system for designating wire gauge in the United States, based on the Brown and Sharpe (B&S) gauge. The larger the AWG number, the smaller the wire diameter.

ampacity   The maximum current that an insulated conductor can safely carry without exceeding its insulation and jacket limits. *See* current-carrying capacity.

ampere (A)   A standard unit of current measurement. The amount of current that flows through a conductor when one volt is applied across one ohm of resistance, in accordance with Ohm's Law. Also, the current produced when one coulomb of charge passes a point in one second.

amplitude modulation (AM)   Impressing a variable signal on the amplitude of a carrier for modulation. It is used in the standard broadcast band (530 to 1700 kHz).

analog signal   A continuously varying audio-, video-, or radio-frequency signal that is proportional to the source that generates it.

analog transmission   The transmission of a signal in analog form, as opposed to that of a signal in digital form.

anneal   The process of heating a solid material (such as metal or glass) just below its melting point and then gradually cooling it to soften the material and relieve stresses. Metal or glass can become brittle during drawing or rolling. Annealed copper has a lowered tensile strength, but an improved ability to withstand repeated flexing.

ANSI   *See* American National Standards Institute.

anti-oxidant   A material that prevents or delays oxidation of material exposed to air (e.g., paint, oil, and metal plating).

Appliance Wiring Material   *See* AWM.

ASCII   *See* American Standard Code for Information Interchange.

ASME   Abbreviation for American Society of Mechanical Engineers.

ASTM   *See* American Society for Testing and Materials.

asynchronous   A form of information or data transmission that is not synchronized with other signals.

attenuation   The decrease in magnitude of an electromagnetic wave as it travels through any transmitting medium (such as air, plastic, ceramic, or metal). Attenuation is measured in decibels (dB) per unit length.

attenuation constant   A rating for a cable that designates the relative rate of voltage or current amplitude decrease in the direction of travel. It is measured in decibels per unit length of cable.

audio frequency (AF)   The range of frequencies from 20 to 20,000 Hz, which are audible to the human ear.

AWG   *See* American Wire Gauge.

AWM   Abbreviation for the Underwriters Laboratories designation for Appliance Wiring Material.

balanced line   A cable that contains a pair of conductors in which the impressed voltages in each are equal in magnitude, but opposite in polarity with respect to ground.

balun   An acronym for balanced/unbalanced, which refers to a circuit element, typically a transformer, that matches an unbalanced coaxial transmission line to a balanced two-wire transmission line. It allows a balanced source of power (coaxial cable) to be connected to an unbalanced load (antenna), or vice versa.

band marking   Bands of color which are printed at regular intervals along the length of an insulated conductor, to contrast with the insulation color for circuit identification.

bandwidth   A range of frequencies in the electromagnetic spectrum. It is determined as the difference between the high and low frequencies of a signal at specified values of attenuation below the midband in decibels and measured in hertz.

baseband   The total frequency band, which is occupied by the aggregate of all the information signals used to modulate a carrier.

baud   A unit of data transmission speed, which is equal to the number of discrete signal events per second. It is usually equal to the bit rate in bits per second (b/s).

bend loss   In optical fibers, it is additional attenuation caused by a sharp bend.

bend radius   The radius of curvature that an optical fiber or metal conductor cable can bend without increasing losses.

binder   Tape or thread that is wrapped in a spiral around two or more conductors to clamp them prior to jacketing a cable.

bit   A contraction of binary digit, the smallest unit of information. A bit can represent a one or a zero.

bit rate   The common measure of data transmission speed, expressed in bits per second (b/s).

block   A group of bits or characters, that is treated as a complete unit.

bond strength   A measure of adhesion between surfaces that have been bonded.

braid   Textile threads or metal strands that are interwoven to form a tubular structure. Braid can be used for insulation or shielding. Copper braid can be flattened to form flexible ground straps.

braid angle   The smaller of two angles formed by the shielding strand and the axis of the cable being shielded.

braid carrier   A spool or bobbin on a braiding machine, which holds one group of strands or filaments. The carrier revolves during the braiding operation.

braid ends   The number of strands used to make up one carrier. The strands are wound side by side on the carrier bobbin and lie parallel in the finished braid.

breakdown voltage   The voltage that, when exceeded, causes the insulation between two conductors to break down.

breakout   The point at which a conductor or group of conductors is diverted from a multiconductor cable to complete intermediate circuits along the main cable route. This divergence might require a local opening in the jacket to permit conductor passage.

British Thermal Unit (BTU)   The amount of heat required to raise the temperature of one pound of water by one degree F.

buffer   A protective covering of resilient material that surrounds a coated optical fiber to provide additional mechanical isolation and protection. In computer technology, a temporary data-storage unit such as a random access memory (RAM).

bunch stranding   Conductors that are twisted together with the same lay and direction, but without following a specified geometry.

buried cable   A cable that is buried directly in the earth without the protection of a separate conduit.

bus-bar wire   Uninsulated tinned-copper wire that is used as a common lead.

butyl rubber   A particular synthetic rubber that has good electrical insulating characteristics.

byte   A series of bits that define a character, now accepted as eight; twice the length of a "nibble" (four bits).

cable   A group of individually insulated conductors that are twisted together or mechanically assembled (bundled) in a parallel configuration.

cable assembly   A length of cable that is terminated with connectors and ready for use.

cable, armored   A cable that has been wrapped with metal wire or tape for mechanical protection.

cable, composite   A cable that contains insulated conductors in differing sizes or styles (such as singles, twisted pairs, triads, or coaxial cables).

cable, fiber-optic   One or more optical fibers or bundles, which have been individually coated, buffered, reinforced with strength members, and jacketed.

cable, filled   A cable whose core is filled with a sealant to prevent the entry of moisture.

cable, switchboard Cable that is used for interconnecting central telephone office equipment.

cabling The twisting together or mechanical assembly of two or more insulated conductors.

cabling factor A numerical value that is used to calculate the diameter of unshielded unjacketed multiconductor cable in the formula:

$$D = Kd$$

Where: D is the cable diameter
K is the factor or multiplier
d is the diameter of one insulated conductor

capacitance The property of conductors that are separated by insulation or dielectric, which permits the storage of electricity when potential differences exist between the conductors. The unit of capacitance is the farad. *See* farad.

capacitance, mutual The capacitance between two conductors when all other conductors, including shield, are short circuited to ground.

capacitance, unbalance A capacitance inequality between two or more conductors, which then receive external-source energy—usually from power lines.

capacitance, unbalance-to-ground An inequality between the ground capacitance of a conductor pair, which then receives external-source energy—usually from power lines.

capacitive coupling Electrical interaction between two conductors that is caused by the capacitance between them.

capacitive reactance The opposition to alternating current as a result of the capacitance of a capacitor, cable, or circuit. This value is inversely proportional to frequency, in accordance with the formula:

$$X_c = \frac{1}{2\pi fC}$$

Where: X_c is in ohms
f is the frequency in Hz
C is the capacitance in farads

capacitor A component with two metallic plates that are separated by a dielectric material. The capacitance in farads is determined by the area of the plates, the dielectric between them, and the spacing.

carrier frequency A frequency higher than the upper limit of the audio-frequency band that might carry audio frequencies as a modulated carrier.

CATV The abbreviation for community-antenna television, also known as cable TV.

CCTV The abbreviation for closed-circuit television.

cellular polyethylene Expanded or "foamed" polyethylene is produced by introducing inert gas into the compound to form individual closed cells. This added gas reduces the dielectric constant.

certificate of compliance (C of C)   A certificate that is issued by a vendor's quality-control department, which states that a particular product meets the customer's specifications.

certified test report   A report that provides actual test data on a particular product.

channel   A line, link, or conducting path for electrical transmission between two or more points. Also, a band of frequencies that are assigned for television transmission.

character   In communications technology, a letter, number, or symbol represented by a specific order of the bits.

characteristic impedance   The ratio of the voltage between the conductors to the current on the conductors at every point along a transmission line without standing waves. A transmission line of any length that is terminated in its characteristic impedance, appears to be infinitely long.

circular mil   A unit for expressing wire cross-sectional area, that is equal to the area of a circle that is one mil (0.001 inch) in diameter (equivalent to 7.85×10^7 sq. in.).

cladding, copper conductor   A method for applying one layer of metal over another to provide a unified bond.

cladding, fiber-optic cable   A transparent part of an optical fiber that surrounds and is immediately adjacent to the core. It has a lower index of refraction than the core and it redirects transmitted light rays so they travel down the core with minimum loss. It can be made of glass or plastic.

coaxial cable   A cylindrical transmission line that is constructed as an inner conductor covered with a dielectric core and surrounded by a metallic tube or shield, which acts as a second conductor. It is usually covered by an insulating jacket.

coil effect   The inductive effect that is exhibited by spiral-wound shields of metal wire or tape, which surround conductor insulation—especially above audio frequencies.

cold flow   The permanent deformation of a plastic material as a result of an externally applied mechanical force or pressure without heat. Conductor insulation can be permanently flattened by cold flow.

color code   A system to identify numerical values with corresponding colors. Wires can be identified by insulation with a range of base colors and contrasting stripes.

common-mode noise   Noise that is caused by a difference in ground potential in a cable. This interference can be reduced by the use of a drain wire with one end grounded at the source.

composite cable   *See* cable, composite.

compound   A mixture of two or more ingredients, such as the resins that are used to prepare primary insulating and jacketing materials.

concentric stranding A group of conductive wires that are twisted together around a central core. Subsequent layers are helically wrapped around the core to form a single conductor.

concentricity In a wire or cable, the location of the center element—with respect to the geometric center of the surrounding insulation or jacket.

conductance The ability of a conductor to carry an electric current. Conductance is the reciprocal of resistance and it is measured in Siemens (S).

conductivity In the wire and cable industry, the ability of a conductor to carry electric current—expressed as a percentage of copper conductivity (designated as 100 percent).

conductor A solid or stranded wire that is suitable to carry electric current.

conduit A tube or trough that is to protect and support wires and cables.

connector A component that makes physical and electrical connections between two or more conductors. Connectors are usually designed for simple manual engagement and disengagement.

connector insertion loss The loss of power as a result of an impedance mismatch or resistance to current passing through a mated set of connectors in a circuit.

contact The element of a connector or relay that carries the electrical current. Contacts are electrically and mechanically attached to conductors and are opened or closed to control current flow.

continuity check A test to determine if electric current will flow continuously in a circuit. It is performed with a power source (typically a battery) and an indicator (lamp or meter).

control cable A multiconductor cable that is intended for use in control or signal circuits.

copolymer A compound that is formed from the polymerization of two different monomers.

copper clad Steel wire or sheets that have a welded coating of copper, as distinguished from a steel wire or sheet that has been copper plated.

Copperweld The trademark of Copperweld Steel Corp. for copper-clad steel conductors.

cord A flexible insulated cable that is used to power appliances and electrical or electronic products from the ac power line.

cord, tinsel A flexible and, in some cases, retractile electric cord that is used between headsets and handsets of telephone equipment. Tinsel conductors are thin, narrow copper-foil ribbons, which are wrapped spirally around textile cords.

core In cables, an insulating sleeve that supports shields or jackets.

core, fiber-optic The transparent light-conducting inner element of an optical fiber with a refractive index that is higher than the surrounding cladding, typically made of the same material.

corona A discharge of electrons as a result of the ionization of air. It typically occurs at a sharp or pointed conductor when the potential gradient exceeds a threshold value.

corona resistance The time that an insulation will withstand a specified level of ionization without breakdown.

corrosion The degradation of a metal surface, caused by a chemical reaction with its environment. Acids and bases cause bare metal corrosion.

coupler In fiber optics, an optical component, with or without connector mating faces, that is used to interconnect three or more optical fibers. Also, an electronic component with a photoemitter (transmitter) and a photodetector (receiver) that is coupled by a short length of optical "light pipe" (for circuit isolation).

coupler loss Optical power that is lost through a coupler.

coupling The transfer of energy between two or more cables or components in a circuit.

coverage The percentage of completeness of a metal braid or foil shield that covers the underlying primary insulation, dielectric core, or shielded or unshielded conductors in a cable.

crazing Fine cracks that develop on the surface of plastics as a result of exposure to environmental stresses, particularly ultraviolet light.

creep The change in contour of a material over time after being subjected to load.

cross-linked Intermolecular bonds that are formed between long-chain thermoplastic polymers by chemical reaction or electron bombardment. Cross-linked thermoplastic resins have some of the properties of thermosetting resins.

crosstalk Originally this term applied to audio-frequency noise or unwanted voice coupled from one conductor into an adjacent conductor. Now, it refers to cross-coupled energy at all frequencies.

crosstalk, far-end Crosstalk that is measured by applying an interfering signal on the near end of one conductor of a pair and measuring the disturbing signal at the far end of the other.

crosstalk, near-end Crosstalk that is measured by applying an interfering signal on one conductor of a pair and measuring the disturbing signal on the other conductor at the same end.

CSA An abbreviation for Canadian Standards Association, a nonprofit, independent organization that operates a certification service for electrical and electronic materials and equipment. The Canadian counterpart of the Underwriters Laboratories.

curl The tendency of a wire to loop after it has been removed from a spool.

current-carrying capacity The maximum current that an insulated conductor can safely carry without exceeding the temperature limitations of its insulation and jacket.

cut-through resistance The ability of a material (such as a cable jacket) to withstand the shearing or cleaving action of a sharp edge without separating or opening.

decibel (dB) A unit that expresses differences of power level, such as power gain in amplifiers or power loss in cables. It is equal to 10 times the common logarithm of power ratios or 20 times the common logarithm of voltage or current ratios.

delay line A transmission line or equivalent circuit that provides a specified time delay when transmitting electrical signals. The delay is caused by the lower velocity of propagation in a cable than in free space.

derating factor A multiplying factor that is used to reduce the current-carrying capacity of an electronic component or conductor when it is exposed to environmental conditions that exceed design values. An example is high ambient temperature.

dielectric An insulating or nonconducting material between two conductors that prevents electrical conduction, but permits electrostatic attraction and repulsion.

dielectric constant (K) The ratio of the capacitance that is obtained with any given dielectric material to that which is obtained when the dielectric is air. A low dielectric constant material causes low capacitance for cables of all sizes.

dielectric loss The dissipated power in a dielectric as a result of friction that is produced by molecular motion when an alternating electric field is applied.

dielectric strength The voltage an insulation or dielectric can withstand before breakdown occurs, expressed as volts per mil.

dielectric test A test to verify the adequacy of product insulation at a rated voltage. A higher-than-rated voltage is applied for a specified time interval under standard conditions.

digital A representation of data with binary characters.

DIN standard An abbreviation for Deutche Industrie Normenausschuses standard (Germany).

direct burial cable A cable suitable for direct installation in the earth.

direct capacitance The capacitance measured directly between conductors through a single layer of insulation.

direct current (dc) An electric current that flows only in one direction.

direct-current resistance (DCR) The resistance offered by a circuit to the flow of direct current.

direction of lay As viewed from the end of a bundle of conductor strands or a bundle of insulated conductors in a cable, the clockwise or counterclockwise direction of the strands or conductors.

dispersion A broadening of input light energy along the length of a fiber-optic cable. It is caused by two factors:

- Differences in path length in an optical fiber that will support more than one mode of transmission (multimode).
- Differences in speeds of the components of the light as a result of their different wavelengths.

Excessive dispersion will degrade the transmitted signal and cause errors.

dissipation factor The tangent of the loss angle of the insulating material. It is also referred to as loss tangent (tan δ) and approximate power factor.

distribution cable In a CATV system, the transmission cable from the transmitter to the subscribers' drop cables.

drain wire An uninsulated wire that is in contact with a conductive shield throughout its length for terminating or grounding the shield. It is widely used with aluminum-polyester foil shields.

drawing The pulling of a metal rod through a die or series of dies to obtain a wire of specified diameter.

drop cable In a CATV system, the cable from the distribution cable to the receiver.

duct An underground or overhead tube for carrying electrical wires and cables. *See* plenum.

eccentricity A measure of the center of a conductor, with respect to the circular cross section of the insulation. It is expressed as a displacement percentage of the inner circle with respect to the outer circle.

EIA Abbreviation for Electronic Industries Association.

elastomer A rubber-like material that returns to its original dimensions after being stretched or distorted.

electromagnetic A reference to the combined electrical and magnetic fields that are caused by electrons moving through a conductor.

electromagnetic coupling The transfer of energy by an alternating magnetic field (also called inductive coupling).

electromotive force (EMF) A term for voltage.

electrostatic Electricity at rest that has an electric charge.

elongation The increase in the length of a material that is stressed in tension or stretched.

EMI Abbreviation of electromagnetic interference.

ends In braiding, the number of essentially parallel wires or threads on a carrier.

EPDM Abbreviation for ethylene-propylene-diene monomer rubber, a material with good electrical insulating properties.

EPR Abbreviation for ethylene-propylene copolymer rubber, a material with good electrical insulating properties.

equilay More than one layer of helically laid wires with the length of lay the same for each layer.

Ethernet   Xerox's trademark for a Local Area Network (LAN) concept.

ETPC   Abbreviation for electrolytic tough pitch copper with a minimum conductivity of 99.9 percent.

external interference   Interference to a signal in a conductor caused by an outside natural or man-made source. *See* EMI.

farad   A unit of electrical capacitance, equal to the amount that permits the storage of one coulomb of charge for each volt applied.

FDDI   Abbreviation for Fiber Distributed Data Interface. *See* Fiber Distributed Data Interface.

feeder cable   In a CATV system, the transmission cable from the transmitter to the trunk amplifier.

FEP   Abbreviation for a melt-extrudable form of fluorinated ethylene propylene, a fluorocarbon resin. It is sold under the DuPont trade name of Teflon FEP. A thermoplastic compound, it has outstanding electrical properties and resistance to chemicals and heat.

ferrous   Iron or an alloy of iron that exhibits magnetic characteristics.

fiber distributed data interface (FDDI)   An American National Standards Institute (ANSI) and International Standards Organization (ISO) standard configuration for a token-ring structure operating at 1300 nanometers with a capacity of 100 Mb/s using duplex 62.5 micron core diameter fibers in standard transceivers.

fiber-optic communication   The technology of using light transmitted through optical fibers for communication.

filled cable   A cable constructed so that its core material will prevent moisture from entering or passing through the cable.

filler   **1.** A nonconducting material that is used in multiconductor cables to fill spaces between adjacent insulated and cabled conductors to round out the shape of the cable, improve its flexibility, and add tensile strength. **2.** An inert substance that is added to a compound to improve its mechanical or electrical properties (e.g., glass-filled nylon).

film   A thin sheet of plastic that might also be metallized.

flat cable   A multiconductor cable with parallel conductors that lie in essentially the same plane. *See* ribbon cable.

flat conductor   A conductor with a rectangular cross section, rather than a round or square cross section.

flat conductor cable   A multiconductor flat cable with the conductors arrayed in parallel and bonded to lie in the same plane.

flame resistance   The ability of a material to avoid combustion.

flammability   The ability of a material to support combustion; the opposite of flame resistance.

flex life   The ability of a conductor or cable to withstand repeated bending without breaking.

flexibility   The ability of a conductor or cable to bend under the influence of an external force. Flexibility contrasts with rigidity and stiffness, despite external force and limpness or bending without external force.

foamed plastic   Insulation material that has been injected with gas to form closed cells and reduce its unit weight.

FR-1   The designation for a vertical flame test that has been replaced by VW-1. *See* VW-1.

frequency   The number of complete periodic actions that occur in a unit of time, expressed in hertz. *See* hertz.

frequency modulation (FM)   A method for transmitting information by modulating the frequency of a radio carrier (e.g., the FM broadcast band and television audio.

gain   The increase in voltage, current, or power over a reference value, expressed in decibels.

gauge   The wire diameter. *See* American Wire Gauge.

giga   A numerical prefix for one billion (10^9) abbreviated as *G*.

GPIB   Abbreviation for general-purpose interface bus cable.

graded-index optical fiber   An optical fiber whose cladding has a graded, rather than a sharp decline in value of the refractive index, with respect to the center of the core. It provides wider bandwidth and lower-loss transmission than stepped-index fiber. *See* step-index fiber.

ground   A conductive connection between an electrical circuit and the earth or other large conducting body to form a complete electrical circuit.

hard-drawn copper wire   Copper wire that has not been annealed after drawing.

harness   A bundle of insulated conductors that has been bound together with cord or plastic-locking ties, which permit multiple breakouts.

hash mark stripe   A noncontinuous contrasting helical stripe that is printed on conductor insulation for circuit identification.

heat distortion   Distortion or alteration of the shape of material, such as a thermoplastic compound as a result of heat.

heat endurance   The time for a material to fail during exposure to a heating test.

heat seal   A method for sealing material by thermal fusion.

heat shock   A test to determine the thermal stability of a material by exposing it to a high-temperature step function.

heat shrinkable   The property of certain thermoplastic materials to shrink around objects when heat is applied. Heat-shrinkable tubing is used to seal exposed conductors.

henry (H)   A unit of inductance that is equal to a drop of one volt when the current changes at the rate of one ampere per second.

hertz (Hz)   A unit of frequency measurement that is equal to one cycle per second.

high frequency   The part of the electromagnetic spectrum that extends from 3 MHz to 30 MHz.

hi-pot Abbreviation for high potential, in reference to a test to determine the highest voltage that can be applied to a conductor before the insulation breaks down.

high-speed channel (HSC) An ANSI standard that defines the mechanical, electrical, and signaling protocol requirements of a simplex high-performance point-to-point channel between units of data-processing equipment. It is designed to transmit digital data at peak rates of 800 or 1600 Mbit/s between data-processing equipment with multiple twisted-pair copper cabling at distances up to 25 meters.

high voltage In the wire and cable industry, an operating voltage that is greater than 600 volts.

hook-up wire Wire that is used for low-current, low-voltage electronic applications within an equipment enclosure.

hygroscopic The property of a material for absorbing moisture from the air.

Hypalon DuPont's trade name for chlorosulfonated polyethylene, an ozone-resistant synthetic rubber for jacketing cable.

HSC Abbreviation for high-speed channel. *See* high-speed channel.

IEEE Institute of Electrical and Electronic Engineers, an organization that sponsors industry-accepted standards, such as RS-232 and RS-449.

impact strength A test to determine the amount of abuse that a cable can withstand without physical or electrical breakdown. A specified weight is dropped on the cable from a specified height in a controlled environment.

impedance The opposition that a circuit or circuit element offers to the flow of alternating current at a particular frequency. It is the vector sum of resistance (R) and reactance (X), which are measured in ohms and designated by the symbol Z. In cables, high impedance is considered to be 25,000 ohms or higher; low impedance is considered to be 600 ohms or less.

impedance characteristic The ratio of the applied voltage to the resulting current at the point where the voltage is applied in an infinitely long transmission line. This value, when connected across the transmission line's output terminals, makes the line appear infinitely long.

impedance match A condition in which the impedance of a circuit, cable, or component is the same as that of the circuit, cable, or component to which it is connected.

inductance The property of a conductor or circuit, measured in henries (H), that opposes a change in current flow. It causes current changes to lag behind voltage changes.

induction The transfer of voltage, magnetic field, or electrostatic charge by the lines of force from the source of these fields.

inductive coupling Crosstalk that results from the action of an electromagnetic field, which surrounds one conductor on another conductor of a pair or in close proximity.

injection laser diode A semiconductor laser that is used as an emitter in long-haul fiber-optic communications systems. Lasing occurs at the junction of the n- and p-type semiconductor materials.

insertion loss A measure of the attenuation that is caused by the insertion of a component in a transmission line.

insulation A material with high resistance to the flow of electric current, which is used to separate electrical conductors. It is customarily called a *dielectric* in radio frequency cable.

insulation resistance The ratio of the applied voltage to the total current between two electrodes, which are in contact with a specific insulation, expressed in megohms-M feet.

intelligent peripheral interface The ANSI standard for the mechanical, electrical, and bus protocol requirements for a high-performance interface for peripheral devices that are attached to computers. The physical interface can be operated at rates greater than 50 Mbytes/s on a 16-bit bus over distances of up to 75 meters, depending on circuit and cable choices. The width of the bus can be expanded in increments of 16 bits if higher transfer rates are required.

interconnecting cable The cable between two units of an electronic system.

ionization The formation of ions that occurs when compounds are dissolved in a solvent or when a liquid, solid, or gas is caused to lose or gain electrons as a result of an electric current.

ionization voltage The impressed voltage that is required to cause an atom to give up an electron or to ionize.

IPCEA Abbreviation for Insulated Power Cable Engineers Association.

IPI Abbreviation for Intelligent Peripheral Interface. *See* intelligent peripheral interface.

irradiation With respect to wire and cable insulation, the exposure of a material, typically a thermoplastic compound, to electron bombardment, which alters the molecular structure by cross-linking molecules. *See* cross-linked.

ISO Abbreviation for the International Standards Organization.

jacket An outer nonmetallic protective covering that is applied over insulated conductors or cable for mechanical protection and additional insulation.

jumper cable A short length of flat cable that is used to interconnect two circuit boards or components.

kilo A prefix that means 1000 (e.g., kilovolts).

laminated tape A tape that consists of two or more layers of different materials, typically insulator and conductor, that are bonded together.

LAN Abbreviation for Local-Area Network. *See* Ethernet.

laser A source of coherent light with a narrow beam and a narrow spectral bandwidth. For fiber-optic communications, the laser is usually a solid-state device. *See* injection laser diode.

lay   The axial distance for a single strand of a stranded conductor or an insulated conductor of a cable to complete one turn around the axis of the conductor or cable.

lay direction   The twist in the cable as indicated by the top strands while looking along the axis of the cable away from the observer. It can be right-hand or left-hand lay.

lead dress   The placement or routing of wiring and component leads in an electrical circuit.

lead-in   The cable that provides the path for radio-frequency energy between the antenna and the receiver or transmitter.

leakage   The undesirable passage of current over the surface of or through an insulator.

LED   *See* light-emitting diode.

life cycle   A test to determine the length of time a conductor or cable performs satisfactorily before failure, usually under accelerated conditions.

light-emitting diode (LED)   A semiconductor diode that emits incoherent light when voltage is applied across the p-n junction. For short-haul fiber-optic communication (under one kilometer distances), infrared LEDs or IREDs are widely used emitters.

limpness   The ability of a cable to conform to surface contours or bend under its own weight (e.g., microphone cable). *See* flexibility.

line equalizer   A reactance that is connected in series with a transmission line to correct the frequency-response characteristics of the line.

line level   The amplitude of a signal at a specified point on a transmission line, expressed in decibels.

line voltage   The utility ac power-line voltage.

load   A component that consumes power from the source and generally uses that power to perform a function.

longitudinal shield   A flat or corrugated tape shield that is applied longitudinally, with respect to the axis of the core to be shielded.

loss   Energy that is wasted without accomplishing useful work.

loss factor   The product of the dissipation and the dielectric constant of an insulating material.

low frequency   The part of the electromagnetic spectrum that extends from 30 to 300 kHz.

low-loss dielectric   An insulating material with a relatively low dielectric loss, such as polyethylene or Teflon.

magnetic field   The force field around a permanent magnet or electromagnet in which flux lines are present.

magnetic flux   The rate of magnetic-energy flow across or through a surface (real or imaginary).

meg or mega   A prefix that means one million (e.g., megavolt or megohm).

mho   The obsolete unit for conductivity, which is measured as the reciprocal of an ohm.

micro   A prefix for one-millionth (e.g., microfarad).

micron (μM)   One millionth of a meter (10^{-6} meter).

microwave   The designation for the radio frequencies above one gigahertz (1 GHz), which have wavelengths of 30 cm or smaller.

mil   A unit of length equal to one-thousandth of an inch.

mismatch   A condition in which impedances in two different circuits or cables are not matched.

mode   A single electromagnetic wave that travels in an optical fiber.

modem   The abbreviation for modulator-demodulator. A circuit that can convert an analog or digital signal into a format that can be transmitted and received over the public telephone line.

modulus of elasticity   The ratio of stress to strain in an elastic material.

moisture absorption   The percentage of moisture that a material will absorb under specified conditions.

moisture resistance   The ability of a material to resist moisture.

monofilament   A single strand of plastic or glass, as opposed to a braided or twisted filament.

monomer   The basic chemical unit of a polymer.

multiconductor   More than one conductor within a single cable.

mutual capacitance   The capacitance between two conductors when all other conductors (including ground) are connected together.

Mylar   DuPont's tradename for polyethylene terephthalate (polyester) film.

nano   A numerical prefix for one-billionth as in nanosecond.

National Electrical Code (NEC)   A standard code that is compiled by the National Fire Protection Association (NFPA), incorporated in OSHA regulations.

NEC   An abbreviation for the National Electrical Code.

NEMA   An abbreviation for the National Electrical Manufacturers Association.

neoprene   A synthetic rubber that has good resistance to oil, chemicals, and flames.

nibble   One half byte (4 bits).

numerical aperture (NA)   A measure of the angular acceptance of light by an optical fiber that is approximately equal to the sine of the half angle of the acceptance cone.

$$NA = \sin \theta = \sqrt{n_1{}^2 - n_2{}^2}$$

where: n_1 = the refractive index of the core
n_2 = the refractive index of the cladding
θ = acceptance cone half angle

nylon   A family of polyamide polymers that are abrasion-resistant thermoplastics with good chemical resistance.

offgassing   A percentage of gas that is released during the combustion of an insulation or jacketing material.

OFHC   An abbreviation for oxygen-free, high-conductivity copper with 99.95 percent (minimum), copper content. It is considered to have an average annealed conductivity of 101 percent.

ohm   A unit of electrical resistance that is obtained when a potential difference of one volt can maintain a current of one ampere.

OSHA   Abbreviation for Occupational Safety and Health Act, which covers all factors that relate to safety and disease prevention in the workplace.

overlap   The amount that the trailing edge laps over the leading edge of a spiral tape wrap.

oxygen index   The percentage of oxygen that is necessary to support combustion in a gas mixture.

ozone   A reactive form of oxygen that is produced by electrical discharge.

pair lay   The distance between the peaks of one complete spiral of one conductor in a single pair. Pair lay is normally 25 times the outside diameter of one insulated conductor, expressed in inches.

patch cord   A flexible section of cable that is terminated at both ends with plugs.

percent conductivity   The conductivity of a material, expressed as a percentage of that of copper.

permittivity   *See* dielectric constant.

pick   The distance between two adjacent crossover points of braid filaments. The measurement of picks per inch indicates the degree of coverage.

pico   A prefix that means one billionth (one millionth of one millionth). This prefix is equivalent to micro-micro (e.g., picofarad).

pigtail   Fine-stranded extra-flexible lead wire that is attached to a shield for termination.

pitch   In flat cable, the nominal distance between the index edges of two adjacent conductors.

pitch diameter   Diameter of a circle that passes through the center of the conductors in any layer of multiconductor cable.

plastic deformation   The change in shape of an object under load that does not recover when the load is removed.

plasticizer   A chemical that is added to plastics to make them softer and more pliable.

plenum   The air return path of a central air-conditioning system, either a duct or the space between the framing and a suspended ceiling, of commercial or industrial buildings.

plenum cable   A cable with no protective metallic covering or conduit, which is approved for installation in plenums by an agency that sets standards, such as UL and NEC.

plug   The part of two mating halves of a connector that can be moved when not coupled to its mating half.

ply   The number of individual strands or filaments that are twisted together to form a single thread.

point-to-point wiring   Connections that are made between components by routing continuous conductors between the connecting points.

polarization   A fitting within a connector that permits it to be connected only with the proper orientation.

polishing   The process of finishing the ends of fiber-optic cable cores with abrasives to provide abutting surfaces that are optically smooth and aligned at right angles to the core axis.

polyester   Polyethylene terephthalate is used as a moisture-resistant core wrap. When metallized with aluminum, it can be used as a shield.

polyethylene (PE)   A thermoplastic material with excellent electrical properties.

polyhalocarbon   A general name for polymers that contain atoms of the halogen family: fluorine, chlorine, bromine, and iodine.

polymer   A material formed by the chemical union of monomers.

polyolefin   Polymers and copolymers of the ethylene family of hydrocarbons.

polypropylene   A thermoplastic material that offers excellent electrical properties. Polypropylene is similar to polyethylene, but it is stiffer and has a higher softening temperature.

polyurethane   A class of polymers with good abrasion and solvent resistance, which can be produced in a solid or cellular form.

polyvinyl chloride (PVC)   A general-purpose thermoplastic that is widely used for primary conductor insulation and cable jacketing.

potting   To seal a cable termination or other component with a liquid material that cures at room temperature to form an elastomer.

power factor   **1.** The ratio of resistance to impedance. **2.** The ratio of the actual power of an alternating current to apparent power. **3.** Mathematically, it is the cosine of the phase angle between the applied voltage and the resulting current that passes through the load.

primary insulation   The first layer of insulating material that is applied over a conductor.

propagation delay   Time required for a signal to pass between two points on a transmission line.

propagation velocity   *See* velocity of propagation.

pulling eye   A fitting that is attached to a cable to pull it into or out of a duct.

pulse cable   A coaxial cable that is built to transmit high voltage pulses without degradation.

PVC   *See* polyvinyl chloride.

quad   A group of four separately insulated cables that are twisted together in pairs.

rated temperature   The maximum temperature for the operation of an electronic or electrical component over an extended period without loss of specified performance.

rated voltage The maximum voltage at which an electrical or electronic component can operate over an extended period without losing performance or becoming a safety hazard.

reactance The opposition that is offered to the flow of alternating current by a combination of inductance or capacitance of a component or circuit. The reactance of a capacitor decreases with frequency; the reactance of an inductor increases with frequency.

redraw The consecutive drawing of wire through a series of dies to reach a desired wire gauge. *See* drawing.

reference edge The edge of a cable or conductor from which measurements are made. It can be indicated by an identifying mark, such as a stripe or printed legend. Conductors are identified by their sequential positions from the reference edge: number one is closest to that edge.

reflection The change in direction or return of electromagnetic waves after striking a surface. Reflections occur in copper cables at an impedance mismatch, which causes standing waves. They also occur in fiber-optic cores if the angle of incidence of the incident light exceeds the angular acceptance or the numerical aperture of the fiber. *See* numerical aperture.

reflection loss The part of the signal that is lost as a result of power reflection at a line discontinuity. *See* mismatch.

refraction The bending of light waves or rays as they move from a material with one refractive index to a material with a different refractive index.

refractive index The ratio of the velocity of light in a vacuum to the velocity of light in the transmitting medium.

repeater A combined receiver and transmitter that is located in a copper or fiber-optic transmission line to regenerate an attenuated signal.

resin A synthetic organic material that is formed from one or more monomers (polymerization).

resistance The property in materials that opposes the flow of electric current when voltage is applied, measured in ohms.

retractile cord A cord with a helical elastic jacket that returns to its original contracted shape after being extended.

return wire *See* ground.

RFI *See* radio-frequency interference.

RG/U Abbreviation for Radio Guide, Universal, the military designation for utility-grade coaxial cable.

ribbon cable A flat cable made up of individually insulated conductors that run in parallel and are held together by weaving, bonding to a substrate, or both. Generally, each conductor will have a different color.

ridge marker One or more ridges that run laterally along the outer surface of plastic-insulated wire for identification.

rigid coaxial cable Coaxial cable that is armored with a rigid metal tube.

ringing out   To check continuity through specific conductors of a cable by passing current through them.

rip-cord   A webbed cable construction in which individual insulated conductors can be separated, leaving the insulation intact.

riser cable   A cable that is suitable for use in a vertical building shaft or from floor to floor.

RMS   *See* root mean square.

rockwell hardness   A test to determine hardness based on the penetration of a hardened steel ball or diamond point into the material under test.

root mean square   The effective value of an alternating current or voltage.

rope lay conductor   A conductor that is composed of a central core, surrounded by one or more layers of helically laid groups of wires.

rope unilay   A group of stranded conductors that are assembled in a unilay arrangement.

routing   The path that is followed by a cable or conductor.

Rulan   DuPont's trade name for its flame-retardant polyethylene-insulating material.

rupture   The point at which a material separates in a breaking- or tensile-strength test; it is the limit of elongation.

SAE   Abbreviation for Society of Automotive Engineers.

SBR   Copolymer of styrene and butadiene, a commonly used type of synthetic rubber.

SCSI   *See* small computer systems interface.

self-extinguishing   The property of a material to suppress combustion after the igniting flame is removed.

semi-rigid   **1.** A cable that contains a flexible core inside a relatively inflexible jacket. **2.** A reference to a form of insulation, such as semi-rigid PVC.

separator   A layer of insulating material (textile, paper, or plastic) that is placed between a conductor and its dielectric, between a cable jacket and the conductors it covers, or between various conductors of a multiconductor cable. With separators, the cable is easier to strip, more flexible, and stronger.

serve   Textile fibers or wires that are wound tightly around a central core.

sheath   The outer covering of a multiconductor cable or jacket.

shield   A metallic tape, serve, or braid that is placed around a conductor or a group of conductors of a cable. It prevents electrostatic or electromagnetic interference from being received by or transmitted from the enclosed conductors. A cable can have individual and overall shields made of the same or different materials.

shield percentage   The percentage of a cable that is actually covered by a shield.

signal   A current that conveys information in analog or digital form (audio, video, or radio frequency).

signal cable   A cable that is intended to carry low-level current of less than one ampere per conductor.

silicone   A material made from silicon and oxygen that can be a liquid or thermosetting elastomer.

single-mode fiber   An optical fiber with a small core diameter of approximately eight microns that permits only one mode to propagate. A single-mode fiber permits extremely high-bandwidth transmission and generally uses an injection laser as a transmitter. This fiber is used in military and public-utility systems.

skew ray   A light ray that enters the fiber core at an angle greater than the angle of acceptance or numerical aperture.

skin effect   The tendency of electric current to travel closer to the surface of the conductor as frequency increases.

sleeve   A braided, knitted, or woven tube used to insulate a conductor.

small computer systems interface (SCSI)   An ANSI standard that defines mechanical, electrical, and functional requirements for interfacing and interconnecting small computers and intelligent peripherals, such as rigid disk, floppy disk, magnetic disk, and optical disk drives, printers, and scanners. Two alternatives exist: single-ended and differential cables. Provisions are made for cable lengths up to 25 meters with differential drivers and receivers. A single-ended driver and receiver configuration is defined for cable lengths of up to six meters and is primarily intended for internal applications.

solid conductor   A single wire conductor.

spacing   The separation distance between the closest edges of two adjacent conductors.

span   In flat cables with flat conductors, the distance between the reference edges of the first and last conductors. In those with round conductors, the distance between the centers of the first and last conductors. It is expressed in inches or centimeters.

spark test   A test that finds pin holes in the insulation of a conductor by applying a voltage for a short period as the wire is being drawn through the electrode field.

specific gravity   The ratio of density (mass per unit volume) of a material, with respect to the density of water.

spectral response   In a fiber-optic system, the response of the detector over different wavelengths.

spiral shield   A metallic shield that is formed from wires served spirally over the conductor or conductors.

spiral wrap   The helical wrap of tape or wire over a core.

stability factor   The difference between the percentage power factor at 80 volts/mil and at 40 volts/mil measured on wire that is immersed in water at 75 °C for a specified time.

standing-wave ratio (SWR)   The ratio of the amplitude of a standing wave at an antinode to the amplitude of a node, a figure of merit that is used to express the efficiency of a transmission line.

step-index fiber   A multimode optical fiber with a core that has a uniform refractive index surrounded by a cladding with a sharp decrease in the index of refraction. *See* graded-index optical fiber and single mode fiber.

strand   One of the wires in a stranded conductor.

stranded conductor   A conductor that is formed by twisting groups of strands together.

strand lay   The advance distance of one strand of a spirally stranded conductor, in one turn, measured axially.

strip   To remove insulation from a cable.

strip force   The force that is required to remove a small section of insulating material from the conductor it covers. Strip force is measured in pounds.

surface resistivity   The resistance of a material between two opposite sides of a unit square of its surface, measured in ohms per square.

sweep test   A test in which a radio-frequency signal applied to a length of cable is swept repeatedly through a frequency range to verify the frequency response of the cable. The cable's response (showing any losses) can be viewed on an oscilloscope and recorded.

tank test   A voltage dielectric test in which the test sample of insulated wire or cable is submerged in water and voltage is applied between the conductor and water, which acts as a ground.

tape wrap   A tape that is spirally applied over an insulated or uninsulated conductor.

TCP/IP   Abbreviation for Transmission Control Protocol/Internet Protocol.

tear strength   The force that is required to initiate or continue a tear in a material, such as insulation, under specified conditions.

Teflon   DuPont's trade name for fluorocarbon resins. *See* TFE and FEP.

Tefzel   DuPont's trade name for a fluorocarbon insulation material.

temperature coefficient of resistance   The amount of resistance change of a material per degree of temperature rise. The temperature coefficient of resistance is expressed in parts per million per degree C (ppm/°C).

temperature rating   The maximum temperature at which an insulating material can be used in continuous operation without losing its basic properties.

tensile strength   The pull stress that is required to break a wire or conductor.

TFE   Abbreviation for tetrafluoroethylene, a thermoplastic material with good electrical insulating properties and resistance to chemicals and heat. It is sold commercially as DuPont's Teflon TFE. *See* Teflon.

thermal rating The specified temperature range for satisfactory material performance.

thermal shock A test to determine the ability of a material to withstand the extremes of heat and cold by subjecting it to rapid and wide temperature changes.

thermoplastic A material, typically a plastic resin, that softens and flows when it is heated and subjected to pressure. It becomes rigid when cooled. Two thermoplastics are polyvinyl chloride (PVC) and polyethylene.

thermoset A material that is initially set or cured when heated, but after curing it will not soften, flow, or distort (e.g., natural rubber, neoprene, and Teflon TFE).

tinsel wire A low-voltage stranded electrical conductor with each strand a very thin conductive ribbon of copper or other metal spirally wrapped around a textile yarn. This material is used in thin cord assemblies, such as for telephone and microphone cords, which require limpness and extra long life.

transducer A device that converts mechanical energy to electrical or acoustic energy and vice versa (e.g., microphones, speakers, and piezoelectric crystals).

transfer impedance For a specified cable length, transfer impedance relates a current on one surface of a shield to the voltage drop that is generated by this current on the opposite side of the shield. Transfer impedance is used to determine shield effectiveness against both the reception and transmission of interfering signals. Cable shields are designed to reduce the transfer impedance. Shields with lower transfer impedance are more effective than shields with higher transfer impedance.

transmission line An assembly of two or more conductors or a waveguide with controlled electrical characteristics to transfer signal energy from one location to another.

transmission loss The loss of power during energy transmission from one point to another, expressed in decibels.

transmitter An electronic circuit that converts electrical energy into radio frequency energy for transmission over cables or in free space. It also applies to the transmission of light energy in an optical fiber or in free space.

tray A rigid structural assembly, typically made of metal, that is used to support wires and cables within a building.

tray cable A multiconductor control, signal, or power cable that is approved by the National Electrical Code for installation in trays.

triaxial cable A three-conductor cable with one inner conductor that is surrounded by two cylindrical conducting shields, each of which is concentric with the inner conductor. All conductors are insulated from each other and the cable is usually jacketed.

triboelectric noise Noise that is generated in a shielded cable as a result of the variations in capacitance between the shield and conductor as the cable is flexed.

trunk cable *See* feeder cable.

tubing An extruded plastic tube that is used as insulation. It might be heat shrinkable.

twin cable A pair of insulated conductors that are twisted, sheathed, or held together, but are not identifiable from each other, in a common jacket.

twin coaxial cable A cable configuration that contains two separate complete parallel coaxial cables or two cables that are twisted around each other in one jacket.

twin lead A transmission line with two parallel conductors that are separated by a web of insulating materials. The impedance of the line is determined by the diameter and spacing of the conductors and the insulating material.

twisted pairs A cable with two small insulated conductors that are twisted together without a common jacket.

UHF *See* ultra-high frequency.

UL *See* Underwriters Laboratories.

ultra-high frequency (UHF) The range of electromagnetic frequencies that extend from 300 MHz to 3 GHz.

unbalanced line A two-conductor transmission line with the voltages on each conductor that are unequal with respect to ground (e.g., coaxial cable).

Underwriters Laboratories (UL) A not-for-profit independent product certification laboratory that establishes test programs, issues safety standards and tests, inspects and lists products.

unidirectional concentric stranding Stranding of conductors in which each successive layer has a different lay length. These different lengths give it a circular cross section without strands migrating from one layer to another.

unidirectional stranding A stranding in which all conductors have the same direction of lay.

unilay strand A conductor with a central core that is surrounded by more that one layer of helically laid wires. All layers have a common length and direction of lay.

VA An abbreviation for volt-amperes. A designation of power in terms of voltage and amperage (current).

velocity of propagation The transmission speed of electrical energy in a length of cable compared with its speed in free space, considered to be a constant (C). Measured as a percentage of C, the velocity of propagation is the reciprocal of the square root of the dielectric constant of the cable insulation.

vertical tray fire   A reference to UL's Vertical Flame Test. The test flame is supplied by a strip or ribbon-type propane gas burner, which subjects the cable to 23,000 BTU.

very high frequency (VHF)   The range of electromagnetic frequencies from 30 MHz to 300 MHz.

video   Reference to the frequency bands that are used to transmit television pictures.

video pair cable   A transmission cable that contains low-loss pairs with an impedance of 125 ohms for applications such as closed-circuit TV (CCTV) and telephone carrier circuits.

volt (V)   A unit of electrical pressure. One volt is the electrical pressure that will cause one ampere of current to flow through one ohm of resistance.

voltage   A term for electromotive force or electrical potential, expressed in volts.

voltage drop   The voltage drop across a conductor as a result of the current flow through the resistance or impedance of the conductor.

voltage rating   The highest voltage that can be applied continuously to a conductor to conform with standards or specifications.

voltage standing-wave ratio (VSWR)   The ratio of the maximum electric field strength to the minimum electric field strength along the length of a radio-frequency transmission line.

volume resistivity (specific insulation resistance)   The electrical resistance between opposite faces of a one centimeter cube of insulating material, expressed in ohms/centimeter.

vulcanization   A change in the physical properties of an elastomer by reacting it with sulfur or other cross-linking chemicals. The process makes the elastomer tougher and more durable.

VW-1   A flammability rating that was established by Underwriters Laboratories for wires and cables that pass a specified vertical flame test, described in UL Standard 758 (formerly designated FR-1).

wall thickness   The thickness of the applied insulation or jacket.

water absorption   A test to determine the amount of water absorbed by a material after being immersed for a specified period.

watt   A unit of electrical power that is equal to the product of one volt and one ampere.

waveform   A graphic presentation of a varying quantity, such as is seen on an oscilloscope or oscillograph. Time is represented as the horizontal or X axis and the variable (current, voltage) is represented by variations on the vertical or Y axis.

wavelength   The distance measured between successive peaks or nodes of a complete wave cycle.

wicking   The longitudinal flow of a liquid in a conductor or cable as a result of capillary action.

wire   A bare or insulated conductor.

wire wrapping   A solderless method to terminate the bare end of a conductor by wrapping it around a square terminal post under tension with a power or hand tool. The post penetrates the surface of the conductor to form a gas-tight seal.

yield strength   The minimum stress at which a material will start to deform without additional load.

zumbach closed-loop system   A process for controlling the outer diameter of insulation on a conductor.

Zytel   DuPont's trade name for nylon resins.

Index